CliffsNotes®

Praxis II®: Fundamental Subjects Content Knowledge (0511)

by

Jocelyn L. Paris, M.Ed.
Judy L. Paris, M.Ed.

WILEY

Wiley Publishing, Inc.

Authors' Acknowledgments

To my mommy,
Thanks for being a good one.

—Jocelyn

To my parents, Shirley and Ellsworth, who are the very reason I have accomplished my dreams. There could not have been a better childhood or more support as an adult.

—Judy

Publisher's Acknowledgments

Editorial

Project Editor: Kelly Dobbs Henthorne

Acquisitions Editor: Greg Tubach

Composition

Proofreader: Joni Heredia

Wiley Publishing, Inc. Composition Services

CliffsNotes® Praxis II®: Fundamental Subjects Content Knowledge (0511)

Published by:
Wiley Publishing, Inc.
111 River Street
Hoboken, NJ 07030-5774
www.wiley.com

Copyright © 2009 Wiley, Hoboken, NJ

Published by Wiley, Hoboken, NJ
Published simultaneously in Canada

Library of Congress Cataloging-in-Publication Data
Paris, Jocelyn L., 1977–
  CliffsNotes Praxis II : fundamental subjects content knowledge / by Jocelyn L. Paris, Judy L. Paris
    p. cm.
  Includes index.
  ISBN-13: 978-0-470-44855-7
  ISBN-10: 0-470-44855-5
  1. Teachers--United States--Examinations--Study Guides. 2. National teacher examinations--Study guides. I. Paris, Judy L. II. Title. III. Title: CliffsNotes Praxis two.
  LB1762.P375 2009
  370.76--dc22

                                                    2009010852

ISBN 978-0-470-44855-7 (pbk), ISBN 978-0-470-50668-4 (ebk), ISBN 978-1-118-15406-9 (ebk), ISBN 978-1-118-15321-5 (ebk)

Printed in the United States of America

10 9 8 7 6 5

Note: If you purchased this book without a cover, you should be aware that this book is stolen property. It was reported as "unsold and destroyed" to the publisher, and neither the author nor the publisher has received any payment for this "stripped book."

WILEY

About the Authors

Jocelyn has had a colorful and enriching life centered around teaching. She graduated with a B.A. from the University of Arizona and obtained her Master's in Elementary Education at Northern Arizona University. She has taught preschool through high school students ranging in all abilities from severe to profound, mentally retarded to deaf to gifted and to emotionally and behaviorally challenged. Jocelyn has taught in a multitude of settings as well: public school, charter school, residential school for the deaf and blind, private school, and Montessori school. She also is author of *Idioms*, published by Butte Publications, Inc. Jocelyn loves to coach sports and has coached basketball, volleyball, and soccer for elementary through high school varsity teams. One of her true passions lies with Camp Abilities, a fundamentally appropriate sports camp for the Visually Impaired. She has been involved in these camps for the past six years in Arizona, New York, and Alaska.

For more than 35 years, Judy has been professionally involved in the field of education as a teacher, a special education director, a principal, a superintendent, a consultant, an author, a mentor, and currently serves as adjunct faculty for several universities. She holds degrees and certifications in special education, early childhood education, elementary education, and educational leadership/administration. She was Teacher of the Year and currently develops college courses and exams, teaches in summer enrichment camps, conducts professional development workshops, and writes educational materials. She passionately endorses early childhood education as a means to improve the capacity of our world by providing children with the foundations to be successful in life. She believes children should learn through discovery and experience the world's wonders every day. This has led her to a new endeavor of establishing a children's museum in her community.

Table of Contents

PART II: PRACTICE EXAMINATIONS WITH ANSWER EXPLANATIONS

Introduction

Education is a profession that requires knowledge, skill, and dedication. Educators are expected to conduct on-going self-assessments, review personal philosophies, identify personal teaching styles, select methods of instruction, and accommodate diverse learners. The education field requires that individuals consistently increase their overall knowledge of the education field and be accountable to society for their instruction to children.

The Praxis II Fundamental Subjects exam has been identified as one method of ensuring that teachers have the basic and fundamental subject knowledge necessary to support this profession. Teachers who desire a promising career study and prepare for it on a regular basis. Using this study guide and taking this exam are just the beginning of pursuing this profession.

Effective educators work in a variety of educational settings using their content knowledge and applying that knowledge and the principles to classroom environments. This elementary Praxis II Fundamental Subjects exam is focused on the most basic content knowledge necessary for these teachers to better understand elementary students and the educational process.

Getting Started

Whether you are a recent college graduate or an experienced teacher, taking this Praxis II Fundamental Subjects exam accommodates certain state certification and licensure requirements. The final score on this exam will reflect what you have gained from teacher preparation courses and from utilizing instructional practices in the classroom. To prepare for the Praxis II 0511 exam, you may also want to review college texts, conduct Internet research, visit the library, or speak with other professionals.

Remember that the practice exams offered in this guide provide additional information about the questions and content included in the actual Praxis II Fundamental Subjects examination. After taking one of the practice exams in this guide, use those answers and detailed explanations to further study specific topics. Then take the second practice exam to determine areas that need additional review. The practice exams and the actual exams differ in both content and difficulty.

Format of the Exam

The Praxis II exam focused on within this guide refers to the elementary education Praxis II exam, 0511 Fundamental Subjects: Content Knowledge. It is intended to help examinees assess their own general content knowledge regarding instruction of elementary students. This exam has 100 multiple-choice questions. The exam questions are based on key indicators of general knowledge and understanding specific to the education of elementary students. The questions found within each subject area are designed to require that examinees utilize basic and fundamental skills, which are predicated upon broad concepts of each subject.

Multiple-Choice Questions

Multiple-choice questions are designed to assess detailed knowledge of the specific subject material. They include a *stem* (statement), which may be written in one of several formats, and four answer options with the correct answer being called the *key*. The four possible selections that follow the stem are identified by letter selections A, B, C, and D. The three *distractors*, the incorrect selections, may be related to the correct answer in some way, but examinees should select only the **best** possible answer.

Multiple-choice questions are factually written and generally do not include opinion statements. The examination questions reflect *best practices* recommended and utilized in elementary education.

In both the practice tests and the actual exam, some of the multiple-choice questions are based on possible classroom situations. Examinees should read the brief excerpts and think about how the posed question should be answered in reference to only the information that is provided. Consider what an educator should do if placed in this particular circumstance and think carefully when making final answer selections.

Multiple-Choice Strategy and Formats

Strong reading skills are a basic requirement for answering discrete multiple-choice questions correctly on an examination. Comprehending the basic premise of each question and retrieving content knowledge of the area tested is essential.

When taking an exam with multiple-choice questions, an examinee should read and then reread each question. The individual should think about the answer before looking at the four options provided. The examinee then may check to see whether her choice is listed in the four options, which will make selecting the best answer an easier task. If the information in the question is unknown, an examinee should look at all of the options and use the process of elimination to choose a response. In this situation, to help an examinee select a correct answer from fewer choices, she might first remove any choices that seem impossible or not probable. When an examinee is unsure of the correct response for a multiple-choice question, she should still select an answer to the question as there is no penalty for guessing an answer.

Following are the types of *multiple-choice* formats.

Fill-in-the-Blank or Complete the Statement

This type offers information through the delivery of a partial sentence that must be completed by the examinee using one of the proposed options. An individual should select the best option that completes the sentence, using facts, data, and knowledge about elementary education.

---

1. Graphs and tables are used to record _____ and specific historical information.

   A. mathematical
   B. statistical
   C. scientific
   D. economic

---

1. B. Statistical information is used on graphs and tables to aid an individual in obtaining factual content. Often, tables and graphs are used to record populations, weather temperatures, historical dates, and events.

---

2. President Lyndon Johnson became president when

   A. President Kennedy was assassinated.
   B. The Cold War ended.
   C. President Lincoln died.
   D. The Civil War concluded.

---

2. A. President Kennedy was assassinated during a visit to Texas, by Lee Harvey Oswald. Lyndon Johnson was the vice president at the time of Kennedy's death and by law was immediately sworn in as president.

Question/Statement or Which of the Following?

This type poses a short question or delivers a statement that must be answered by selecting one of the four options provided. The most frequently used phrase is the question that begins with "Which of the following . . ." To answer these questions, examinees should read the question or statement carefully and think about all the given options, finally choosing the one that is **best** suited as an answer.

> **1.** Which of the following fractions is equal to 55%?
>
>   A.   11/20
>   B.   1/2
>   C.   5/11
>   D.   3/5

1. A. In order to find the percentage that a fraction yields, divide the numerator (top number) by the denominator (bottom number) to obtain the decimal and then multiply by 100 to calculate the percent. 11 divided by 20 equals 0.55 and then 0.55 multiplied by 100 equals 55%.

Least/Not/Except

This type requires that an examinee select an answer that is considered *incorrect*, or *least likely* to be correct. These questions place a negative slant on the outcome of the answer, so examinees should be particularly careful in choosing a response. These questions require the examinee to first decide which of the three options provided are correct answers and then eliminate those options in order to determine the one that is incorrect, which is the answer being sought. One strategy to use is to restate the question in a positive way to help select the three correct answers, thereby leaving the fourth choice as the best answer.

Following are examples of least/not/except formats:

- Which of the following is NOT included on . . .
- Which is the LEAST likely to . . .
- All of the following are true EXCEPT . . .
- Which choice is NOT a component of . . .

The multiple-choice questions that use the terms "Least," "Not," or "Except" are included on the actual Praxis exams, but samples of these questions are **not** included in this study guide. It is important that examinees study only the most accurate information in preparation for the Praxis II Fundamental Subjects exam. This type of question, used on the actual exam, should be considered tricky, so use caution when selecting an answer.

Time Frame

The amount of time permitted to take the Praxis II Fundamental Subjects exam is based on the specific format of the test. Examinees are allowed up to 2 hours to answer 100 multiple-choice questions.

Examinees should use the practice exams to pace themselves in preparation for the actual exam. When taking the Praxis II Fundamental Subjects exam, examinees will need time to read each question, consider an answer, and review the final answers before submitting the test for a score.

Content of the Exam

The Fundamental Subjects exam covered in this guide is comprised of four content categories. The actual Praxis II exam assesses an examinee's understanding of the concepts and applications of the concepts that are related to these specific categories.

This list outlines these four broad topics, the number of questions, and the percentages of the final score that are dedicated to each of these sections.

English Language Arts	25	25%
Mathematics	25	25%
Citizenship and Social Science	25	25%
Science	25	25%

Frequently Asked Questions

As an examinee prepares to take a Praxis II exam, questions may arise. Some of the most common questions have been answered here. However, if you need further assistance, contact the Educational Testing Services at 1-800-772-9476 or check their website at www.ets.org.

Q: What are the Praxis II exams?

A: The Praxis II exams were developed by the Educational Testing Service (ETS) to measure the general knowledge in specific education subject areas of prospective teachers. Many states require these examinations in order to complete the certification or licensure process for professional practice, and some professional organizations require the completion of a Praxis II exam for membership.

Q: What is the best method for registering to take a Praxis II exam?

A: Many individuals find that registering online is easy since it is available 7 days a week; however, it is not intended for those who may need special accommodations due to a disability or primary language need or for those with religious or military requirements. Registration may also be conducted via U.S. mail or by calling the company. Registration must be finalized prior to taking a Praxis II exam, and it is recommended that examinees complete this 1–3 months ahead of the proposed testing date. For further information, contact the Educational Testing Services on their website or at the telephone number listed previously.

Q: Where should an examinee take a Praxis II exam?

A: Testing locations have been identified in many states and several regions across the country. A list of these centers is available online.

Q: What if an examinee misses the registration period for a test date?

A: Late registration may be allowed, but there could be an additional fee for late registration. Examinees should expedite their registration in order to be considered for the correct exam and obtain a seat at the specific testing location. Check for information about late registration on the ETS website.

Q: Can the registration date be changed if needed?

A: Contact ETS as soon as possible if a conflict or problem arises with a confirmed registration date; however, changes in dates may impose an additional fee.

Q: Which states require the Praxis II exams for certification or licensure?

A: Contact a specific state department of education or check the ETS website to determine which exams are required in each state. Some states use examinations developed by that state and may not require the use of the Praxis II exams. Checking with a specific state department of education would offer the most up to date information.

Q: How does an examinee know which particular Praxis exam should be taken?

A: States that mandate Praxis II examinations for certification or licensure do not always require the same tests. Examinees should research the state requirements by contacting the specific department of education. The teacher certification office in each state should have information to help examinees select the correct exam or combination of exams.

Q: What scores are considered as passing for teacher certification or licensure?

A: Acceptable scores differ in each state, so contacting a state department of education would provide the most accurate score information. If an examinee took a Praxis II exam in one state and then moved to another state, she should ask whether the current score may be acceptable. Most states allow the transfer of a score as long as it is recent and meets the requirement in that state.

Q: When might an examinee expect to receive the scores?

A: ETS provides the scoring results for examinees. They try to expedite this information and scores may be expected within 4 to 6 weeks, pending no major holidays. A list of scoring dates is available on the ETS website, as well as an informational guide on how to interpret an individual's scores.

Q: Are accommodations allowed for an examinee with a documented disability?

A: For individuals with disabilities, reasonable accommodations may be provided and the process to apply for these accommodations is identified online at the ETS website, under Resources for Test Takers with Disabilities. This supplemental guide is available to aid an examinee in registration and apply for support. For telephone contact, examinees may call 1-866-387-8602 Monday through Friday (8:30 A.M.–5 P.M. EST).

Q: On the day of the examination, what should an examinee plan to bring to the testing site?

A: Examinees must bring the following:

- Proof of registration—the admission ticket
- Identification that includes name, a photo, and signature
- Several sharpened soft-lead (No. 2 or HB) pencils and good eraser
- Blue or black ink pens for some exams

Other considerations include the following:

- An additional form of identification
- A watch
- Extra clothing as room temperatures may vary

Other personal belongings may not be allowed in the testing center, so examinees should be careful of the items they bring.

Q: In what ways should an examinee prepare to take a Praxis II exam?

A: This study guide was designed to help an examinee improve the chances of receiving a passing score on a specific Praxis II exam(s). An examinee should review the testing format, and the practice exams, as well as study the content of the guide to reinforce an overall general base of knowledge.

Using this Study Guide

CliffsNotes Praxis II: Fundamental Subjects Content Knowledge (0511) includes several supports to help guide examinees.

1. **Introduction**: Included for overall information that supports the fundamental subject areas of elementary education.
2. **Subject Area Review**: A comprehensive section for each content area that includes these four major subjects: English language arts, mathematics, citizenship and social science, and science. The headings are designed as guides to those select topics identified in the examination. This section should be the focus of intense study and review.
3. **Practice Exams:** Sample full-length tests provided as a guide to the content and format of the actual Praxis II exam. In addition to the practice exams are answers with detailed explanations as an added study tool.
4. **Final Thoughts and Tips:** A summary of the test-taking strategies provided, along with tips for test preparation, which should aid an examinee in achieving exam success.

PART I

SUBJECT AREA REVIEWS

English Language Arts

Mathematics

Citizenship and Social Science

Science

English Language Arts

This portion of the Praxis 0511 exam assesses skills and understandings in the broad content knowledge area of English Language Arts. This exam includes questions that pertain to a variety of texts, the effects of literary passages, basic reading comprehension, and the key elements of writing and speaking. This exam does not include questions of specific vocabulary terms, although this study guide includes several English and language arts terms and definitions to increase an examinee's familiarity in the field.

Reading Literature

Literature is an essential subject area in schools, as it is considered the art of written works and is utilized in other subjects as well as daily life. The most basic types of literature include **fiction** and **non-fiction** literary pieces.

Literary works have evolved during each period in history and reflect the people, their ideologies, and the society of the times. Authors in these time periods assert their own beliefs and values in their works, and the works demonstrate their biases. It is because of the influences of the authors that literature can be easily linked to certain periods in history.

Literature is a unique form of written materials. Literature does not deliver a direct message for the reader but more often provides a discreet or concealed message. The reader has the responsibility of deciphering, uncovering, analyzing, and interpreting the meaning of the literary selections being read.

There are four critical stages in the interpretation of literature:

- **Initial** (construction stage)—Reader has contact with content, structure, genre, and the language of the text, using prior knowledge to build an understanding of the elements.
- **Developing** (extending stage)—Reader delves into the text, using background knowledge to build an understanding of the literary piece with new information being absorbed and used to ask questions.
- **Reflection/response** (extension of reading stage)—Reader uses text knowledge to connect to personal knowledge of the reader's life, the lives of others, and the human condition.
- **Critical analysis** (examining stage)—Reader reflects and reacts to the literary work by judging, evaluating, and relating to the literature.

Literary Selections

Making literary selections depends on a student's knowledge of the types of literature. They may be selecting a literary work based on the topic, the genre, or merely for a pleasurable experience. Knowing the various types of literary texts or genres helps students prepare or anticipate the characteristics of each before reading. This aids in their comprehension of the materials. There are two basic categories of literature: expository and narrative.

Expository

Includes reference or resource works, textbooks, and informational materials most often used in subject or content areas and regularly used in schools. Students need training in how to read and interpret expository text, since later grades depend heavily on this type of literary selection.

Narrative

Other types of literature that may be used in subjects but is often for pleasure or based on the reader's interest. Narrative literature includes these genre (literary forms):

- **Autobiography**—About an author's own personal life
- **Biography**—About someone's life written by another person
- **Epic**—A narrative poem about historical or legendary characters
- **Fantasy**—A story with imaginary setting, plot, or characters, some of whom may have special powers
- **Folktales**—Stories passed down from generation to generation that include fables, myths, legends, folktales, and tall tales
- **Historical fiction**—Although it might be altered to some extent, the setting, time, event, and characters are based on history and facts
- **Mystery**—Tales that relate to the unknown and revealed through human or worldly dilemmas or situations that include horror, fantasy, crime-solving, secret events, and the supernatural
- **Play**—A story written for the purpose of performance
- **Poetry**—A story written in certain form or rhyme and rhythm with imagery
- **Realistic fiction**—A theme or plot that could happen in life
- **Science fiction**—Focuses on a mix of reality and the imaginary

Themes and Purposes

A **theme** is the main idea or the fundamental meaning of a literary work that can be either plainly stated or implied. An author may weave a complex theme or one that is related to societal morals throughout a literary piece. Often, a theme has to be extricated from the story as the reader studies the text and deciphers the use of the literary elements and characters in the work. When a reader is able to decipher a theme, he is better able to determine the author's purpose for writing the work. A theme is categorized either as a major theme or a minor theme. If the author repeats the theme or the same important idea regularly throughout the written work, it is considered a major theme. A minor theme is one that appears only once in a while.

Themes may be used by writers in several ways.

- Themes may articulate or highlight emotions. When an author shares the feelings of the main character, a reader can study the thoughts and ideas in the character's mind.
- Themes convey ideas, thoughts, and comprise conversations. When an author uses character conversations to repeatedly share thoughts and ideas, the author may be delivering the theme and sharing the purpose of the story.
- Themes are intertwined in the characters. An author may use the main character to illustrate the main theme and secondary characters to share a lesser theme.
- Themes may be found in the actions or events of a story. An author may use the characters to express ideas and feelings through their actions.

It is essential that individuals understand that there is a difference between the *theme* of a literary work and the *subject* of a literary work. Although not every literary work has a theme, they all have a subject, which is the topic that the writer has chosen to write about. A theme differs from the subject (topic) of a piece as it delivers a purpose, a statement, or opinion about the topic.

Types of Literature

There are many types of literature, each possessing unique characteristics. A reader must be familiar with various types of literature in order to accurately interpret the meaning of the text or selection read. Understanding the basis and definition of the type of literature will help the reader decipher meaning and interpret purpose. Following is a brief list of the most common forms of literature.

Allegory—A narrative in which the characters and events represent an idea or truth about life in general.

Autobiography—A narrative in which the author writes about his/her own life.

Biography—A narrative in which an author writes about another person's life.

Comedy—A genre of literature in which life is dealt with in a humorous manner, often poking fun at people's mistakes.

Drama—A play that uses dialogue to present its message to the audience and is meant to be performed.

Essay—A nonfiction piece that is often short and used to express the writer's opinion about a topic or to share information on a subject.

Fable—A short story, often with animals as the main characters, that teaches a moral or lesson to the reader.

Fantasy—A genre of literature in which the story is set in an imaginary world, involving magic or adventure, in which the characters often have supernatural powers.

Folktale—A story that has been passed down orally from one generation to another; the characters usually follow the extreme (all good or all bad) and in the end are rewarded or punished as they deserve.

Myth—A story that was created to explain some natural force of nature, religious belief, or social phenomenon. The gods and goddesses have supernatural powers but the human characters often do not.

Novel—A fictional narrative of book length in which characters and plot are developed in a somewhat realistic manner.

Parable—A simple short story that is used to explain a belief, a moral, or spiritual lesson.

Poetry—A literary work that uses colorful, concise, rhythmic language and focuses on the expression of ideas or emotions.

Prose—A literary work that is in ordinary form and uses the familiar structure of spoken language, sentence after sentence.

Realism—A writing in which the reality of life is shown.

Science fiction—A genre of literature in which real or imaginary scientific developments and concepts are prevalent and is often set in the future.

Short story—A narrative that can be read in one sitting. Has a few characters and often one conflict or problem. The characters often go through some sort of change by the end of the story.

Tall tale—A humorous and exaggerated story often based upon the life of a real person. The exaggerations increase and build until the character can achieve impossible tasks.

Tragedy—A genre of literature in which there is a downfall of the hero due to a tragic flaw or personal characteristic; often ends with an unhappy ending.

Elements and Relationships

Literary elements refer to the specific and recognizable characteristics of the text or literary work. Every literary form includes a theme, a setting, a conflict, a point of view, characters, and so on. Students must be able to determine these elements and analyze their importance to the author's intent and purpose. Some of these elements are explained here, and others are found in separate sections.

Pace is how the details of a narrative are placed and how transitions are made within the narrative. The pace of a narrative helps the story move forward and is made up of scenes.

Tone is the feeling or attitude that is conveyed by a narrative or selection. The tone is often expressed through characters, word choice, and the writing style. It can be humorous, tragic, serious, satiric, and so on.

Plot is the sequential order of events within a narrative. The plot implies the reason that the events occur in a story. Through the plot, the reader will become involved in the lives and situations of the characters. Eight elements comprise the plot.

- **Exposition**—Introduction of the story in which the reader is introduced to the setting, the tone, the characters, and purpose of the story.
- **Inciting force**—Characters or events trigger the central conflict.

- **Conflict**—Event that comprises the plot. There are five types of conflicts:
  1. Man v. Man: One person is pitted against another.
  2. Man v. Nature: A person(s) battles with the forces of nature.
  3. Man v. Society: Societal values (customs) are challenged by person(s).
  4. Man v. Self: Internal struggles, or test of values of a character.
  5. Man v. Fate: Problem or struggle appears to be far beyond the person's control.
- **Rising action**—A string of events that builds up from the conflict, which then moves toward the climax.
- **Crisis**—As the conflict reaches a turning point (its most intense point), the two opposing forces in the story meet (producing a climax).
- **Climax**—The outcome of the conflict can be forecasted. This is the peak of the story and often included the greatest emotion.
- **Falling action**—A series of events occurring after the climax that bring the story to a conclusion.
- **Resolution**—The conclusion of the story and the completion of the action.

Characters are the people, animals, or objects that participate in the sequence of events within a narrative. Characters are presented to the reader in a variety of ways such as physical traits, dialogue, actions, behaviors, responses to situations, beliefs, and the point of view.

Setting is the physical location and/or time of the narrative or events of the narrative. The setting can be developed directly through description or can be inferred through context clues, word choice, and dialogue of characters.

Theme is the view or belief that is an underlying message of the narrative. Theme is not directly stated but is left up to the reader to extract it from what has been read.

Historical and Cultural Contexts

Language, written and spoken, has played a critical role in the development of societies, cultures, and nations. Literature has long had historical and cultural connotations that are relevant to present day.

From a historical standpoint, literature has evolved through the years and to this day has provided us with a rich literary base. The very early themes of literary works (2700 B.C.E.) revolved around heroism, friendship, religion, and the search for eternal life. During the Middle Ages, morals, religion, and romance were present and continued into a historical period that provided literature with shared themes in national and philosophical epics. Later in history, popular folk literature developed and brought readers into the nineteenth century with themes of realism and nature. The twentieth century brought forward literary studies with symbolism and detailed character development. Students now study all these types of literary works and themes.

Customary stories and oral traditions that use a variety of themes from cultural literature provide children with the exposure and awareness of other people and their backgrounds. Students learn to appreciate multicultural aspects of society and teachers can begin with literature that has cultural representations pertinent to the classroom or school. The literature that is chosen should be accurate, factual, and current about the people and the cultures reflected. Teachers should share and discuss customs, beliefs, heritage, and the impact of the various cultures on the world.

Comparisons of Literary Texts

Research shows that when students are able to use strategies that activate their use of prior knowledge, they comprehend better than those students who cannot use it. Students must learn to comprehend and apply what they read, which is possible by using the schema theory. **Schema** is the background knowledge or experiences that students may bring with them into the reading of a text. This may include their emotions, opinions, feelings, ideas, and understandings as they read a literary piece and make connections or applications. This helps students make sense of what they read, especially challenging materials, but may be exactly what some poor readers lack.

When writing a literary comparison one cannot examine thoroughly two or more aspects, but instead must take one characteristic as a starting point and lead the criticism and the investigations to that single aspect of the text. These aspects may include plot, character (background, actions, motivations), setting, or theme. Readers may relate their interpretations of literary texts to prior readings or experiences by making meaningful connections of text-to-text, text-to-self, or text-to-world.

The **text-to-text** (T-T) connection is defined as the comparison between what is currently being read to that of other literary works that have been read in the past. Students may connect the similarities between two texts (literary works) that are by the same author, have a similar theme, are in a related genre, or have the same subject.

For example, when reading *Into the Wild* by John Krakauer, the reader draws a comparison to the character's loneliness and self-examination to that of the old fisherman in *The Old Man and the Sea* by Ernest Hemmingway.

The **text-to-self** (T-S) connection occurs when students can relate their own lives or make very personal connections (schema) to what is currently being read. They may be reminded of an activity or event in their life that a character is experiencing in the text or the topic or issues may be similar to something happening in their family.

For example, when reading *Saturdays and Teacakes* by Lester Laminack, the reader remembers a time when he went to his grandmother's house and learned how to make homemade cookies just like the protagonist.

The **text-to-world** (T-W) connections are on a larger, broader scale, and this happens when students are able to relay what occurs in a literary work to what ensues in the world, such as the economic, business, or financial occurrences. Educators may enhance these connections through readings of certain genre, such as those subjects of science, social studies, or literature that encompass worldly things. Students may then refer to something they learned through a magazine, the television, on a vacation, or in an article.

For example, while reading *Sing Down the Moon* by Scott O'Dell, the reader may remember and compare information that she learned from watching a documentary on the Navajo Tribe and Kit Carson in Canyon de Chelly.

Students may learn to make connections as described through teacher modeling and practice in each area. Although these three types of connections may be taught separately, students should understand that sometimes literary texts may relate to any combination of the three. Making connections helps students in their comprehension of the literary work. Teachers may prompt students to make the connections by using questions such as "What did that make you feel like?", "What do you remember from the story we read last week?", "Has anything happened to you like the event in the story?"

The reasons these connections help readers are

Readers are able to understand how characters feel.

Readers are able to figure out the motivations of the characters' actions.

Readers become more actively involved and engaged in the materials.

Readers can determine the purpose, figure out the theme, and remain focused on the concepts.

Literary Methods and Effects

Literary methods and effects include literary techniques and devices. These devices played a critical role in showing the reader the author's style, along with plot, setting, and theme. Literary techniques/devices collectively form the components of the work being read. These also allow the author to create meaning through language and establish style as well as help readers gain an understanding of and an appreciation for the works being read. These devices may include figures of speech, conventions, and structure.

Point of View

The **point of view** is the perspective from which a story is told or a literary piece is written. It varies depending on the author or the type of work being provided. It may be a certain type of judgment, an attitude, or an opinion shared by the author through the characters, which may include their feelings or motives. It delivers the events and activities of a story-line from the writer through a narrative to the reader. Readers must learn to understand and recognize the point of view as it is an essential skill in knowing how to interpret or comprehend literature.

In literature, the point of view may be defined in three ways (see the following) and sometimes writers combine several *points of view* within the same piece of work.

1. **Physical point of view**—refers to the position in time and space in which an author describes his views or material.
2. **Mental point of view**—describes a writer's feelings or attitudes toward the subject.
3. **Personal point of view**—focuses on the manner in which the writer describes, discusses, or narrates a subject.
   - **First person**: The author takes the point of view of a character providing personal thoughts or feelings and shares what other characters do and say. This is the "I" narrator. For example, *I was strolling down the dirt road yesterday on my way home when I saw a man approaching me. He had a bit of a swagger to his step and was wearing a brimmed cap. I wondered why he was wearing such a large hat. I slowed my pace in order to gauge my options. He glanced at me and smiled.*
   - **Second person:** The writer tells the story to another character addressing him as "you." It appears to the readers as if they are the characters being told what to do and what to feel. For example, *You are a talented detective. While preparing to leave your office late on Friday evening, the phone rings. You decide to stay an extra five minutes and answer the phone. A mysterious voice trickles through the line asking you for help. Your caller ID traces the caller's name and location.*
   - **Third person:** The author tells the story from an outside voice. The narrator is not one of the characters in the story but informs the reader about the characters. There are three types of third-person narrators: *objective* (the story is told through actions and dialogues), *omniscient* (the narrator is all knowing and knows the inner thoughts of the characters), and *limited omniscient* (the narrator has limited knowledge of only one character's thoughts and feelings).

Character

The **character** in a literary piece is a person who is identified by the author as being responsible for the thoughts and actions within the story or poem. Characters are critically significant to a piece of literature, as readers often draw information from them. Each character has his own personality, which aids in establishing the plot of a story or defining the mood. Character development is fundamental to an author. Character presentations, their attitudes, mannerisms, thoughts, and appearances impact the other essential elements of a piece of literature, such as the setting, tone, and theme.

Characterization refers to the manner in which an author presents characters in a story. This may be accomplished through **direct presentation,** in which a character is portrayed by the author, the narrator, or the other characters, or through **indirect presentation,** in which a character's traits are exposed by actions and speech.

Characters are divided into two groups:

- **Protagonist**—The primary or main character in a piece of literature, but may not be the hero or heroine.
- **Antagonist**—A character or force (nature, society, a person, and so on) that may oppose the protagonist in a piece of literature.

Major characters are the characters that dominate the story. They are often considered dynamic, round, or three-dimensional characters and may possess both good and bad qualities. Major characters may change themselves, their goals, ambitions, or values based on what happens in the story. Dynamic characters may grow or progress to a more advanced level of understanding as the story unfolds.

Minor characters are the characters that also are referred to as flat, static, or two-dimensional as they do not change with the story line. They may have only one or two prominent qualities, and in general, those qualities are not balanced by a reverse quality. These characters are most often either good or bad, and although they lack depth, they may be fascinating or humorous as an addition to the overall story.

Setting, Tone, and Mood

Other literary elements that contribute to the presentation of a literary work include the setting, the tone, and the mood. Most authors carefully analyze their development of these three elements and attempt to capture their readers' attention and interest by creating mental pictures.

The **setting** includes the time, the place(s), the physical details, and the circumstances or events in which a situation occurs. A setting allows the reader to visualize how a story will unfold. Settings can be created as simple or elaborate and are used to generate the ambiance of the material and to emphasize, organize, or divert the reader while lending credibility or realism to the events. A setting includes the background or physical environment in which the characters function and if the author uses intricate details, it helps the reader get drawn in and to keenly envision characters and actions in the story.

Tone is described as the writer's attitude toward a subject, the materials, or the readers, and it may be stated or implied. An author sets the tone of a literary work by the choice of words and details used. Attitudes that may be delivered in literature include playfulness, seriousness, humorous, pessimism, optimism, outrage, bitterness, depression, and joyfulness.

Mood is defined as the sense of feeling(s) in literary works. How the author presents or selects the setting, images, objects, and words in a story are all factors in creating the mood. Writers develop stories of mystery, humor, and romance based on how they incorporate the literary elements and describe the story.

Imagery and Figurative Language

Imagery is a specific use of language that appeals to the readers' senses. It may be used to describe people or objects and is influenced by the use of the five senses. Imagery is the act of forming mental pictures by the reader and to form these pictures while reading. Students need instruction and practice in the technique. When students use imagery, they increase their retention of the materials. However, to gain the necessary skills, they must have the ability to understand literal information, use prior real-world images and experiences, analyze details, comprehend author's purpose, predict upcoming content, and maintain a long-term memory of known images and information.

Methods that help teach the skill of imagery include providing background information to students, sharing concrete words and short sentences while making mental pictures, pointing out familiar words in stories, and teaching poetry and art.

Figurative language is the use of words, phrases, or other language structures that change the literal meaning of the words used. Figurative language uses the literal or ordinary words and constructs them in an imaginary way to add beauty, strength, or a different context to the structure. The use of figurative language may compare a person, place, thing, idea, concept, or characteristic to another in order to improve, magnify, strengthen, refine, and clarify meaning. The use of figurative language aids the reader in comprehension as it relates an unknown to a known entity.

Specific types of figurative language structures include the following:

Alliteration—The use of language in which the consonant sounds are repeated, generally at the beginning of a word or within words. This use develops the mood, creates melodic language, and helps the reader focus on important words, pointing out similarities and differences. For example, *The sneaky snake was snoring loudly as she slept soundly.*

Hyperbole—An exaggeration or use of a statement that enhances the effect of the words, which may or may not be realistic. A hyperbole is not meant to be taken literally or to confuse the reader, but rather to place emphasis on a particular point. For example, *It was such a hot summer that even the saguaro cactus was sweating.*

Idiom—A group of words with a special, more figurative meaning instead of the literal meaning. For example, *steal one's thunder* (to take the credit away from someone else). *Chandra planned a presentation on water resources, but Jack stole her thunder when he told the boss it was his idea.*

Metaphor—A figure of speech used as a comparison of two unrelated objects, concepts, or ideas without using the words *like* or *as*. For example, *The girl was a hog when it came to ice cream.*

Onomatopoeia—The use of words that are appealing to the sense of hearing and mimic sounds that aid in the description for the reader. For example, *boom, sizzle, tinkle, hiss, chiming, tolling, moan, groan, purr, squeak*

Oxymoron—A pair of words that when combined have the opposite meanings. For example, *found missing, exact estimate, tragic comedy, old news, small fortune, pretty ugly, jumbo shrimp*

Personification—The use of descriptive words in such a way as to give human characteristics to a nonhuman thing such as an object, idea, or animal. It helps to convey a particular feeling or attitude toward the item and allows the reader to form their own perception. For example, *The dog danced with joy when she was given a bone.*

Simile—A figure of speech that is a comparison of two unrelated objects, concepts, or ideas through the use of the words *like* or *as*. For example, *My words trickled off my tongue like raindrops on a windshield.*

Other Literary Devices

Authors use a variety of techniques, and methods to add interest and details to their narratives and stories. Listed here are some of the most common literary devices employed by authors.

Analogy—The comparison of similar objects, which suggests that since the objects are similar in some ways that they will probably be alike in other ways. For example, *Dogs are like babies. If you give them a lot of care and attention they will grow strong, healthy, and happy. If you neglect them, they will become weak, depressed, and sick.*

Dialogue—The use of conversation between characters in order to provide readers with insight into the characters' behaviors, motivations, and human interactions. Authors use this device to move the narrative along, to provide the personality of characters, to make the story flow naturally, and to make the story enjoyable.

Dramatic monologue—A speech or poem spoken by one character in order to share their innermost thoughts and feelings, which have been hidden throughout the story. The monologue comes at a climatic moment in the narrative and often reveals hidden truths about the character. For example, *In Shakespeare's tragedy* Hamlet, *Hamlet struggles with whether it is better to be alive or dead, to fight and suffer or to give up, which is an internal struggle that comes to light for the reader through his soliloquy "To be or not to be . . ."*

Exaggeration—The overstatement or the stretching of the truth in order to emphasize a point. For example, *The music was so loud it shattered my eardrums.*

Flashback—The device in which an author interrupts the story or narrative to go back and explain an earlier event or recall an earlier memory of a character. This allows the author to provide readers with insight to character motivation or behavior. For example, *In* Death of a Salesman *by Arthur Miller the character Willy Loman flashes back to memories of his dead brother, even talking to the dead brother during a card game.*

Foreshadow—A hint or clue that the author provides to the reader to suggest what will happen next or at sometime in the future in the story or narrative. For example, *When an author describes a setting in which a loaded gun hangs on the wall and then later in the narrative the gun is used.*

Irony—A device in which a word or phrase is used to mean the exact opposite of its normal meaning. Irony can also be used to show that a person, situation, statement, or circumstance is not as it usually appears. There are a variety of different types of irony, but the most common are verbal, dramatic, and situational. **Verbal irony** is when an author says one thing and means something else; **dramatic irony** is when an audience perceives something that a character in the literature does not know (tragic irony is a type of dramatic irony); and **situational irony** is a discrepancy between the expected result and actual results. For example, *In* Romeo and Juliet *(Shakespeare), when Romeo finds Juliet in a drugged death-like state, he believes that she is dead and kills himself. Then when Juliet awakes and finds Romeo, her love, dead, she kills herself with his dagger. This is an example of tragic irony (situational irony).*

Motif—The use of a recurring object, concept, element, word, phrase, or structure in order to draw the readers' attention to a specific point the author wishes to make. For example, *In "The Raven," by Edgar Allan Poe, the word "nevermore" is a motif.*

Symbol—A real or concrete object that is used to represent an idea or concept. For example, *The eagle due to its ability to fly often represents freedom; a dove stands for peace; and the raven in the poem by Poe stood for death.*

Reading and Communication Skills

Reading skills are critically important for individuals to have success in school as they are necessary for learning in all subject areas. They are also a necessity for functioning well in the daily activities of life. Students need instruction on reading a variety of expository and nonexpository text materials. As they mature and become adult consumers, they can make better decisions and be more informed in keeping themselves and their family safe if their reading skills are adequate. They will need to understand warnings on product labels; read materials to help care for their home, health, and family; and be able to access information in many venues. In modern society, they will also need to acquire a set of reading skills that focus on the technology age.

Promoting an interest in reading is a primary factor in developing future reading skills. The purpose of teaching reading is to instill in students that they may gain information from text, they can improve their communication skills with knowledge, and they may read for pleasure. There are many steps in the development of reading skills. If the instructor lacks motivation, students become disinterested in being better readers. Research suggests that students must advance from decoding skills to meaningful reading, but the longer this transition takes, the more probable it is that learning to read for pleasure will disappear.

Children learn to read and write through modeling, and many opportunities are available at home and at school on a regular basis. Parents who read aloud and use reading and writing in the home demonstrate the importance of these skills, and children absorb the purpose indirectly. When teachers encourage vocabulary growth and allow interactions with books and writing materials, children become interested in learning to read and write.

Children need a combination of continued structured and unstructured experiences with reading and writing, so they may use this previous knowledge in the application of their skills. Children must acquire knowledge about the printed word, with an understanding that letters become words, words become sentences, and sentences have meanings.

Creating a curriculum that focuses on reading and integrates other subject areas can be a challenge for educators. Educators must be cognizant of the scope and sequence established for the school curriculum as well as the standards set at the state level and the requirements at the district level. A reading program requires that teachers use a variety of strategies and methods and base their instruction on conducting individual diagnostics on all students. Curriculum development for reading and language arts should include instruction in phonemic awareness, phonics, spelling, reading fluency, grammar, writing, and reading comprehension strategies. A curriculum is a guide and not a substitute for a well-trained and effective teacher.

Developing **decoding skills** is the process of understanding that letters in text represent the sounds (phonemes) in speech. In order to learn how to decode words, a student must understand that letters in text represent the phonemes in speech. Some students have difficulty developing decoding skills as they lack phonological processing skills. Some students have problems developing decoding skills as they may not have received adequate instruction in the domains that are essential for acquiring decoding skills (print concepts, letter knowledge, alphabetic principle).

Essential skills that are indispensable in school and daily life include those related to reading examination directions, school work instructions, recipes, newspapers, telephone books, labels, community or traffic signs, and computer-related text. Students will be faced with reading map directions, application directions, product labels, insurance forms, and other important documents as they mature. Each of these types of readings require that students possess certain reading skills.

Following directions is an important life skill and requires that students possess special reading skills. Directions, whether specific or general, must be read carefully and completely to fully understand them, gain knowledge on how to use them, and provide the reader with confidence to finish the task or follow instructions. Students must learn direction reading skills in order to complete assignments, operate equipment, prepare meals, assemble materials, understand warnings, find locations via maps, follow sequential steps, read for fact or opinion, and so on.

Labels on products vary as does the vocabulary. They may offer information about the dose or side effects of a medical product or provide cautions or warning on a cleaning product. Labels include directions, abbreviations, and warnings specific to a product; therefore using special words, or unique vocabulary that may not be learned directly or used everyday. Understanding these words and knowing how they are used in context will make a difference in the interpretation by the reader.

Completing forms with personal information, such as work applications, insurance documents, or medical question-naires also pose the need for specific reading skills.

Communication is the ability to impart and share knowledge, opinions, ideas, feelings, and beliefs. Communication is present in a variety of formats in various cultures and our society. It may be spoken or written, explicit or implied, simple or complex, positive or negative, and passionate or reasonable. Socially, humans gather together according to understandings and beliefs about the things and events around them. People have the capacity to respond to these situations and events, and social bonding is generated through discussion and understanding. Communication is strong before, during, immediately after, and long after an event occurs. The ability to talk, discuss and respond to such events develops social, cultural, and community cohesion. There are four ways in which a society or culture communicate, which include:

- **Encounters**—Daily communications that happen as people interact with one another in their common environment. These relations may occur in the home, at work, in school, in the community, or on the computer.
- **Rituals**—These communications occur as part of a tradition, or established meeting or time when certain groups come together for discussions or in response to activities. This may include religious communications, holiday gatherings, rallies, protests, weddings, funerals, or scheduled meetings.
- **Crisis**—When society is faced with an issue of concern or a situation, people must be cooperative and make successful responses. During these times, communication is critical, and attention is vital. This may include a community fire, an earthquake, a flood, war, or other community or society emergency.
- **Deviants**—Societies must deal with people who are considered misfits or deviants, as they stray from societal norms and laws. Communication is important in outlining the requirements and in resolving situations.

Students learn to communicate through their models, explicit teaching, and their experiences. Their ability to communicate is often representative of their reading and writing abilities, since oral language development plays an essential role in both.

Means of Communication	
Mean	**Definition**
Symbolic names	Names identify people and places with groups, differentiate communities, and declare known and recognizable groups.
Specific vocabulary Jargon Lingo	Cultures and communities develop characteristic vocabulary. Being able to use this specific vocabulary demonstrates membership within the culture and society.
Heroes and villains	People in groups tend to single out certain people to talk about. Some are praised, and their actions endorsed (hero). Others are condemned, and their actions reprimanded. Both reflect societies' values and beliefs.
Proverbs	A set of values or sayings that impart wisdom within a culture and guide the society in their actions. ("A penny saved is a penny earned.")
Stories Myths Histories	Every culture, society, and community has symbolic narratives. Knowing the stories identifies a person as a member of the group. Most tell tales of success in crisis or the growth of a hero or the defeat of a villain.

Summaries and Paraphrases

Research demonstrates that when readers can compose **summaries** of the materials they read, active thinking, comprehension, and retention all increase. Using summaries helps individuals remember information, and they are better able to make applications in their daily lives.

There are several strategies suggested for the instruction of summary skills. One strategy taught to enhance student summarizing skills is called K-W-L. Students identify what they already know (K), prior to reading a passage and what they want (W) to find out. Then they decide what they learned and what else they want to learn (L) after reading. Another way to instruct students on summarizing is to guide them through specific steps, and scaffold these until they are independent:

- Select main ideas from sentences and paragraphs.
- Group ideas together that refer to the same subject.
- Paraphrase using only a few words.
- Restate using words that pertain to the summary ("in conclusion" and "so on").
- Eliminate those details that do not pertain to the main topic.

When summarizing, students should be able to do the following:

- Pull out main ideas.
- Focus on key details.
- Use key words and phrases.
- Break down the larger ideas.
- Write only enough to convey the general idea in brief.
- Take succinct but complete notes.

Students may also learn summarizing skills by constructing a graphic map to organize information in summary fashion. Students can use a story map to review what they have read or to retell the story. When students use maps, they can increase comprehension and make connections of the story elements.

Informational content, such as that found in school textbooks, may require additional types of strategies, as students may need to remember facts and apply concepts. Teaching students to summarize using an expository text may require a study strategy known as SQ3R (survey-questions-read-recite-review).

Full text: Earth's outer shell, called the lithosphere, was long thought to be a continuous and unbroken covering. However, the crust is actually a fluid arrangement of many irregular plates. These plates are made up primarily of solid rock 4 to 40 miles thick, which vary in size and shape, and have definite borders that cut through both continents and oceans. There are nine large plates and a number of smaller plates. These plates move constantly upon the mantle and are the cause of volcanic activity, landform development, and the creation of new crust.

Summarization: The earth's crust is made up of separate plates that move across the mantle. As these plates move, they help form the Earth's surface.

Knowing how to **paraphrase** (restating in different words) is a skill students need to acquire so they may use it when a literary work is too complicated to read or too difficult to understand in its original state. They may learn to review shorter segments or repeat a few sentences and paragraphs about what was read. They would then be able to make connections between the sentences and paragraphs to identify the author's styles, purpose, main ideas, and the concepts of the piece.

There are six steps to consider when paraphrasing:

1. Read and reread the original passage until the full meaning is understood.
2. Write the paraphrase on a separate sheet while not looking at the original.
3. Jot down a few key words.
4. Check the paraphrase with the original to make sure it accurately expresses all essential information in a new form.
5. Use quotation marks to identify any terms or phrases that have been copied exactly from the original source.
6. Record the source in order to give credit to the original.

Full text: Earth's outer shell, called the lithosphere, was long thought to be a continuous and unbroken covering. However, the crust is actually a fluid arrangement of many irregular plates. These tectonic plates are made up primarily of solid rock 4 to 40 miles thick, which vary in size and shape, and have definite borders that cut through both continents and oceans. There are nine large plates and a number of smaller plates. These plates move constantly upon the mantle and are the cause of volcanic activity, earthquakes, landform development, and the creation of new crust.

Paraphrase: The lithosphere is the outer covering of the Earth and is broken into plates. The tectonic plates are different sizes and shapes with varying thicknesses and move on top of the mantle. Mountains, valleys, volcanic activity, earthquakes, and new crust are all results of the tectonic plate movement.

Summarizing and paraphrasing serve many purposes. Writers may use them to do the following:

- Refer to work that leads up to the work now being written.
- Give examples of several points of view on a subject.
- Call attention to a position with which the author wishes to agree or disagree.
- Expand the breadth or depth of the writing.

Language and Words in Context

Language is the essence of communication and understanding words in context. To be able to understand language passages, whether written or spoken, individuals must first comprehend words or the vocabulary being used. Vocabulary is particularly important to reading success in school:

- When students know word meanings, their comprehension improves.
- When students have a proper vocabulary, their overall communication skills improve (speaking, listening, reading, writing).
- When students increase their word skills and communication abilities, they improve their self-confidence and social abilities.
- When students can adequately communicate, using appropriate vocabularies, and have success in reading, they improve in all areas of their school, work, and life.

According to research, students need vocabulary skills taught systematically and explicitly, through specific categories of words to help with acquisition and memory and for gaining success in reading, writing, speaking, and listening. These categories include the following:

- Subject or content area words, such as those related to science and math. These are words that may be used across the disciplines and found in different genres and glossaries.
- High-frequency or basic words, such as those used regularly in writing or reading. These may include words like *and, the, is, are,* and so on.
- Connector words or signal words that help students understand cause-and-effect relationships and related ideas. These may include words like *therefore, because, furthermore, although, additionally,* and so on.
- Difficult, challenging, or multiple meaning words that are new or related to a specific subject, like *phenomenon* (science), *attributes* (English), and *factors* (math or social studies). In teaching children to decode words or find the root word in more complex words, they will begin to develop work attack skills and apply previous learning to new words they face.
- Infrequent or unusual words that are encountered only when reading or listening to specific genres. For example, words that are more historically generated (time-related vocabulary) such as *carriage, dirigible,* or *asylum.*

Students should be provided vocabulary instruction in every subject area taught in school and not just through the reading teacher. Several methods are essentially effective in school programs:

- Pre-teach new vocabulary related to each lesson, concept, or subject area.
- Provide a variety of reading materials (genres) to support access to new words.
- Expose students to extended reading periods, so they have time in text.
- Talk, formally and informally, to students using new vocabulary or more complex sentences as models.
- Study the origin of words and explain the multiplicity of root words and how those change with the addition of a prefix or suffix.
- Play with multiple meanings of words and use resources such as dictionaries for independent searches.
- Allow time for discussion to enhance knowledge of words used in context.

Students gain vocabulary skills when they are faced with the task of deciphering the meaning of words based on the context given. Word context skills aid individuals in learning to decode words, extract meaning, and comprehend text. While reading passages, individuals may gain skills in the context clue area in five different ways:

Clue	Definition	Key Vocabulary	Example
Antonym clue	Words or phrases that indicate the opposite of an unknown word or concept	but, however, unlike, yet, in contrast, instead of	*Instead of* singing in a *mellifluous* voice, she sang with a *harsh* and *grating* voice.
Synonym clue	Words or phrases that have a similar or the same meaning as the unknown word or concept	that is, in other words, sometimes called, or, known as	The *ursine, commonly known as the bear,* tore through the camp's garbage.
Definition clue	Words or phrases that explain or define the unknown word or concept	means, the term, is defined as, can be delineated as a phrase by commas, italics, or boldface	*Raucous sounds, loud and harsh noises,* can be heard in the jungle.
General knowledge	Meaning is acquired from background knowledge or prior experience of the reader	The information is either familiar or common.	The *plethora* of balloons floated in the sky. There were a *myriad of colors* in the atmosphere.
Word analysis	Breaking down words into roots, prefixes, and suffixes to determine meaning	the meanings of individual roots, prefixes, suffixes (*un-* = not, *-able* = having a quality of)	The home team was undefeatable in their tournament play. *un – defeat – able* *not having the quality of being beaten*

Grammar

Because writing and reading are based on language, having a firm grasp of language is a fundamental skill for all readers and writers. There are many rules and guidelines that are employed when reading and writing, and each must be understood in order to develop a clear and concise ability to communicate. Grammar is a key factor in this communication development. Grammar can be defined as the rules and guidelines that are followed to write and speak in an acceptable manner. In the English language, parts of speech assist in the understanding of words and how to use the words.

Parts of Speech

There are eight parts of speech in the English language. Every word is a part of speech.

A **noun** is a word that names a person, place, thing, concept, idea, act, or characteristic. Nouns give names to everything that exists, has existed, or will exist in the world.

Common nouns refer to general ideas, objects, places, and concepts and are *not* capitalized. For example, girl, man, house, bridge, class.

Proper nouns refer to specific ideas, people, concepts, places, and objects and *are* always capitalized. For example, Haley, Chip, Arizona, Statue of Liberty, English.

Concrete nouns name things that are physical and can be touched. For example, table, bed, computer, truck.

Abstract nouns name something that cannot be seen or touched but can be thought or felt. For example, love, desire, distain, Buddhism, happiness, sickness.

Collective nouns name a group or collection of people, things, places, concepts, or characteristics. For example, family, team, flock, pod, group, bunch, dozen.

Compound nouns are made up of two or more words. For example, basketball, middle school, mother-in-law, toothpaste, blackboard.

Singular nouns refer to only one thing, person, place, idea, concept, or characteristic. For example, dog, teacher, leg, quiz, giraffe, boxer, happiness, sorrow.

Plural nouns refer to more than one thing, person, place, idea, concept, or characteristic. For example, butterflies, dogs, bikes, leaves, keys, volcanoes, religions, theories. There are rules for making nouns plural:

- Most words, simply add "s."
- If a word ends in "ch", "s", "ss", "x", "z" add "es."
- If a word ends in a "y" preceded by a consonant, change the "y" to "i" and add "es."
- If a word ends in "o" with a vowel right before the "o", add "s."
- If a word ends in "o" with a consonant right before the "o", add "es."
- If a word ends in "f" or "fe" in which the final sound is a *v* sound, change the "f" or "fe" to "ve" and add "s."
- If a word ends in "f" and the final sound remains the *f* sound, add "s."

A **verb** is a word that shows action(s) or a state of being. Verbs can also be known as linking verbs, which link the subject to the words that describe it. For example, jump, hop, skip, scream, throw, call, divide, is, has, been, was.

Action verbs are those that state a behavior or activity that can be done. For example, throw, eat, sleep, scream, cry, jump, enjoy, love, hug.

Linking verbs are those that do not express an action but connect the subject of the verb to additional information. For example, is, are, were, has been, have been, be, become, am.

Helping verbs are those that aid in the formation of tense and also voice of the main verb. For example, shall, will, should, would, could, must, can, may, have, had, has, do, did, is, are, was, were, am, being, been.

There are three principle *verb tenses*: past, present, and future. Verbs must be conjugated into these different tenses depending upon the time that the action is taking place. Verbs in a sentence should agree with one another and should coincide or match time sequences. If an action happened at the same time as another action, then the verbs must have the same tense. This holds true within sentences and also within paragraphs and narratives.

- Present tense—shows the action is happening now. For example, climb.
- Past tense—shows the action happened in the past or before (uses "ed"). For example, climbed.
- Future tense—shows that the action will happen (uses "will"). For example, will climb.

Verbs can also be *regular* and *irregular*. Regular verbs follow a distinct pattern and are predictable: past = ed, future = will. Irregular verbs have their own, individual form for each tense, which does not follow a pattern. Some irregular verbs are listed in the following table.

present	past	future (are preceded by the word "has", "had", or "have")
am, is, are	was, were	been
begin	began	begun
break	broke	broken
bring	brought	brought
catch	caught	caught
choose	chose	chosen
do	did	done
eat	ate	eaten
give	gave	given
go	went	gone
grow	grew	grown
know	knew	known
lay	laid	laid
lie	lay	lain

An **adjective** is a word used to describe a noun or pronoun. For example, green, courageous, minuscule, gigantic, colorful, sweet, sleepy, chaotic, unwary, slimy.

There are different types of adjectives, which are used in specific instances. Here are a few types and forms of adjectives.

- *Demonstrative adjective* singles out a specific noun; this, that, these, those (a noun must immediately follow). For example, *This* house is old, but *that* house is new and sturdy.
- *Compound adjective* is made up of two or more words and is hyphenated. For example, The *action-packed* movie held my dad's attention for two hours.
- *Indefinite adjective* gives the reader approximate information and does not tell exactly how much or how many. For example, *Some* students do not understand grammar.
- *Predicate adjective* follows a linking verb and describes the subject. For example, Mabel was *energetic*, but she is now *tired*.
- A *proper adjective* is formed by a proper noun and is always capitalized. For example, The *San Francisco* Bridge stretches a long way.
- A *common adjective* is any adjective that is not proper and is not capitalized. For example, The *lengthy* bridge stretches for miles across the *wild* sea.
- *Positive adjective* describes a noun or pronoun without comparing it to anyone or anything else. For example, Kayaking is an *exciting* sport that requires strength and balance.
- *Comparative adjective* compares two or more people, places, things, ideas, concepts, or characteristics. The adjective usually ends in *–er*. For example, Kayaking is *better* than canoeing.
- *Superlative adjective* compares three or more people, places, things, ideas, concepts, or characteristics. The adjective usually ends in *–est*. For example, Kayaking is the *most exciting* water sport. Mountain biking is the *hardest* type of biking.

- *Two-syllable adjective* shows comparison by the suffixes (*er/est*) or modifiers (*more/most*). For example, quicker, quickest or the most athletic or more athletic.

- *Three (or more) syllable adjective* requires the words *more/most* or *less/least* to express comparison. For example, more terrifying, most terrifying, less terrifying, least terrifying.

- *Irregular adjective* uses a completely different word to express the comparison. For example, good, better, best and bad, worse, worst.

An **article** is a word placed before a noun, which introduces the noun as specific (the) or nonspecific (a, an).

"The" delineates a specific person, place, thing, concept, idea, characteristic, or a plural noun. For example,

> Please get *the* brown coffee cup from *the* shelf.
>
> *The* stack of books is on the desk.
>
> I love *the* grey sweater Chip has.

"A" or "an" delineates a nonspecific person, place, thing, concept, idea, or characteristic. "An" is used for nouns that begin with a vowel. For example,

> Pick *a* ripe apple from the bin.
>
> Pick *an* apple off the tree.
>
> *A* space shuttle can travel faster than *an* airplane.

A **pronoun** is a word used in place of or to replace a noun. Pronouns include I, me, myself, you, yours, yourself, we, us, ours, he, she, his, her, hers, they, their, theirs, it, its. For example, "As the football sailed over the goalposts, *it* spun to the left (*it* replaces *ball*)."; "Haley finished the paper for *her* class as soon as *it* was assigned (*her* refers to *Haley,* and *it* replaces to the *paper*)."; "The children walked into *their* classroom late (*their* replaces *children*)."; "The dog chased *its* tail (*its* replaces *dog*)."

The *antecedent* is the noun that the pronoun replaces or is referring to. Every pronoun has an antecedent. The antecedent can be in the same sentence as the pronoun or in the previous sentences. All pronouns must coincide and agree with their antecedent in person, number, and gender. For example,

> Shirley painted her ceramic bowl a variety of colors. It was the most colorful in the class. She was very proud of it. (Shirley is the antecedent for *her* and *she* and ceramic bowl is the antecedent for *it*).

Personal pronouns replace nouns in a sentence. There are three types of personal pronouns: *Simple pronouns* such as I, you, we, it, he, she, they; *compound pronouns* such as myself, herself, himself, itself, ourselves, themselves, yourself; and *phrasal pronouns* such as one another, each other.

Singular pronouns express one person, place, thing, concept, idea, or characteristic. For example, I, you, he, she, and it.

Plural pronouns express more than one person, place, thing, concept, idea, or characteristic. For example, we, you, they, us, you all, and them.

Pronouns can function in many ways within a sentence. They can represent a subject, an object, or can show possession. There are three functions of pronouns:

- **subject**—When the pronoun is used as the sentence's subject (*I, you, he, she, it, we, they*). For example, *I* like to eat peanut butter and jelly sandwiches. (*I* is the subject.)

- **object**—When the pronoun is the object of a verb or prepositional phrase (*me, you, him, her, it, us, them*). For example, Don't kick *me*! (*me* is the object pronoun because it receives the action *kick*) For example, That food is way too spicy for *him* to eat (*him* is the object pronoun of the preposition "for").

- **possessive**—When the pronoun shows ownership or possession (*my, mine, our, ours, his, hers, their, theirs, its, your, yours*). For example, The pink lunchbox was *hers* (*hers* shows ownership of the *lunchbox*).

An **adverb** is a word that modifies a verb, an adjective, or an adverb. Adverbs tell how, when, where, why, how much, and how often. (Many adverbs end in -*ly* but not all.) For example,

> The snake slithered *quickly* across the floor. (*quickly* modifies the verb *slithered*)
>
> Mohave rattlesnakes are *very* deadly. (*very* modifies the adverb *deadly*)
>
> Rattlesnakes are *extremely* dangerous. (*extremely* modifies the adjective *dangerous*)

There are three types of adverbs.

Positive adverbs describe a verb, adjective, or adverb. For example, "She skipped *happily* on the playground."

Comparative adverbs compare two things. For example, "He plays the drums *more loudly* than his brother."

Superlative adverbs compare three or more things. For example, "The blue-ringed octopus is the *deadliest* cephalopod in the world."

There are also many uses for adverbs that can help a reader better comprehend the text and assist a writer in conveying their messages more clearly.

Time adverbs occur when the adverb tells how often, when, or how long. For example, "She will go mountain biking *tomorrow*."

Place adverbs occur when the adverb tells where, to where, or from where. For example, "The opossum hid *inside* the cardboard box."

Manner adverbs occur when the adverb tells how something is done (often ends in –*ly*) For example, "The tri-athlete trained *carefully* for the upcoming race."

Degree adverbs occur when the adverb tells how much or how little. For example, "I eat at my favorite restaurant *often*."

A **preposition** is a word or group of words that tells position, direction, or how two ideas are related to one another. Prepositions may be located at the beginning of the sentence or in the middle. For example, "The computer fell *off* my lap"; "The beard grew *around* Chuck's face"; "She danced wildly *across* the floor"; and "*During* the game, Ali shot eight free-throws."

Common prepositions include above, below, except, off, since, across, beneath, for, on, through, after, beside, from, on top of, to, against, between, in, onto, together with, along, beyond, inside, opposite, under/underneath, among, but, into, out, until, apart of, by, like, outside, up/upon, around, down, near, over, with/within, at, during, of, regarding, without.

A *prepositional phrase* contains the preposition, the object of the preposition, and the modifiers of the object. The phrase can function either as an adjective or adverb. For example, "Andrea swam *through the powerful undercurrent*." (Within the prepositional phrase, through = preposition; powerful = modifier; undercurrent = object.)

A **conjunction** is a word that joins together words or groups of words. Some examples include *when, and, but, so, or, because*. There are three types of conjunctions:

- *Coordinating* is when a conjunction joins a word to a word, a phrase to a phrase, or a clause to a clause; the words or phrases or clauses joined must be equal or of the same type. They include *and, or, but, for, nor, yet, so*. For example, "We should go see a movie *or* get coffee."

- *Correlative* is when a conjunction is used in pairs. For example, "*Either* you eat your cereal at the table, *or* you may not eat it at all."

- *Subordinating* is when a conjunction connects two clauses that are not equal or the same type; it connects a dependent to an independent clause. They include *if, although, as, when, because, since, though, when, whenever, after, unless, while, whereas, even though*. For example, "I like to mountain bike *because* it is challenging."

An **interjection** is a word or phrase used to show strong emotion or surprise. Interjections are usually delineated in a sentence by an exclamation point or a comma. For example, Hey!; Oh, no, a shark!; Look, a shooting star!; Yeehaw! I won the lottery!; Quick, get out of the way!; and Yea, it's time for lunch!

Sentence Types

Sentences are made up of one or more words and express a complete thought. Sentences begin with a capital letter and end with a punctuation mark (period, question mark, or exclamation point). Understanding how to construct and deconstruct a sentence helps readers comprehend meaning and helps writers by promoting structural sound writing. There are four sentence forms.

Simple sentences express one complete thought (independent clause). For example, "My back aches."

Compound sentences contain two or more simple sentences which are joined by a conjunction and/or punctuation. For example, "I usually workout in the morning, but this morning I had no time."

Complex sentences have one independent clause and one or more dependent clauses. For example, "Since my back aches, I think I should stretch out and do yoga today."

Compound-complex sentences possess two or more independent clauses and one or more dependent clauses. For example, "On Sunday Todd wants to play ping-pong, but I need to do my homework before I can go over to his house."

There are four major type categories into which sentences can be divided. The type of sentence helps the reader recognize voice and mood of the text as well as determine meaning and lends to the overall comprehension of text.

- *Declarative (.)*—A sentence that makes a statement or tells something and ends with a period. For example, "Writing a book is a lot of hard work."
- *Interrogative (?)*—A sentence that asks a question and ends with a question mark. For example, "Will you ever try to write a book?"
- *Imperative (.)*—A sentence that gives a command, often with you as the understood subject, and ends with a period. For example, "Study this book well."
- *Exclamatory (!)*—A sentence that expresses strong feeling or shows surprise and ends with an exclamation point. For example, "Wow, that book was great!"

Organization of Selection

Structure is the way writing is organized. Authors must construct what they have to say in a pattern or form in order to convey their message to the reader. Understanding the organization of a piece of writing helps the reader comprehend the text.

Specific patterns can be found within fiction, poetry, and nonfiction. The structure often can be used as a type of formula when reading various forms of literature. If the reader understands the organization of the literature, he may better understand the message that is being portrayed by the author.

Fiction	*Poetry*	*Non-Fiction*
story and plot	poetic devices	description and details
theme and meaning	rhythm	main idea and supporting details (introduction of the subject and the support to prove it)
conflict and climax	alliteration	
resolution and epiphany	metaphor	compare and contrast
assonance	simile	chronological order (time pattern)
	verses	cause and effect (situations/events and the reasons it occurs)
	stanzas	process (describes how an event happens)
	diction	

A **narrative** is a story. Sequence or time is found within a narrative along with description. Characters are an important ingredient within the sequence of events of the narrative. Every narrative has a beginning, middle, and end. There are certain components that must be present in order to make a piece of writing a story. These essential components are the elements of a narrative: pace, tone, point of view, characters, setting, theme, and plot.

Nonfiction is writing in which the information is presented as fact or as a truth. This does not necessarily mean that the information is accurate or valid. Some examples of nonfiction writing include, but are not limited to essays, journals, scientific papers, biographies, textbooks, user manuals, historic papers, encyclopedias, dictionaries, almanacs, book reports, memoirs, literary critiques, menus, and letters.

Poetry is written in groups of lines called stanzas. Poetry is a creative form of writing and employs many ingredients. Poems are meant to be read aloud and, therefore, must utilize many devices to ensure aesthetically pleasing reads. Poetic devices include rhyme, meter, alliteration, assonance, consonance, foot, onomatopoeia, repetition.

Rhyme is a scheme of how words are organized into patterns. There are two common types.

Internal rhyme—The rhyming of words within the line (<u>Peter</u>, <u>Peter</u> pumpkin <u>eater</u>).

End rhyme—The rhyming of words at the end of a line (What <u>now</u>/Brown <u>cow</u>)

Within poetry there are structural elements as well. These include verse and stanzas.

Verse—A verse is what a line of poetry written in meter is called. A verse is named based upon the number of feet per line. There are eight common types of verse: monometer, one foot; dimeter, two feet; trimeter, three feet; tertameter, four feet; pentameter, five feet; hexameter, six feet; heptameter, seven feet; octometer, eight feet.

A foot is one unit of meter. There are five basic feet in poetry:

1. *iambic*: an unaccented syllable followed by an accented syllable
2. *trochaic*: an accented syllable followed by an unaccented syllable
3. *spondaic*: two accented syllables
4. *anapestic*: two unaccented syllables followed by an accented syllable
5. *dactylic*: an accented syllable followed by two unaccented syllables

Stanza—How poems are broken up into sections/lines. There are six common stanzas: couplet, two lines; triplet, three lines; quatrain, four lines; sestet, six lines; septet, seven lines; octane, eight lines.

Fact versus Opinion

Students must learn to distinguish between fact and opinion in literature, so they are better able to decipher what information is reliable or true and what information is based on someone's personal ideas. They may also gain skills to better express their ideas and opinions in their speaking and writing. Students will learn these skills through the types of literature selected and explicit instruction. They have the responsibility of making an informed assessment about the materials they use to gain facts, opinions, and ideas.

	Definition	*Key Vocabulary*	*Examples*
fact	Statements or ideas that are indisputable and able to be verified and supported with evidence. Facts are often used in conjunction with research and studies in which information is gathered and analyzed.	demonstrated, according, confirmed, discovered	census studies, scientific laws, statistics, reviews, and research findings
opinion	Based upon a belief or a view and is not based upon evidence that can be verified.	claims that, believes, argues, view of, suspects that	letters to the editor, editorials, interpretations, and commentary

Information is available through many sources in our society. Students have access to television, Internet, newspapers, magazines, libraries, and so on. Students must learn to appraise the information provided as to its reliability and trustworthiness. To evaluate a resource, students should ask key questions that include the following:

What type of source is this? Whether the source is a primary or a secondary one can play a large role in determining the validity and reliability of the information. Did the source actually witness or experience the information, or are they simply relating it to the reader second hand?

Who is the source? Anyone can write literature or essays and post it on the Internet, claiming the information is valid. Check to see whether the source is an expert or authority on the subject or topic before judging the validity. Explore the background of the individual providing the information.

Is the information accurate? The information provided needs to be clear, concise, and of high quality. Check to see whether there are other sources that express similar information.

Is the information up to date? Make sure that the information given is the most current. Information that is out of date and/or out of touch with the times may not be accurate or may be obsolete.

Is the source biased? Check to see whether the source is an objective observer/participant or whether the source has something to gain by using the facts and providing the information (for example, politicians, TV infomercials, drug company findings, and so on).

The use of resource materials is one way to point out the facts and reliable information that may be present in written work. When students use resource materials, they will also study alphabetical order; they will learn to read for a purpose; they will discover how to retrieve information; and they will develop study skills. Determining the type of resource materials to use depends on the need, and students will learn to make these choices.

Many types of resources and ways to obtain information are available throughout the world. Students must learn to seek the proper resources and consider the validity and reliability of the source. The two categories for source information are *primary* and *secondary*.

Primary sources provide the reader with first-hand knowledge, ideas, and details of an event or activity. This allows the reader to get closer to the truth about a subject or event. Primary sources can be easily traced back to the author.

Five major types of primary sources include the following:

1. **Interviews**—Allows a person to talk directly with a person who has expert knowledge about a subject or topic.
2. **Presentations**—Use of lectures, displays, and exhibits provide first-hand information.
3. **Surveys**—Use of questionnaires help gather opinions and preferences directly.
4. **Diaries, journals, letters**—Supply information first hand through personal writings.
5. **Observation and participation**—Furnishes a person with a first-hand account and experience by watching an event or activity directly.

Secondary sources provide information gathered from a primary source. The facts and data are collected from a variety of primary sources and then organized and presented in a different format. Secondary sources can be traced to the author and at least one other person. Examples of secondary sources are magazines, newspapers, television news programs, and encyclopedias.

Inferences and Conclusions

Research suggests and practice concurs that making inferences and drawing conclusions from literary selections are two essential reading skills. Both of these skills have been added to high stakes criterion-referenced tests and are necessary in almost every subject area. Learning to infer, predict, conclude, or interpret are not single and independent skills, but are developed through a complex process and combination of skill building. When students are able to make inferences and draw conclusions, this enables them to transfer ideas from text into and from their knowledge and experience base, which is developing critical thinking skills useful in making daily informed decisions. Making inferences and drawing conclusions helps students to remain engaged in their learning, to process literal information, and to gain skills making predictions in other areas. Ellin Keene, author of *Mosaic of Thought*, states "To infer as we read is to go beyond literal interpretation and to open a world of meaning deeply connected to our lives."

Inferences are conclusions reached on the basis of evidence and reasoning. Inferring is a skill taught in many ways. Asking questions about a text can help instill inference making in readers. A reader is able to connect to a text when personal ideas, experiences, and prior knowledge are drawn upon to comprehend a text. A reader should have some background knowledge of the subject matter being read in order to read inferentially. Without some background knowledge, the reader may be lost and/or unable to comprehend the text fully. Context clues may be helpful to readers in making inferences. Proficient readers are also able to visualize and imagine the text that they have read. If a reader is able to visualize a text, then she can create precise and distinctive interpretations of the text, which allows the reader the ability to recall specific details read, draw conclusions, and recall the information. Inference also allows readers to absorb what is read, interpret what is read, and incorporate what is learned into one's life in the form of ideas, beliefs, and knowledge.

Types of Inference		
Type	**Definition**	**Example**
Location	The reader decides the place or setting, which helps the reader make connections and understand the situation.	The skyscrapers looked upon the sunset in awe. The flow of the Sears Tower was muted by the brilliance of the dying sun. (The reader can determine that the "place" is Chicago.)
Agent	The reader decides the role or occupation of the character or author, which helps the reader understand the implications of the character.	She meticulously scrubbed her hands before entering the operating room. Her fear of an infection attacking the patient rose as she saw a nurse cough before entering the sterile operating room. (The reader knows that the character is a doctor, but more specifically, probably a surgeon.)
Time	The reader decides when actions/things occurred, which can help the reader understand the situation.	Sir Pephen swung his sword with great vigor at the approaching knight. (The reader can conclude that the time of the text is during the medieval era.)
Object	The reader decides what item is being discussed, which helps the reader understand the implications of the object	George swung with such force that his hands slipped, and he lost control. The pitcher, seeing the impending situation, ducked quickly to avoid the flying mass. (The reader can reason that the object being discussed is a baseball bat.)
Action	The reader decides the activity taking place, which helps the reader understand implications and results of the action.	Haley ran her fingers across the strings creating a beautiful, melodic sound. (The reader concludes that Haley must be playing a guitar or another string instrument.)
Cause - effect	Reader decides the reason for something occurring, which helps the reader understand the implications of the situation.	Andrea and Justin were flopping on the ground in a spasmodic manner. Broken glass littered the ground and a puddle of water saturated the floor. The two gasped for air as their fins fluttered up and down. (The reader can infer that a fish bowl broke, and two fish are lying on the floor.)
Problem - solution	The reader decides how to solve the predicament, which forces the reader to draw upon past experience and knowledge and understand the results of actions.	Eric had a sore throat but was unable to see his doctor due to the holiday. His throat had been getting progressively worse since he had gotten up in the morning. (The reader knows that the problem is Eric has a sore throat and cannot reach his doctor. Now the reader will ask "What should Eric do? How can he solve this?")

(continued)

Types of Inference *(continued)*		
Type	*Definition*	*Example*
Feelings - attitudes	The reader decides why or how characters react or behave, which allows the reader to connect to and understand the characters.	After Oddie came back from the war, he felt tired and found that he had little patience for everyday toils. He struggled to remain calm during stressful situations and often found himself worrying about the well-being of his friends who did not come home. (The reader can assume that Oddie is having difficulty fitting back into everyday life due to the experiences of war.)

Following are the steps in teaching inferences:

- **Modeling**—The teacher shows how to do the skill. First the teacher explains the strategy being used. Then she demonstrates how to apply the skill to everyday life or various situations. Finally the teacher thinks aloud while reading to solidify the process of the skill.

- **Think-aloud**—The teacher states the steps and strategies being used as she reads a text. She states aloud the process of questioning, predicting, concluding, and judging.

- **Guided practice**—The teacher leads the students in practicing the skills taught. This is done in large group or small group so that each student has the same text. Students will follow the teacher's lead in producing the skill desired.

- **Independent practice**—This is the final stage in developing inference skills. The teacher monitors individual, paired, or small group practice of the skill learned. Students are encouraged to discuss their findings with one another and also to question each other's interpretations of the text.

Fiction and poetry enable readers to have a wide array of interpretations. These are difficult genres for readers to make inference within. Nonfiction and content area texts provide readers with a narrow range of interpretations. These are the best types of genre for making predictions, drawing conclusions, and making inferences.

Conclusions are the summing up of a text. Conclusions are reached when a reader combines the knowledge and information in their head with the knowledge and information received from the text read. Reaching conclusions is a learned skill important to reading skill development. It aids readers in realizing the main ideas or purpose of an author's intent. Individuals learn to make decisions based on presented information and answer their own questions about text. Being able to draw conclusions requires the skill of critical reading, which is acknowledging and understanding facts.

For example,

I start life green but when I grow I can turn yellow.

I am slightly curved most of the time.

I wear a protective "coat" that you must open to see my insides.

I can be made into bread or pie or used with ice cream.

What am I?

The reader knows bananas go from green to yellow as they ripen; bananas are curved slightly; bananas have peels; you must peel a banana to eat it; banana bread and banana pie and banana splits are all made with bananas. Therefore, the reader can safely conclude that this is a banana.

I am portable.

I store a lot of information.

I can help you with work documents, music, and pictures.

I often fit onto your lap.

What am I?

The reader knows phones, computers, calendars, water bottles, and so on are all portable; computers, phones, and calendars store a lot of information; phones and computers can help with work documents, music, and pictures; laptops fit onto a lap. Therefore, the reader can identify the object as a laptop computer.

When students can adequately make inferences or draw conclusions, they will demonstrate the abilities to also decipher meaning, relate to facts, identify author's intent, and generalize and summarize the information.

To be well-versed in using inference skills, students need to be active readers, possess appropriate vocabulary, have strong memory skills, and possess varied background knowledge.

Activities used to build upon inference and conclusion skills include the following:

- Promote word-level work.
- Enhance vocabulary development.
- Practice decoding skills.
- Conduct text-level work.
- Ask questions.
- Use working memory.
- Make predictions.
- Use prior knowledge and experiences.
- Improve listening skills and communications.
- Select cross-discipline texts.
- Present proper genre.
- Use aural tasks.
- Learn to paraphrase.
- Refer to graphics and photos.

Purposes for Writing and Speaking

To enhance writing and reading skills, students need multiple opportunities within their environment that are full of symbolic play and oral language experiences. Whether using listening skills to attend to a speaker or using the language in their own spoken words, young students learn the meanings and use of words and how to combine words to make sense of thoughts. Being exposed to sounds, words, gestures, and so on enable children to build upon their vocabularies.

When stories are read aloud, listening skills are improved and language skills are increased, both critical to speaking and writing well. Reading books aloud and allowing adequate time for discussion and contemplation helps children to internalize aspects of the stories. They need time to talk about and analyze the pictures with the stories. They also need time to talk about the books and stories so they can determine their feelings and learn how to respond to the knowledge gained from the readings, as this aids them in making connections.

When students are learning to write, it is essential that they talk about their ideas, activities, experiences, and opinions. By discussing ideas with another, the student is better able to place their own words into print form.

Speaking requires the speaker to be knowledgeable and clearly state ideas, facts, or opinions. Listening skills are necessary in conversational speaking. Listening is an active process that requires the listener to hear, understand, and judge what a speaker presents.

Being a good listener and an expressive speaker depends on a person's grasp of language.

Three components of listening that are essential to comprehension are as following:

- **Hearing**—Able to repeat a piece of information previously stated
- **Understanding**—Able to process information heard, asking pertinent questions, and forming responses
- **Judging**—Able to form opinions and analyze information stated

When presenting information, a speaker should consider the following:

- **Subject**—What information is presented (informative, persuasive, entertaining) and how (direct or indirect)
- **Audience**—What are the background, needs, and wants of the audience
- **Themselves as a speaker**—What preparations should be made
- **Occasion**—What is the time and place of the speech or presentation

Writers must consider many things when writing: audience, topic, purpose, and mode. Each of these considerations will help convey the author's motivation and message. There are four modes of writing with which writers should be familiar.

Modes of Writing			
Mode	**Definition**	**Verb**	**Example**
Descriptive	Used to create a detailed and vivid picture in the reader's mind. Descriptive writing follows this pattern: • elaborate use of sensory details that enhance or define the central idea • details that go beyond the general • details that allow the reader to picture or experience the story	describe elaborate expand show	cookbooks, poems, narratives, character profiles
Expository (informational)	Gives information about a topic, is often objective and nonemotional. Expository writing follows this pattern: • development of a main idea • support of the main idea using examples, details, and/or facts • presentation of logically organized information	explain provide clarify define instruct	letters, definitions, guide-books, newspaper/magazine articles, pamphlets, comparison/contrast essays, cause-effect essays, reports, research papers, literary analysis
Narrative	Recounts a personal event or experience and tells a story based upon a real or imaginative occurrence. Narrative writing follows this pattern: • the use of POV (1st, 2nd, or 3rd) • develops plot, characters, setting • dialogue occurs • showing, not telling • the events are organized in time-order sequence	tell spin report relay relate account	poetry, short stories, novels, personal essays, tall tales, folk tales, plays

Mode	Definition	Verb	Example
Persuasive	Attempts to convince the reader of a certain point of view or opinion or belief or to take a specific action. Persuasive writing follows this pattern: • topic or issue stated • position of writer clearly stated • argument supported by reasons, examples, and/or facts	convince state argue	letters to the editor, editorials, advertisements, advice columns, award nominations, pamphlets, petitions, opinion writing

Writing Process

The development of writing consists of eight stages, and in order for writers to fully understand language and its usage, they must progress carefully through each stage. Teachers and other educators must be cognizant of these stages in writing development in order to clearly aid students in acquiring their writing skills.

1. **Scribbling:** Is a random collection of marks on a paper used by a young writer to express ideas, which may be large and circular, and in some ways resemble drawing but not letters or print.

2. **Letter-like symbols:** More advanced than scribbling, letter-like shapes and numbers begin to randomly form allowing the emerging writer the opportunity to explain and tell about his "writing."

3. **String of letters:** Now the writer has developed an awareness of sound-symbol relationships, although may not match the letter to the sound. Letters are forming more legibly and often written as capital letters.

4. **Beginning sound emergence:** The writer tends to make more sense in his work and matches the pictures that accompany it. The writer is more able to understand the comparison of a letter and a word.

5. **Consonants represent words**: The writer creates more sentences that express ideas and the spaces become more frequent between words, while lowercase letters appear with uppercase letters.

6. **Initial, middle, and final sounds:** Most words are spelled phonetically, but sight words, familiar names, and environmental print are spelled correctly. The writer tends to have more legible and readable writing.

7. **Transitional phase:** The writing has become more readable and is advancing toward conventional spelling, as the writer is more familiar with standard form and standard letter patterns.

8. **Standard spelling:** The writer is capable of decoding words and correctly spelling most words, as the writer has an understanding of root words, compound words, contractions, and analogies.

With the writing process comes the development of spelling. Young children follow general stages to achieve proper spelling skills and habits. When children first begin to associate marks on paper with words, they use *invented spelling* as they attempt to spell words by using their own judgment about how a word looks or sounds. Sometimes children are able to identify some letters and sounds during this period.

The stages of spelling development include the following:

- **Precommunicative**—Symbols are used to represent the alphabet; however there is no letter-sound correspondence, no deciphering of upper and lowercase letters, and no concept of left-to-right directions.

- **Semiphonic**—Letter-sound correspondence appears, and single letters are used to represent words, sounds, or syllables with sounds helping to spell words in order of initial, final, and medial sounds.

- **Phonetic**—Each sound heard is represented by a letter or group of letters with vowels appearing in this stage.

- **Transitional**—The rules of spelling are learned and influence the use of all letters present in a word but may not be in the correct order and vowels appear in every syllable.

Basic spelling guidelines are as following:

- *i* before *e* except after *c* or when the sound produced sounds like *a* (neighbor). Exceptions to this rule: counterfeit, either, financier, foreign, height, heir, leisure, neither, seize, sheik, species, their, weird.
- Silent *e* at the end of a word means to drop the *e* before adding the suffix that begins with a vowel. For example, state = stating = statement; like = liking = likable; use = usable = useful.
- If *y* is the last letter in the word preceded by a consonant, change the *y* to *i* when adding a suffix. For example, hurry = hurried; happy = happiness; beauty = beautiful.
- One-syllable words ending in a consonant preceded by one vowel, double the final consonant before adding a suffix that begins with a vowel. For example, pat = patting; god = goddess; hum = humming.

Being able to write in an effective manner is a skill that must be continually practiced. There are key traits that effective writing contains. In the **six traits approach,** the key components aid learners of all abilities to access and use good writing. It breaks the difficult process of writing into six smaller processes.

- **Ideas**—The message that presents the purpose, includes the theme, the main idea, and the details to engage the reader and deliver understanding.
- **Organization**—Constructing the piece into the proper format, using a beginning, a middle and an end to pursue the purpose.
- **Voice**—The personal and unique style of the writer that provides the reader a connection and an interest in the piece.
- **Word choice**—The use of words, phrases, and language selected by the writer to create the appropriate meaning.
- **Sentence fluency**—The manner in which the writer composes the sentences and paragraphs to give a flow to the piece that is rhythmic, and easy to read.
- **Conventions**—The grammar, spelling, punctuation, and word use that is considered when the piece is edited to support its meaning and purpose.

Upon acquisition of writing skills, students can then move into the process of writing. Although each writer is different and approaches the task of writing in a different way, there are logical steps that will help a writer. Although these are a set of steps writers may move through in a liquid motion, writers may revisit a previous step as needed throughout their writing. There are six basic steps taught in the writing process:

1. **Pre-writing**—Generate ideas for writing and gather details
2. **Rough draft**—Write ideas on paper and ignore conventions
3. **Reread**—Proof the work, fit the purpose and order details
4. **Revise**—Improve how information is presented and create more details
5. **Edit**—Review writing for mechanics and grammar usage
6. **Final draft**—Prepare a complete and final copy

Stages of the Writing Process		
Stage	*Description*	*Techniques Used*
Prewriting	generate ideas for writing gather details	brainstorm read literature create life maps use webs use story charts examine word banks determine form, audience, voice

Stage	Description	Techniques Used
Rough draft	write ideas on paper ignore conventions	take notes use outlines use webs
Reread	proof the work fit purpose order details	read aloud to self conduct peer edit
Revise	improve how information is presented improve details	remove unneeded words add details and adjectives accept peer suggestions add imagery
Edit	review writing for mechanics and grammar usage	spell check grammar check
Final draft	rewrite final copy type final copy number the pages	publish the work

Terminology

Listed here are some additional language terms with which you should be familiar. This is not a comprehensive list of vocabulary terms and not all terms will be used in the actual Praxis exam.

- **affix**—Attachment to a base or root word. For example, unfit (un), premeditate (pre), teacher (er), department (ment), monkeys (s).
- **alphabetic principle**—A foundation of reading in which the student realizes that letters represent sound and speech.
- **analogy clues**—Readers are able to draw connections between patterns, simple words, and syllables. Being able to compare known words to unknown words helps readers determine sounds and make-up of new words.
- **antonym**—A word having the opposite meaning of another. For example, antonyms of love are hate, despise, detest, abhor, intolerable, loathe, contempt, and so on.
- **assonance**—A poetic device in which a repetition of vowel sounds occurs.
- **comprehension**—A foundation of reading in which the student is critically thinking and processing the content read.
- **consonance**—A poetic device in which a repetition of consonant sounds anywhere within words occurs.
- **context clues**—The ability to use words, meaning, and context to extract meaning of unknown words. Context clues alone are not enough to predict word meaning and therefore must be accompanied by other clues such as phonics or comparison or word structure.
- **digraph**—Combination of two letters possessing a single sound. For examples, head = *ea*, chance = *ch*, ring = *ng*, path = *th*.
- **dipthong**—Two vowels in which the sound begins at the first vowel and moves toward the sound of the second vowel. For example, snout = *ou* and boy = *oy*.
- **fluency**—A foundation of reading in which the student reads with expression, is automatic and flowing (does not require comprehension).
- **grapheme**—A letter or letters that represent one phoneme; the smallest meaningful unit within a writing system. For example, all the letters of the alphabet and cat = c, a, t = three graphemes.

- **homonym**—Words that have the same pronunciation and spelling but different meanings. For example, left (direction, opposite of right) and left (past tense of leave), bear (animal) and bear (to carry), mouse (animal) and mouse (computer component), mean (rude) and mean (average) and mean (to define).

- **homophone**—Words that are spelled differently, pronounced identically, but have different meanings. For example, two, to, too; hour, our; aero, arrow; isle, aisle; ball, bawl; sweet, suite; hear, here; pair, pear; pain, pane; rain, reign; sighs, size.

- **homograph**—Words that have the same spelling but different meanings and may or may not be pronounced differently. For example, read (*past tense*), read (*present tense*), dove (*bird*), dove (*past tense of dive*), close (*shut*), close (*near*), wind (*to turn*), wind (*blowing air*)

- **meter**—A poetic device that is a measure of the rhythm of the poem; the accented and unaccented syllables.

- **morpheme**—Smallest meaningful unit of speech, which can no longer be divided. For example, in, come, on.

- **phoneme**—Distinct unit of sound found within language that helps distinguish utterances from one another.

- **phonemic awareness**—A foundation of reading in which the student realizes that speech is broken into individual sounds; in the English language, there are 44 found within the 26 letters of the alphabet.

- **prefix**—Word or letters placed at the beginning of a root or base word to create a new word or alter the meaning of the root. For example, un-, pre-, non-, a-, tri-, bi-, dis-.

- **print concept**—A foundation of reading in which the student understands that letters have sounds and they form words.

- **repetition**—The stating of a word or phrase more than once which adds rhythm or focus.

- **suffix**—Morpheme added to the end of a root or base word to form a new word or to alter the meaning of the root. For example, -ing, -er, -tion, -fy, -ly, -it, -ous.

- **symbolic clues** (pictures)—Illustrations and graphics can provide assistance in the identification of words.

- **synonym**—A word that means exactly the same or nearly the same as another word. For example, say, speak, tell, vocalize, voice, declare, state, remark, mention, observe, announce, comment, respond, allege, profess, note, and so on.

- **syntactic clues** (word order)—Looking at the order and structure of words the reader can determine meaning based upon the part of speech.

- **verbals**—Words made from verbs and have the power of a verb, but acts like another part of speech.

- **word structure clues**—Recognizing frequent letter groups. Included in this category are prefixes, suffixes, and inflectional endings.

Web Sites

The following web sites are provided to examinees to gather information that may be helpful during study periods and for research related to classroom work.

Note: At the time of the development of this book, the Internet sites provided here were current, active, and accurate. However, due to constant modifications on the Internet, web sites and addresses may change or become obsolete.

http://www.rif.org/	Reading is Fundamental
http://www.ncte.org	National Council of Teachers of English
http://www.readwritethink.org/	Read, Write and Think
http://www.reading.org/	International Teachers of Reading
http://www.eric.ed.gov/	Educational Resources Information Center (ERIC)
http://www.free.ed.gov/subjects	Federal Resources for Education Excellence: Language Arts

Mathematics

Mathematics is a discipline based upon the concepts of change, space, structure, and quantity. It constructs conclusions systematically and clarifies relationships between numbers, problems, solutions, and patterns. Math is rampant within our society and permeates many fields ranging from educational to business to scientific to financial to medical. It is visible in everyday life when individuals must grocery shop, pay bills, calculate costs, balance a checkbook, and determine tax percentages.

Number Sense and Basic Algebra

Number sense is the ability to understand numbers and their relationships. This skill develops gradually through experiencing numbers, exploring numbers, and relating numbers in a variety of contexts. Number sense should encompass all kinds of numbers (whole, fraction, decimal, percent, integer, rational, and so on). It is the ability to progress beyond basic numeration concepts and the reading and writing of numerals. Skills found with number sense include size relationship (lesser than or greater than, smaller or larger, close or the same), real world connections (numbers in life, daily use of numbers, what to do with numbers), and approximations/rounding (estimations).

There are different types of numbers used in mathematics. These may include natural, whole, integer, rational, prime, even, odd, and complex. The most common numbers used in daily computations are rational numbers. Rational numbers include all numbers, all fractions, all decimals, and all negative numbers.

There are four basic operations to be familiar with when computing any math problem: addition, subtraction, multiplication, and division.

Addition

Carrying (regrouping) is the basic process used in addition. Count by ones in the right hand column, tens in the next column to the left, hundreds in the next column to the left, and so forth. After the sum of two numbers in any column exceeds nine (reaches ten) the amount greater than ten is kept, and the rest carried into the next column on the left.

13 added to 59

Adding the units column 3 plus 9 yields 12 or one 10 and two 1s. The 10 is carried to the left and the 2 remains in the units column. Then add the tens column, 1 and 5 and 1, which yields the sum of 7 tens (70). Therefore, the sum of 13 and 59 is 72.

Subtraction

Borrowing (regrouping) is the basic process for subtraction. Subtract the units column first and if the **subtrahend** (number subtracted from another) is larger that the **minuend** (number to be subtracted from), one must be borrowed from the next column to the left. Then subtract the tens column, then the hundreds, and so on, borrowing as needed.

167 subtract 29

First subtract the units column 7 minus 9. The subtrahend is larger than the minuend, so you must borrow from the tens column. 60 now becomes 50, and the ten borrowed is moved to the 7 in order to make 17. Now the units column becomes 17 minus 9, which yields 8. Then move onto the tens column, 50 minus 20 equals 30. Next, move to the hundreds column and take 0 away from 100, which yields 100. The difference of 167 and 29 is 138 (100 + 30 + 8).

Multiplication

The basic process for multiplication is long multiplication or grade school multiplication. When faced with a multiplication problem, multiply the **multiplicand** (the number being multiplied) by each digit in the **multiplier** (the number of times to multiply). After this has occurred, add the results. This procedure is based upon three concepts:

- Place value system
- Memorization of multiplication table
- Distributive property of multiplication over addition

    247 multiplied by 3

247 is 2 hundreds, 4 tens, and 7 units. 7 units taken three times is 21; 4 tens taken three times is 12 tens (120); and 2 hundreds taken three times is 600; therefore, 600 and 120 and 21 added together gives the final product of 741.

Division

The basic process for division is long division and involves the quotient, remainder, divisor, and dividend. The **divisor** (how many times to divide) is placed into the **dividend** (the number being divided) to yield a **quotient** (answer). When dividing, the operation is conducted from largest place value to the smallest place value (left to right). This procedure is based upon three concepts:

- Firm grasp of basic multiplication facts
- Subtraction
- Place value

    7521 divided by 3

The 3 can be put into 7 (in the thousands place) two times, leaving a remainder of 1. The 5 (in the hundreds place) is then dropped down to make 15. 3 goes into 15 three times, yielding 15 with no remainder. The 2 (in the tens place) is dropped down to make 02. 3 can be put into 2 zero times for a product of 0 and leaving a remainder of 2. Finally the 1 (in the units place) is dropped down to yield 21. The 3 can be divided evenly into the 21 seven times with no remainder. Therefore, the quotient is 2307.

Place Value

Place value is based upon groupings of ten. It is the basic foundation for all mathematical operations. As the number progresses from the right of the decimal point to the left, its value increases.

Whole Numbers

Millions	Hundred Thousands	Ten Thousands	Thousands	Hundreds	Tens	Units
1000000	100000	10000	1000	100	10	1
10 hundred thousands	10 ten thousands	10 thousands	10 hundreds	10 tens	10 units	one

For example,

    6782 is 6 thousands, 7 hundreds, 8 tens, and 2 units, or 6,000 + 700 + 80 + 2

    360 is 3 hundreds, 6 tens, and 0 units or 300 + 60

    79 is 7 tens and 9 units or 70 + 9

Place value is also used for decimal concepts. As the number moves further to the right of the decimal, its value begins to decrease in amount. For instance, 0.5 is larger than 0.005, 0.0005, and 0.00005.

Units	Decimal Point	Tenths	Hundredths	Thousandths	Ten Thousandths	Hundred Thousandths	Millionths
1	•	.1	.01	.001	.0001	.00001	.000001

For example,

0.894 is 0 units, 8 tenths, 9 hundredths, and 4 thousandths or $0.8 + 0.09 + 0.004$

3.25 is 3 units, 2 tenths and 5 hundredths or $3 + 0.2 + 0.05$

6.1 is 6 units and 1 tenth or $6 + 0.1$

Place value plays an important role when ordering numbers. The basis of greater than and less than, larger versus smaller, and estimation all rely upon place value. When making judgments on less than or greater than, place value allows the numbers to be ordered and organized. When looking at numbers to order from largest to smallest, you must compare numbers based upon their numeric value as well as their placement of value. And when making estimations that may include rounding, place value guides the structure of the number.

Which is greater in value 18,634 or 18,638?

Evaluate the numbers by place value in order to determine which is greater. Each number has the following in common: 1 ten thousand, 8 thousands, 6 hundreds, and 3 tens. Where the two numbers differ is in the units place. This is where one must look in order to make a judgment of value. Since 8 units is greater than 4 units 18,638 is greater than 18,634.

Place the following numbers in numerical order from largest amount to smallest amount: 2538, 2583, 3528, 3258.

First look at the values of each number (they are each within the thousands). Now look for the largest number by comparing first the thousands place, then the hundreds place, next the tens place, and finally the units place. Since the question asks for the numbers to be ordered from largest to smallest, search for the larger thousand value (**3**,528 and **3**,258). Now look at the hundreds value place to determine the biggest (3,**5**28 and 3,**2**58). Since 500 is larger than 200, there is no need to continue to compare the tens place and units place. There are still two values to be compared in order to answer this question. Again, compare the thousands place value, then the hundreds place value, the tens place value, and units place value. Since each number has 2,000 and 500, the comparison of value must be made at the tens place (2,5**8**3 and 2,5**3**8). Because 80 is larger than 30, the ordering from largest amount to smallest amount can be completed: 3528, 3258, 2583, 2538.

Round to the nearest hundred: 2,890,897.

When rounding a number, two rules must be employed:

1. If the number immediately to the right of the place being rounded is greater than 5, it increases the number by one place value and if the number is less than 5, the number is left as it is.

2. When the number is rounded either up or down, all numbers to the right must be made into zeros.

To complete the problem, find the hundreds place (2,890,**8**97). In order to round to the nearest hundred, the tens place must be evaluated using the rules above (2,8990,**8**97). Since the nine is greater than 5, the number must be rounded up or increased by one place value. To complete the solution, use the second rule and turn all numbers to the right into zeros, yielding the answer 2,890,900.

Estimating to Solve a Problem

Estimations can be used to solve problems or to evaluate the reasonableness of an answer. When faced with the following problem, estimations can help determine the reasonableness of the answer.

1. Shirley has $15,678 in savings that she would like to split between her 4 grandchildren. Would it be wise of Shirley to say that each grandchild will get more than $3,000?

1. Use estimation to determine this answer, as it does not require an exact calculation.

   Round $15,687 up to $16,000.

   Divide this by 4.

   An estimated answer would be $4,000 for each grandchild.

   It would be valid for Shirley to say that each grandchild would get more than $3,000 but less than $4,000.

2. Farmer John needs his chickens to produce at least 500 eggs this year. If the chickens produce an average of 42 eggs a month, will John attain his quota?

2. Use estimation to determine the answer, as it does not ask for an exact calculation.

   Round the average of 42 eggs down to 40.

   Multiply 40 by 12 (months in the year).

   An estimated answer would be 480 eggs produced.

   It would be reasonable to say that Farmer John will not attain his quota based on the average eggs laid each month by his chickens.

3. Sadie makes $7.15 per hour at a local retail store. She wants to save up to buy a plane ticket to visit her brother in Argentina. If the plane ticket costs $845.71, approximately how many hours does Sadie need to work in order to purchase the ticket?

3. Use estimation to determine the answer, as it does not ask for an exact calculation.

   Round her pay to $7 and the ticket to $850.

   Divide 850 by 7.

   7 goes into 850 approximately 121 times.

   Sadie needs to work approximately 121 hours in order to purchase the plane ticket.

Ratios, Proportions, Percents

These three terms are imperative in not only mathematics, but in business and science as well. Each term represents mathematical information in a similar manner yet each is very distinct in its own way.

Ratio

A **ratio** is a comparison between a pair of numbers. For example, if there are six boys and ten girls in a classroom, the ratio of boys to girls is 6:10 or 6/10 or 6 boys to 10 girls.

When writing a ratio, the same unit of measure must be used. For example, to express the ratio of 1 hour to 5 minutes, the ratio cannot be written using both hours and minutes as units. First a conversion must be made from hours to minutes in order to obtain the same unit of measure for both values. One hour is equivalent to 60 minutes, so the ratio may be written as 60:5 or 60/5. This ratio may also be reduced or simplified into smaller terms. Five can be used as a factor to reduce the ratio to 12:1.

Ratios can also be used to interpret illustrations. For example, find the ratio of the shaded portion to the unshaded portion of the following illustration:

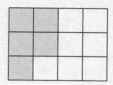

Since there are 5 shaded squares and 7 unshaded squares, the ratio of shaded to unshaded should read 5:7.

Proportion

A **proportion** is a ratio that is written with an equal sign between the two ratios, which are equal to one another. For example, $\frac{6}{8} = \frac{12}{16}$ or 3:4 = 6:8.

> **1.** The ratio of blue shirts to pink shirts in a store is 4:7, and there are 232 blue shirts. How many pink shirts are there?

To solve for an unknown number in a proportion, complete the following steps: (X is the unknown value)

1. Set up a proportion $\qquad\qquad\qquad\qquad$ $4:7 = 232:X$

2. Write the proportion in fraction form $\qquad$ $\frac{4}{7} = \frac{232}{X}$

3. Solve for X using cross multiplication $\qquad$ $(a/b = c/d \rightarrow a*d = b*c)$

$$4*X = 232*7$$

$$4X = 1624$$

$$X = \frac{1624}{4}$$

$$X = 406$$

Therefore, there are 406 pink shirts in the store.

Sometimes proportions are inverse proportions. This means that they will vary in opposite directions; while one term increases, the other decreases. For instance, the more people working on a project, the less time it will take to complete; the greater the demand for a commodity, the less time it will last; the bigger the pizza, the more people it will feed. In this situation, the proportion must be set up much differently to accommodate for the increase of one term while there is a decrease in the other term.

To solve an inverse proportion, complete the following steps:

1. Make a ratio of one type of term (minute, people, volume, etc.).
2. Make a ratio of the other term (weight, distance, time, etc.).
3. Invert one of the ratios (flip it upside down).
4. Cross multiply to solve for X.

> **1.** If 9 people can build a house in 6 days, how long will it take 3 people to do the same job? (This is an inverse proportion because the fewer the people, the longer it will take to build the house.)

1. Set up the proportions to solve (people = days). $9:3 = 6:x$

Write the proportions in fraction forms. $\dfrac{9}{3} = \dfrac{6}{x}$

Invert the first fraction. $\dfrac{3}{9} = \dfrac{6}{x}$

Solve for x using cross multiplication. $(\dfrac{a}{b} = \dfrac{c}{d} \rightarrow a*d = b*c)$

$3*x = 9*6$

$3x = 54$

$x = \dfrac{54}{3}$

$x = 18$

It takes 3 people 18 days to build the house.

---

2. If a corn field can be harvested by 6 machines in 5 hours, how many hours will it take if 2 of the machines break and cannot be used?

---

2. Ratio of machines = 6:4. (There are 4 machines because out of 6 total 2 are broken: $6 - 2 = 4$.)

Ratio of hours = $5:x$

$\dfrac{6}{4} = \dfrac{5}{x}$

$\dfrac{4}{6} = \dfrac{5}{x}$ (invert one of the ratios)

$4*x = 6*5$

$4x = 30$

$x = 7.5$ hours

It will take 4 machines 7.5 hours to harvest the field.

Percent

The term percent, when broken down into its literal components, means "per one hundred." A percent is represented by the % symbol. Percentages can be written in three mathematical expressions; all are equivalent to one another. For example, twenty percent is 20% or .20 or 20/100.

There are many ways to use percentages in calculations. Each calculation requires knowledge of multiplication, decimal, place value, and division concepts.

---

1. What is 45% of 250?

---

1. 45% of "something" requires a set up for cross multiplication. Simply stated this means the percentage multiplied by "the something." The easiest way to calculate this is to change the percentage into a decimal and then multiply the decimal by the number.

45% = 0.45 (To calculate the decimal of a percentage, divide by 100.)

$0.45 * 250 = 112.5$

2. What percentage of 326 is 91.28?

2. Set up the cross multiplication fractions.

$\frac{x}{100} = \frac{91.28}{326}$ (cross multiply)

$326X = 9128$ (divide by 326 to isolate the X)

$X = 28\%$

3. 32 is what percent of 50?

3. Divide the number you have by the number possible and multiply by 100 to obtain the percentage.

$32 \div 50 = 0.64$

$0.64 * 100 = 64\%$

4. A pair of shoes is on a 15% off sale rack. The sale price is $68. What was the original price?

4. The regular price is denoted by x, and the discount is 15% less than x. The sales price is $68. There is enough information to solve. The equation is written as follows:

$x - (0.15)x = 68$ Remember there is an invisible 1 in front of the first x, so it really states $1x - 0.15x = 0.85x$.

$0.85x = 68$ (Divide by 0.85 to isolate the variable.)

$x = 68 \div 0.85$

$x = \$80$

Problem Solving

Methods to solving algebraic equations and problems rely upon the ability to represent unknown and missing quantities. Vocabulary is critical to understanding algebraic representations. Common phrases or key words are the key to determining the operations and skills needed to solve problems.

Addition	*Subtraction*	*Multiplication*	*Division*	*Equals*
more than	less than/fewer than	product	quotient	is
in addition to	decreased by	times	divided	are
exceeds	diminished	twice	separated	was
increased by	take away	of	distribute	were
altogether	difference	multiplied by	per	will be
sum	deduct	increased by	out of	gives
and			percent	yields
extra			ratio of	
combined				
total of				

For example, here are some of the terms in action:

9 more than a number	=	$9 + x$
5 less than 23 times a number	=	$23x - 5$
47 times a number increased by 13	=	$47x + 13$
7 less than a number divided by 5	=	$\dfrac{(x-7)}{5}$

Patterns litter the world around. You use patterns to organize information that you see and hear, analyze data that you receive and evaluate situations that you encounter. Recognizing patterns is an important problem solving skill to help generalize specific concepts into broader solutions. Being able to find, describe, explain, and utilize patterns to make educated predictions is a vital skill in mathematics. Pattern recognition is dependent upon each individual person and individual perceptions. Being able to communicate patterns effectively is an important concept to master. Algebra is a tool used to describe patterns in a universal manner.

Skills that can help determine and recognize patterns include finding (looking for repetition or regular features), describing (communicating clearly and concisely), explaining (determining why and how the pattern occurs), and predicting (foreseeing the next steps or future situation). For example, look at the following sequence:

2, 4, 6, 8, x, 12, 14, 16

Can you find the missing number? Look at the regular feature of evens.

Can you describe the pattern? The numbers are increasing in an ascending order by 2.

Can you explain the pattern? The difference between each number is 2, and every number is an even number.

Can you predict the numbers? After recognizing a pattern, the missing numbers can be solved ($x = 10$).

Algebraic concepts include expressions with numbers, variables, and arithmetic operations. It is a branch of math that studies structures, relationships, and quantities. Algebraic concepts at the elementary level introduce children to the fundamental ideas of adding and multiplying numbers, variables, definitions of polynomials, factorization, and determining number roots.

Algebra uses equations to help solve patterns and problems. An unknown variable is often represented by the letter x but can also be represented as any letter in the alphabet. The variable is what the equation should be set up to solve. When solving algebraic equations, follow this sequence:

1. Eliminate fractions or decimals by using multiplication.
2. Eliminate parenthesis by using the distributive property. One operation may change to another: $a(b+c) = ab + ac$.
3. Combine terms that are similar.
4. Isolate the variable being solved for one side of the equation.
5. Get rid of (usually by dividing) the coefficient (the number connected to the variable) if needed.

To solve for x:

$12x - 3 = 21$	(Isolate the variable by getting rid of the 3.)
$12x - 3 + 3 = 21 + 3$	(Use the inverse of –3, which is +3.)
$12x = 24$	(Get rid of the coefficient by using division.)
$12x \div 12 = 24 \div 12$	(Remember that whatever operation is performed on one side of the equation must also be performed on the opposite side.)
$x = 2$	

To solve for y:

$0.12y + 8.56 = 2.6y$

$0.12y - 0.12y + 8.56 = 2.26y - 0.12y$ (Combine like terms.)

$8.56 = 2.14y$

$8.56 \div 2.14 = 2.14y \div 2.14$ (Isolate the variable by using division.)

$4 = y$

There are a multitude of word problems, all of which require algebraic equations to solve. Some types of word problems are basic problems, consecutive integer problems, geometry problems, mixture/money/percentage/interest problems, theory problems, age/time problems, and distance/rate problems.

Basic problems are considered the most simple of all story problems.

---

1. 8 more than six times a number is ten less than five times the number. Find the number.

Set up algebraic equations piece by piece. (Let x represent the unknown.)

$6x + 8$ is the first part, $5x - 10$ is the second part, and the last part "is" becomes the equal sign.

Write the entire equation as one piece:

$6x + 8 = 5x - 10$

Solve the equation using the rules of equations.

$6x + 8 = 5x - 10$

$6x - 5x + 8 = 5x - 5x - 10$ (Combine like terms.)

$1x + 8 = -10$ (Isolate the variable and coefficient.)

$1x + 8 - 8 = -10 - 8$ (Rules of negativity apply here.)

$x = -18$ (Since the coefficient is 1, there is no need to divide.)

---

2. A 56-inch board is cut into a ratio of 3 to 5. Find the length of each piece.

If the ratio is 3 to 5, then let one piece equal $3x$ and the other $5x$.

Set up the algebraic equation.

$3x + 5x = 56$.

$3x + 5x = 56$ (Combine like terms.)

$8x = 56$ (Eliminate the coefficient.)

$x = 7$

Plug the answer back into your original equations to obtain the length of each piece.

$3(7) = 21$ inches.

$5(7) = 35$ inches.

The two pieces measure 21 inches and 35 inches.

Consecutive integer problems involve numbers that are in order and may have a pattern to their order.

---

3. Find five consecutive even integers so that the sum of the smallest two is two less than three times the largest.

Recognize the even integers: . . . −10, −8, −6, −4, −2, 0, 2, 4, 6, 8, 10, . . .

The difference between consecutive even integers is always 2.

Let x represent the first integer (the smallest), then $x + 2$, $x + 4$, $x + 6$, and finally $x + 8$ (the largest).

Now write equations for each piece of the problem.

$x + x + 2$ is the sum of the two smallest, and $3(x + 8) − 2$ is less than 3 times the largest.

Place the two pieces together to get the complete equation needed to solve.

$x + x + 2 = 3(x + 8) − 2$

Solve for the variable.

$2x + 2 = 3x + 24 − 2$

$2x + 2 = 3x + 22$

$2x = 3x + 20$

$−x = 20$ (Remember that the negative of a variable is the inverse, change the sign.)

$x = −20$

Remember to plug the value into the original equations to obtain all 5 numbers needed to answer the problem.

$x + 2, x + 4, x + 6, x + 8$

$−20 + 2 = −18$

$−20 + 4 = −16$

$−20 + 6 = −14$

$−20 + 8 = −12$

The answers are −20, −18, −16, −14, and −12.

Geometry problems require basic knowledge of geometry principles and are best solved by drawing or sketching out the information.

---

4. The length of a rectangle is 8 inches more than its width. The perimeter is 66 inches. Find the dimensions.

Let x = width and $x + 8$ = length as shown in the following illustration:

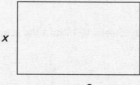

Perimeter means to add up the distance around the shape (add all sides).

$x + x + x + 8 + x + 8 = 66$

Solve for the variable.

$x + x + x + 8 + x + 8 = 66$ (Combine like terms.)

$4x + 16 = 66$ (Isolate the coefficient and variable.)

$4x = 50$ (Eliminate the coefficient by using division.)

$x = 12.5$ inches   (Plug the value into the length equation.)

$x + 8 = 20.5$ inches

The dimensions are 12.5 inches by 20.5 inches

Mixture/money/percentage/interest problems involve a variety of units of measure (be careful to maintain a consistent unit of measure when solving). Setting up tables may also be useful when solving.

---

5. Dale has nickels and dimes in her pocket. She has a total of 40 coins which equals $3.80. How many of each coin does she have?

Develop a theory: The value of a coin times the number of coins equals the total amount of money (5 quarters would be $5*.25 = \$1.25$.)

Set up a table to distinguish data (let x represent nickels).

Coin	Value per coin	Number of coins	Total value
nickels	5	x	$5x$
dimes	10	$40 - x$	$10(40 - x)$
mixture		40	380

Combine each equation piece into one equation.

$5x + 10(40 - x) = 380$

Solve. (Remember the variable is representing nickels only right now.)

$5x + 10(40 - x) = 380$ (Distribute.)

$5x + 400 - 10x = 380$ (Combine like terms.)

$-5x + 400 = 380$ (Isolate the coefficient and variable.)

$-5x = -20$ (Eliminate the coefficient.)

$x = 4$ (There are 4 nickels; solve for dimes now.)

$40 - x = 36$

There are 4 nickels and 36 dimes in Dale's pocket.

---

6. Shedlin invests money at 8% and then a month later he invests another $600 at 6%. If he has $442 interest, how much was invested at each rate?

Develop a theory: The principal amount invested times the rate equals the interest earned ($10,000 at 3% is $10000 * 0.03 = \$300$).

Construct a chart to help organize the data (x represents the first amount).

Money	Principal	Rate	Interest
Amount A	x	0.08	$0.08x$
Amount B	$x + 600$	0.06	$0.06(x + 600)$
Mixture			442

Combine each equation piece into one equation.

$0.08x + 0.06(x + 600) = 442$

Solve. (Remember the variable is representing the first amount only right now.)

$0.08x + 0.06(x + 600) = 442$	(Distribute.)
$0.08x + 0.06x + 36 = 442$	(Combine like terms.)
$0.14x + 36 = 442$	(Isolate the variable and coefficient.)
$0.14x = 406$	(Eliminate the coefficient by using division.)
$x = 2900$	(Plug into amount B equation.)
$x + 600$	(Solve.)

Shedlin invested $2900 at 8% and $3500 was invested at 6%.

Age/time problems can involve more than one variable in order to solve. Units of measure must be consistent and the same in order to obtain a correct solution.

---

7. Poppy is 3 times Finley's age. In 4 years, Poppy will be 2 times Finley's age. How old are they now?

Write equations for each component of the problem. Let x represent the smallest quantity.

Right now Finley is x years old, and Poppy is $3x$ years old.

In 4 years Finley will be $x + 4$ years old, and Poppy will be $3x + 4$ years old.

Combine the components to finish writing the entire equation:

$3x + 4 = 2(x + 4)$	(In 4 years, Poppy will be 2 times Finley's age.)
Solve the equation.	(Remember x represents Finley's age.)
$3x + 4 = 2(x + 4)$	(Distribute.)
$3x + 4 = 2x + 8$	(Combine like terms.)
$3x = 2x + 4$	(Combine like terms again.)
$x = 4$	(The coefficient is one so there is no need to divide.)

$3x$ (Plug the value into Poppy's age equation.)

Poppy is 12 years old, and Finley is 4 years old.

Distance/rate problems involve physical quantity and are the most prolific in daily life. The common equation used to solve these problems is rate times time equals distance ($r * t = d$).

> **8.** A commuter train leaves San Diego heading north. An express train going 30 miles per hour faster leaves San Diego 3 hours later on the same track heading north. 8 hours later the express train collides into the commuter train. What are the speeds of the two trains when they collide?

Create a table or chart to organize the data. The commuter train leaves 3 hours before the express train and the express train travels for 8 hours before colliding with the commuter train ($3 + 8 = 11$).

Train	Rate	Time	Distance
commuter	x	11	$11x$
express	$x + 30$	8	$8(x + 30)$

Both trains leave from the same starting point and end up at the same point (where they crash) even though they travel at different times. The distance traveled is the same for each train.

Place the components together to form the equation.

$11x = 8(x + 30)$

$11x = 8(x + 30)$	(Distribute.)
$11x = 8x + 240$	(Combine like terms to isolate the coefficient and variable.)
$3x = 240$	(Eliminate the coefficient by dividing.)
$x = 80$ mph	(This is the speed of the commuter train, plug into the equation for the express train.)
$x + 30$	(Express train equation.)

The commuter train traveled at a speed of 80 mph, and the express train traveled at 110 mph.

Equivalence

Equivalence is being equal in value or amount. Equivalences can be used in a variety of forms to demonstrate information in a multitude of ways. Fractions, decimals, and percentages are used when computing equivalences.

The following table lists common equivalences.

Simplified Fraction	Fractions	Decimal	Percentage
$\frac{1}{8}$	$\frac{2}{16}, \frac{3}{24}, \frac{4}{32}$	0.125	12.5%
$\frac{1}{5}$	$\frac{2}{10}, \frac{3}{15}, \frac{4}{20}$	0.2	20%
$\frac{1}{4}$	$\frac{2}{8}, \frac{3}{12}, \frac{4}{16}$	0.25	25%
$\frac{1}{3}$	$\frac{2}{6}, \frac{3}{9}, \frac{4}{12}$	$0.\overline{3}$	≈33%
$\frac{1}{2}$	$\frac{2}{4}, \frac{3}{6}, \frac{4}{8}$	0.5	50%
$\frac{2}{3}$	$\frac{4}{6}, \frac{6}{9}, \frac{8}{12}$	$0.\overline{6}$	≈66%
$\frac{3}{5}$	$\frac{6}{10}, \frac{9}{15}, \frac{12}{20}$	0.60	60%
$\frac{3}{4}$	$\frac{6}{8}, \frac{9}{12}, \frac{12}{16}$	0.75	75%
$\frac{7}{8}$	$\frac{14}{16}, \frac{21}{24}, \frac{28}{32}$	0.875	87.5%

Being able to understand equivalent numbers is essential to solving some math problems. Reading graphs, charts, and data can utilize the concept of equivalences. For instance, using the pie graph that follows, you can determine which two outdoor activities roughly half of the children chose.

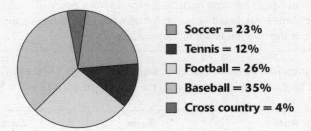

Soccer = 23%
Tennis = 12%
Football = 26%
Baseball = 35%
Cross country = 4%

Based upon the knowledge of equivalences, look for 2 outdoor activities, which add up to 50% or half of the children polled. 23% plus 26% yields 49% which is very close to half (50%).

Geometry and Measurement

Geometry and measurement saturate the world around us. These math topics help develop critical thinking skills, basic reasoning, and spatial relationship concepts. Geometry literally translates to the measurement of the earth and focuses upon two-dimensional (plane) and three-dimensional (solid) shapes. The field of geometry encompasses a wide array of topics and is the study of properties and relationships of points, lines, angles, surfaces, and solids.

Metric Units and Conversions

The most common prefixes used in the world today are the following: kilo-, hecto-, deka-, deci-, centi-, and milli-. It is easy to remember the order by using a simple sentence such as: **K**ing **H**enry **D**oesn't **U**sually **D**rink **C**hocolate **M**ilk

The unit refers to the measurement that is being used: grams (weight), meters (length), or liters (volume/capacity). Metric measurement is usually written using decimals and whole numbers. When converting between the various sized units, simply move the decimal point as the number travels along the chart.

kilo-	hecto-	deka-	unit	deci-	centi-	milli-
0.001	0.01	0.1	1	10	100	1000

---

1. Convert 100 cL to L.

$$1,0,0 \text{ cL}$$

Look at the chart and count the number of moves needed. To convert, 2 spaces must be moved to the left.

1.0 L or 1 L = 100 cL

---

2. Convert 944.06 mm to kilometer.

$$0\,0\,0\,9\,4\,4.0\,6 \text{ mm}$$

Look at the chart and count the number of moves needed to make the conversion. 6 moves need to be made, which means moving the decimal point 6 spaces to the left and then adding 3 zeros for space holders.

0.00094406 km = 944.06 mm

There is another way to convert measurements, which involves proportions.

---

3. Convert 136 centigrams into kilograms use ratios and proportions.

Set up ratios for each component of the problem.

1 Kg = 1000 grams and 1 g = 100 cg and 136 cg = x Kg.

Use dimensional analysis to solve:

1 Kg	1 g	136 cg	
1000 g	100 cg		

Cross reduce all common units of measure.

1 Kg	1 ~~g~~	136 ~~cg~~	
1000 ~~g~~	100 ~~cg~~		

Now solve by using fractional multiplication procedures. (Note the only measurement unit left is the Kg, which is what the problem is asking for.)

$$\frac{136 \text{ Kg}}{100,000}$$

136 cg is equal to 0.00136 Kg.

Customary Units and Conversions

Customary measurement is the system of measurement used in the United States. Customary measurements are usually written in fractions and whole numbers. There are 4 categories for customary measurement: length, weight, volume, and time.

Units of Length

The units of length are inches, feet, yards, and miles.

1 foot (ft. or ') = 12 inches (in. or ")
1 yard (yd.) = 36 inches (in.)
1 yard (yd.) = 3 feet (ft.)
1 mile (mi.) = 5,280 feet (ft.)
1 mile (mi.) = 1,760 yards (yd.)

Units of Weight

The units of weight are ounces, pounds, and ton.

1 pound (lb.) = 16 ounces (oz.)
1 ton (T.) = 2,000 pounds (lbs.)

Units of Volume/Capacity

The units of volume and capacity are fluid ounces, cups, pints, quarts, and gallons.

1 cup (c.) = 8 fluid ounces (fl. oz.)

1 pint (pt.) = 2 cups (c.)

1 quart (qt.) = 4 cups (c.)

1 quart (qt.) = 2 pints (pt.)

1 gallon (gal.) = 4 quarts (qt.)

Units of Time

The units of time are seconds, minutes, hours, days, weeks, months, and years.

1 minute (min.) = 60 second (sec.)

1 hour (hr.) = 60 minutes (min.)

1 day = 24 hours (hr.)

1 week (wk.) = 7 days

1 year (yr.) = 52 weeks (wk.)

1 year (yr.) = 12 months (mo.)

1 year (yr.) = 365 days

Knowledge of how to use each measurement unit is essential to understanding measurement. For instance, to measure distance between cities miles are employed instead of feet or inches, as it would be irrational to use the smaller units. When measuring passage of large increments of time, years or months would be used as opposed to hours or seconds. However, when measuring the speed of an athlete, minutes and seconds are used to obtain a precise measurement. It is also important to be able to convert units within the same systems. Conversion between units of measure requires the use of proportions.

---

1. 9 cups is equal to how many quarts?

Set up the ratios. (Let x represent the unknown value.)

4c. : 1 qt. and 9c. : x qt.

Place ratios in fraction form and create a proportion:

$$\frac{4}{1} = \frac{9}{x}$$

Solve the proportion by using cross multiplication.

$$\frac{4}{1} = \frac{9}{x}$$

$4 * x = 9 * 1$

$4x = 9$ (Eliminate the coefficient using division.)

$x = 9 \div 4$

$x = 2.25$

The answer is 9 cups is equal to $2\frac{1}{4}$ quarts.

2. John wanted to calculate how many weeks would yield 141,120 minutes. What was his solution?

Set up the ratios needed (let x represent the unknown value of weeks).

1hr : 60min   24hr : 1day   7days : 1 week   141120min : x weeks

Place ratios into fraction form and create a proportional chart (dimensional analysis).

1 hr	1 day	1 week	141120 min
60 min	24 hr	7 days	

Remember to place the units so that they will cancel out, leaving only the unit of measure being sought (in this case, weeks)

Multiply using regular fraction multiplication procedures. (All units of measure should cancel one another out except for weeks.)

1 ~~hr~~	1 ~~day~~	1 week	141120 ~~min~~
60 ~~min~~	24 ~~hr~~	7 ~~days~~	

Multiply and divide as needed (remembering the only unit of measure left is weeks).

$$\frac{1*1*1*141120}{60*24*7}$$

$$\frac{141120}{10080}$$

Completing the division process results in the solution to the problem (14 weeks).

The solution John arrived at was 141,120 minutes is equal to 14 weeks.

Measurement as a Tool

Measurement is a tool that mathematicians, scientists, and historians use when analyzing and evaluating data. When studying tables, charts, and graphs, measurement units can range from percent to fraction to number of people to years to groupings of tens. When examining scientific measurement, common units include those used in volume mass, weight, speed, distance, and rate. When researching maps, models, and illustrations, historians use distance, length, and width on a scaled system. Each type of situation requires a specific measurement tool and unit in order to decipher valid and reliable solutions. It is up to the individual to determine what tool or measurement unit best facilitates the outcomes desired.

Use the map and scale to solve the following questions.

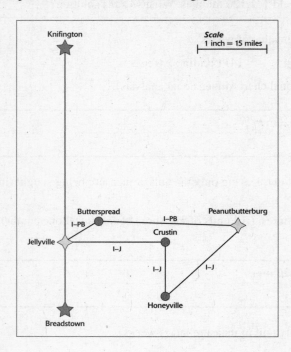

---

1. Determine how far Breadstown is from Knifington.

Using the scale provided, measure the distance between the two cities: 3 inches apart.

Set up a proportion to solve (let x represent the unknown value):

1in : 15 miles   3in : x miles

Set ratios into fraction and solve the proportion using cross multiplication.

$$\frac{1}{15} = \frac{3}{x}$$

$1x = 45$

Breadstown is 45 miles away from Knifington.

---

2. Which route is the shorter distance between Peanutbutterburg and Jellyville, Interstate PB or Interstate J?

Use the scale provided to measure the distances of each interstate:

Interstate PB = from Jellyville to Butterspread is $1\frac{1}{2}$ inches, Butterspread to Peanutbutterburg is 2 inches.

Interstate J = from Jellyville to Crustin is $1\frac{1}{2}$ inches, Crustin to Honeyville is $\frac{3}{4}$ inch, and Honeyville to Peanutbutterburg is $1\frac{1}{2}$ inches.

Calculate the distances using proportions.

1in : 15miles $1\frac{1}{2}$ + 2 in : x miles

$$\frac{1}{15} = \frac{3\frac{1}{2}}{x}$$

$1x = 52\frac{1}{2}$

Interstate PB is $52\frac{1}{2}$ miles.

1in : 15miles $\qquad$ $1\frac{1}{2} + \frac{3}{4} + 1\frac{1}{2}$ in : x miles

$\dfrac{1}{15} = \dfrac{3\frac{3}{4}}{x}$

$1x = 56\frac{1}{4}$ miles

Interstate J is $56\frac{1}{4}$ miles.

Interstate PB is the shorter distance between Jellyville and Peanutbutterburg.

Perimeter, Area, Volume

When discussing perimeter, area, and volume, you must be familiar with the following formulas.

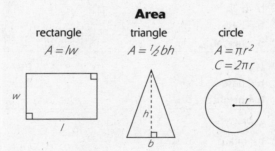

The **perimeter** of a **rectangle** is twice the length plus twice the width:

$P_{rect} = 2l + 2w$

The **area** of a **rectangle** is the length time the width:

$A_{rect} = lw$

The **perimeter** of a **triangle** is the sum of the three sides:

$P_{tri} = s_1 + s_2 + s_3$ or $a + b + c$

The **area** of a **triangle** is half the base times the height:

$A_{tri} = \frac{1}{2}bh$

The Pythagorean Theory states that $a^2 + b^2 = c^2$.

The angles of a triangle add up to 180 degrees: $\angle_1 + \angle_2 + \angle_3 = 180°$.

The **perimeter** of a **square** is the sum of the four sides:

$P_{sqr} = 4s$

The **area** of a **square** is the square of one side:

$A_{sqr} = s^2$

The **circumference (perimeter)** of a **circle** is $2(\pi)r^2$ or πd, where r is the radius and d is the diameter:

The **area** of a **circle** is πr^2:

(π is the number approximated by 3.14159 or in fraction form $\frac{22}{7}$.)

Volume

The volume of an object is measured in cubes and is the amount of cubes that is required to fill the object completely.

Shape	Formula
Cube	s^3 (side · side · side)
Rectangular prism	l · w · h l = length w = width h = height
Prism	b · h b = base h = height
Pyramid	⅓ b · h b = base h = height
Cylinder	$\pi\, r^2 h$ r = radius h = height π = 3.14 or $^{22}/_7$
Cone	⅓ $\pi\, r^2 h$ r = radius h = height π = 3.14 or $^{22}/_7$
Sphere	⅘ $\pi\, r^2$ r = radius π = 3.14 or $^{22}/_7$

Volume

rectangular solid

$V = lwh$

right circular cylinder

$V = \pi r^2 h$

In order to solve geometrical problems, the concepts of area, perimeter, and volume must be understood and able to be applied correctly. Common problems include determining the area of a room, perimeter of a quadrilateral, volume of specific containers, and other such daily living applications.

1. Haley wants to retile her rectangular kitchen with Mexican tiles. Each tile is 1 square foot and costs $6.49. If Haley has a kitchen that measures 12 feet by 14 feet, how much money can she plan to spend retiling the floor?

This problem requires two steps in order to obtain the answer: First solve the area to be covered and second determine the price based upon that area.

Come up with equations for each step of the problem: Length times width equals area of the kitchen and price of a single tile times the area will give the total price of retiling the kitchen.

Solve the area of the kitchen by using $l \times w = A$.

$l = 12$ ft $w = 14$ ft   (Plug into the formula.)

12 ft $*$ 14 ft $= 168$ ft^2 (It must result in squared feet – feet $\times$ feet $=$ feet^2)

Now plug the area into the equation for determining cost of retiling

$6.49 * 168 = \$1,090.32$

It will cost Haley $1,090.32 to retile her kitchen floor.

2. Eric needs to treat his cylindrically shaped pool with chlorine. His pool is 7 feet deep (height) and 12 feet across (diameter). Each cubed foot of the pool requires 4 gallons to fill it. If the bottles of chlorine are sold by the gallon, and each gallon treats 6 gallons of water, how many bottles does Eric need to buy? (No partial bottles are sold.)

Again this problem requires multiple steps to obtain a solution. Set up each component of the problem: determine volume of the pool, the number of gallons within the pool, and the amount of chlorine needed to treat the pool.

Set up equations for each component.

π r^{2}h $=$ Volume of pool

Volume $*$ Gallons $=$ total gallons

Total gallons $\div$ gallons treated by one bottle

Solve the volume of the pool.

$V = \pi$ r^{2}h   (Since the problem gives the diameter, the radius must be calculated by
                                          dividing the diameter by 2. 12 ft $\div$ 2 $= 6$ ft.)

$V = (3.14)(6$ft$)^2(7$ft$)$ (Don't forget to square the radius.)

$V = (3.14)(36$ft$^2)(7$ft$)$

$V = 791.28$ ft^2 (The volume of the pool.)

Solve for the amount of water (measured in gallons) needed to fill the pool.

Volume $*$ Gallons $=$ Total Gallons

$791.28 * 4 = 3,165.12$ gallons   (total gallons in the pool)

Solve for the total number of chlorine bottles needed.

$3,165.12 \div 6 = 527.52$

Eric will need to buy 528 bottles of chlorine in order to treat his cylindrical pool.

3. The Montessori Children's Room wants to fence in their new playground area. The playground is shaped like a rectangle with a triangular-shaped swing area attached to the rectangle to create a pentagon shape. If the rectangle is 25 yards by 40 yards and the triangular area measures 12 yards on each side and has a base of 25 yards how much fencing will the school need?

Determine the information known.

Rectangle shape = 25 by 40 and triangular shape = 12 by 12 by 25.

It may help to draw a picture of the playground.

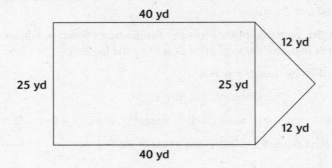

Calculate the perimeter by adding up all the sides. Remember that the base of the triangle and one side of the rectangle should not be used to calculate the perimeter. Perimeter is the measurement of the outer sides.

25yds + 40 yds + 40 yds + 12yds + 12yds

25 + 80 + 24

129 yards

The school needs to purchase 129 yards of fencing for the new playground.

Rates

The rate explains a relationship between a pair of numbers. It is the amount of one thing needed to find the amount of another. To find the **rate,** divide distance by time (r = d ÷ t).

Rate is written as a fraction with the distance units as the numerator and the time units as the denominator. (For example, miles/hour or meters/second, yards/minute). Be sure to keep the units organized and consistent. Sometimes time will need to be converted in order to make the units match.

To find **time,** use time = distance / rate (t = d ÷ r).

To find **distance,** use distance = rate * time (d = rt).

---

1. Two trains leave the station at the same time heading in opposite directions. The Blue train travels at a speed of 50 mph, and the Green train travels at a speed of 70 mph. In how many hours will the trains be 480 miles apart?

Organize the data into a chart:

Train	Rate	Time	Distance (rate · time)
Blue	50 mph	x hours	$50x$
Green	70 mph	x hours	$70x$

Write the equation using all components.

$50x + 70x = 480$ (Combine like terms.)

$120x = 480$ (Eliminate the coefficient by using division.)

$x = 4$ hrs

In 4 hours the trains will be 480 miles apart.

2. Chip can kayak 45 miles downstream in 5 hours but when he kayaks back upstream the same distance it takes him 9 hours. Find Chip's rate in still water and the rate of the current.

Set up a chart to organize the data. (Let x represent Chip and y represent the water).

Direction	Rate	Time	Distance
Downstream	$x + y$	5 hours	45 miles
Upstream	$x - y$	9 hours	45 miles

Construct equations for the components of each problem:

$(x + y)5 = 45$ $(x - y)9 = 45$ (Eliminate the coefficient in each equation by using division.)

$x + y = 9$ $x - y = 5$

Combine (add) the equations to solve for Chip's rate (x).

$$x + y = 9$$
$$+x - y = 5$$
$$\overline{}$$
$$2x = 14$$

$x = 7$ mph   (Plug this back into an equation to obtain the value of y.)

$7 + y = 9$ (This yields the rate of the current.)

Chip kayaks at a rate of 7 mph in still water and the current has a rate of 2 mph.

Data Analysis and Probability

Graphics (visual displays) are used to reveal data, often in a more precise and direct manner than conventional computations. The most common visual representations used in math are the graph, chart, table, and spreadsheet.

There are different types of graphs, which are used to display information in a specific manner. Some types of graphs are:

Line graph uses either vertical or horizontal lines to connect plotted data points and shows change or information over a period of time.

Bar graphs can be displayed vertically or horizontally and each bar represents a specific set of information in which the value is based upon the height or length of the bar.

Pie graphs have the shape of a circle and display the information in relation to a whole. Data is usually shown in percentages.

Pictographs have pictures or symbols that are used to represent numbers of specific items. Value of items is obtained by counting the pictorial representation.

Data Interpetation

Interpreting and analyzing the data is what occurs once the data has been collected, organized into an appropriate format, and all investigations are over. Interpretation and analysis helps develop conclusions from data. There are three steps to data interpretation:

1. **Interpretation**—Identifying the trends in the various variables
2. **Correlation**—Identifying how one factor effects another
3. **Analysis**—Understanding what the data represents

Determining the relationship between two variables is the purpose of investigation. Data is used and interpreted to see if a correlation exists. Trends and patterns can often be found when analyzing data on charts and graphs. A pattern on a graph can be used to draw conclusions (make **inferences**). Understanding the pattern on a graph can help communicate information and data in a clear and concise manner, allow comparisons to be made, and predict future patterns. Sometimes the information displayed can develop an upward trend and sometimes it can develop a downward trend. Trends can fluctuate and remain constant, peak, or subside. A trend on a line graph demonstrates more than merely a connection between the two variables. It also implies that tinkering with one of the variables will cause a change in the other variable.

Common and universally accepted vocabulary can be used to describe trends: gradually, smoothly, fluctuated, erratically, slowly, reached a peak, regularly, became, constant, unevenly, leveled off, rapidly, steadily, subside, continue, increase, decrease, upward, and downward.

When describing a trend or pattern, many mathematicians use a comparison such as: When the first variable *increased/decreased*, the second variable *increased/decreased/stayed constant*.

1. Based on the chart, explain how the light affects photosynthesis.

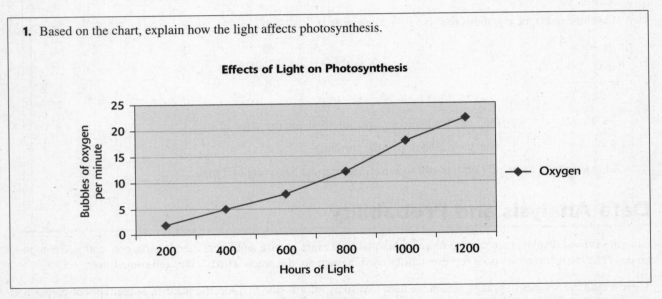

The trend is an upward movement in production of oxygen bubbles. Looking at the *x*-axis (hours of light) when compared to the *y*-axis (oxygen bubbles), a pattern arises. As the time of light increases, the production of oxygen bubbles increases.

Mean, Median, Mode, Range

Mean, median, and mode are used in math to determine three kinds of averages. The range measures the amount of values the information covers. Generally, these four concepts are seen together in math problems or sets of data.

Mean is the average of a set of numbers. To calculate mean add up all the numbers in the set and divide the sum by the number of numbers.

1. What is the mean of 2, 12, 22, 27, 38, 64?

2 + 12 + 22 + 27 + 38 + 64   (Add up all the values.)

Divide 164 by 6.   (There are 6 numbers in the set.)

The mean is 27.5.

Median is the middle value in a set of numbers. To find the median, list the numbers in numerical order. If the set of numbers is an even set, add the two middle numbers and divide by two to obtain the median.

2. Find the median of these numbers: 37, 89, 17, 34, 99, 56, 72.

Place in numerical order:

17, 34, 37, 56, 72, 89, 99   (There are 7 values, so the middle value is the 4th one.)

The middle value is 56.

The median is 56.

3. Find the median of these numbers: 45, 66, 13, 80, 32, 20.

Place in numerical order:

13, 20, 32, 45, 66, 80

There is an even number of values. Add the middle two together and divide by two.

$(32 + 45) \div 2$

$77 \div 2$

The median is 38.5.

Mode is the number that occurs most often. If there is no number that is repeated, there is no mode.

4. Find the mode of this set of numbers 1, 132, 12, 80, 33, 12, 132, 12, 33, 12.

It may help to place the values in numerical order:

1, 12, 12, 12, 12, 33, 33, 80, 132, 132

The mode is 12. (It is the number that is most repeated.)

Range is the difference between the largest and smallest value.

5. Find the range of this set of data: 48, 78, 31, 987, 123.

Find the smallest and largest values: 31 and 987.

Find the difference between the two values:

$987 - 31 = 956$

The range is 956.

6. Find the mean, median, mode, and range of Class A from the following table of test scores:

Class A	Class B
68	90
79	85
90	78
94	95
82	73
79	65
70	69
95	96
84	90
88	89
97	86
60	75
98	73
79	81
82	

Mean = (68 + 79 + 90 + 94 + 82 + 79 + 70 + 95 + 84 + 88 + 97 + 60 + 98 + 79 + 82) ÷ 15

Mean = 1245 ÷ 15

Mean = 83

Median = 60, 68, 70, 79, 79, 79, 82, 82, 84, 88, 90, 94, 95, 97, 98

Median = 82

Mode = 79

Range = 98 − 60

Range = 38

7. Find the range of scores for both A and B combined.

The lowest score between the two classes is 60.

The highest score is 98.

Range = 98 − 60

Range = 38

8. Mabel has been racing road bikes for the past six years. She needs to maintain an average race time of 97 minutes to qualify for the finals. In her last seven races, she has received 92, 102, 91, 100, 98, 93, and 99 minutes. What time does she need to get on her last race to maintain her qualifying average of 97 minutes?

Recognize needed information (average time needed and past times) versus unneeded (racing six years). Let x represent the unknown value that is needed.

Write an equation:

$(92 + 102 + 91 + 100 + 98 + 93 + 99 + x) \div 8 = 97$

$(675 + x) \div 8 = 97$

$(675 + x) \div 8 * 8 = 97 * 8$ (Multiply each side by 8 to isolate the variable.)

$675 + x = 776$ (Subtract 675 to solve for x.)

$101 = x$

Mabel needs to ride the race in 101 minutes or less in order to maintain her qualifying time of 97 minutes.

9. Three sixth grade classes take a standardized test and as a collective whole need to maintain an average score of 80 to meet annual yearly progress. If the scores of 41 children have a mean of 83, but there is one more student that must take the test, what is the lowest score this student can get to maintain the passing average of 80 for the group?

Recognize needed information versus unneeded information.

Unneeded	Needed
6th grade class	Mean of 83
41 students	Average of 80 needed

Let x represent the unknown score needed.

$(83 + x) \div 2 = 80$ (Multiply by 2 on each side of the equation.)

$(83 + x) \div 2 * 2 = 80 * 2$

$83 + x = 160$ (Isolate the variable by subtracting.)

$x = 77$

In order to maintain the group average (80), the minimum score needed by the last student would be 77.

10. Find the range of cars sold and the range of trucks sold from the following data:

Vehicle Sales

Locate the lowest value and the highest value of cars sold as well as for trucks sold. (Remember the values are measured in thousands.)

Cars = 30 (lowest), 100 (highest)

Trucks = 20 (lowest), 95 (highest)

Use the range equation to solve for each.

Cars = 100 – 30

Trucks = 95 – 20

The range for cars is 70,000 and the range for trucks is 75,000.

Simple Probability

Probability is the measure of the likelihood that an event will occur. Probabilities are expressed as fractions, ratios, decimals, or percentages. To calculate the probability of an event, count the number of times the event is true (favorable) and divide that number by the possible (total) number of outcomes.

$$\text{Event} = \frac{\text{number of favorable outcomes}}{\text{number of possible outcomes}}$$

$$P_{event} = O_f / O_p$$

Outcomes

An outcome is the result of a single trial of an experiment. It is also the end result or the consequence. A possible outcome is one of three things:

1. a choice
2. a possibility
3. a result

A **favorable outcome** is what someone wants to happen.

A **total outcome** is all the things that could happen.

Outcomes must be delineated between favorable and total in order to calculate the correct probability. For instance: At a restaurant, there are the following choices of pie: cherry, apple, pumpkin, mud, and peach. What are the outcomes? The outcomes are the five choices of pie. The favorable outcome is the one type of pie chosen or desired.

---

1. What is the probability of rolling an odd number on a standard 6-sided die?

What are the outcomes?

Outcomes: odd numbers (1, 3, 5) and all numbers (1, 2, 3, 4, 5, 6)

Therefore, there are 3 "favorable" outcomes and 6 "possible" outcomes.

The probability of rolling an odd number is $\frac{3}{6}$ or reduced is $\frac{1}{2}$ or .5 or 50%.

---

2. What is the probability of rolling a 5 on a standard six-sided die?

There are 6 possible total outcomes = 1, 2, 3, 4, 5, 6.

There is only 1 favorable outcome = 5.

Therefore, the probability of rolling a 5 is 1:6 or 1/6 or 1 to 6 or 0.167 or 16.7%.

3. If a coin is flipped twice, calculate the probability that it will land on heads both times.

Favorable outcomes = 1 (HH)

Possible outcomes = 4 (HH, HT, TH, TT)

Solve: $P_{heads} = \dfrac{favorable\ outcome}{possible\ outcome}$

Therefore, the probability that the coin will land on heads each time is $\dfrac{1}{4}$ or 1:4 or 25%.

4. A marble jar contains 12 green marbles, 10 blue marbles, 8 yellow marbles, 14 red marbles, and 4 orange marbles. If a single marble is chosen at random from the jar, what is the probability of choosing a green marble? Blue marble? Orange marble? Yellow marble? Red marble?

Organize what is known:

Outcomes: green (12) blue (10) yellow (8) red (14) orange (4)

Total number of possibilities: 12 + 10 + 8 + 14 + 4 = 48 marbles.

Write equations for each probability

Probability of Green: $P_g = \dfrac{\#\ of\ green\ marbles\ to\ choose\ from}{total\ \#\ of\ marbles}$

Probability of Blue: $P_b = \dfrac{\#\ of\ blue\ marbles\ to\ choose\ from}{total\ \#\ of\ marbles}$

Probability of Yellow: $P_y = \dfrac{\#\ of\ yellow\ marbles\ to\ choose\ from}{total\ \#\ of\ marbles}$

Probability of Red: $P_r = \dfrac{\#\ of\ red\ marbles\ to\ choose\ from}{total\ \#\ of\ marbles}$

Probability of Orange: $P_o = \dfrac{\#\ of\ orange\ marbles\ to\ choose\ from}{total\ \#\ of\ marbles}$

Solve each probability:

Green = $\dfrac{12}{48} = \dfrac{1}{4} = 0.25 = 25\%$

Blue = $\dfrac{10}{48} = \dfrac{5}{24} = 0.208 = 20.8\%$

Yellow = $\dfrac{8}{48} = \dfrac{1}{6} = 0.167 = 16.7\%$

Red = $\dfrac{14}{48} = \dfrac{7}{24} = 0.292 = 29.2\%$

Orange = $\dfrac{4}{48} = \dfrac{1}{12} = 0.083 = 8.3\%$

The outcomes in this example are not equally likely to occur due to the different values. The most likely outcome is red marble and the least likely outcome is orange marble.

Events

An event is the set of outcomes found within a probability; it is the occurrence (one or more outcomes) of a probability.

The probability of an event is written: $P_{event} = \dfrac{\#\ of\ ways\ an\ event\ can\ occur}{total\ \#\ of\ possible\ outcomes}$

> **1.** Justin grabs a pen from his desk drawer at random. The drawer has 4 blue, 2 black, 1 red, 2 green, and 1 purple pen. What is the probability he will grab a secondary colored pen?

One event of this probability is grabbing a black pen.

Another event of this probability is grabbing a blue pen.

Another event of this probability is grabbing a red pen.

Another event of this probability is grabbing a green pen.

Another event of this probability is grabbing a purple pen.

Another event is grabbing a primary colored pen (red or blue).

Another event is grabbing a secondary colored pen (green or purple).

Understand the possible events that could occur as well as the outcomes desired.

Secondary pens are desired: 2 green + 1 purple (number of ways secondary can occur).

Total possibilities: 10 pens

Set up an equation for this problem

$$P_{event} = \frac{\text{\# of ways a secondary pen can occur}}{\text{total \# of possible outcomes}}$$

$P_{event} = 3 \div 10$

$P_{event} = 0.3$ or 30%

There is a 30 % (1 in 3) chance that Justin will grab a pen that is a secondary color.

Terminology

The subject of mathematics offers many opportunities for refined and numerous experiences with vocabulary. The acquisition of math terms elevates the student's core knowledge of not only foundational math but also higher level mathematics. The following list of terms, although not exhaustive, provides additional words that perhaps were not defined or mentioned in this content area. Remember that each grade level, preschool to eighth grade, has specific terms most suitable for instruction due to the specific mathematical topics covered in those age groups.

angle—the union of two rays with a common point

average—same as the arithmetic mean

bisect—to divide into two equal parts (line, angle, shape, etc)

circumference—the distance around a circle (a circle's perimeter)

congruent—identical in form (lengths and angles are the same)

diagonal—a line joining two opposite corners of a parallelogram

diameter—a straight line passing through the center of a figure from side to side

dividend—the number that is to be divided by another number

equation—a statement that the values of two expressions are equal

estimate—an approximate calculation

exponent—a quantity that expresses the power to which the base number or value must be raised

factor—a number that goes evenly into another

improper fraction—when the numerator is larger than the denominator

mean—the average of a given set of numbers

median—the middle term in a series of numbers

midpoint—the exact middle of a line segment

mode—the number that occurs most frequently in a set of numbers

multiplicand—the number that is to be multiplied

multiplier—how many times to take the multiplicand

numerator—the top number in a fraction

parallel—lines, planes, segments, figures that rest side by side and maintain the same distance continuously between them

perimeter—the distance around the outside of a figure

perpendicular—being at an angle of 90° in relation to another line, figure, or plane

probability—the likeliness that something will occur

radius—line segment from the center of a circle to the arch

ratio—comparison between two amounts that shows the amount of times one amount is contained within the other amount

slope—the degree at which a line rises or falls on a given plane

solution—the answer to a puzzle, equation or problem

symmetry—being made up of exactly the same parts which are arranged around a axis or are facing one another

variable—a letter than represents an unknown value

Web sites

The following web sites are provided for additional study and research. Examinees may want to review national mathematics standards, reflect on the various specific topics in math education, study some of the units and lessons, and consider the strategies and methods of math education for the elementary level found on these sites.

Note: At the time of the development of this book, the Internet sites provided here were current, active and accurate. However, due to constant modifications on the Internet, web sites and addresses may change or become obsolete.

http://www.nctm.org/	National Council of Teachers of Mathematics
http://www.ed.gov/about/bdscomm/list/mathpanel/factsheet.html	U.S. Department of Education-National Mathematics Advisory Panel
http://www.education-world.com/standards/national/math/index.shtml	Education World-Mathematics information
http://www.maa.org/	The Mathematical Association of America
http://www.ams.org/	American Mathematical Society

Citizenship and Social Science

Key concepts and various aspects of the social sciences are reflected in the Praxis II exam questions from this content area. Examinees are assessed on their knowledge and skills related to four specific areas:

- Historical Continuity and Change
- People, Places, Geographical Regions
- Civics and Government
- Scarcity and Economic Choice

Also assessed is an examinee's understanding of the connections and comparisons related to major historical events and ideas, which may also be referenced to contemporary events and issues. Knowledge in this area aids examinees in making logical and informed decisions as citizens in a richly diverse society and as participants in the greater global society.

The National Council for the Social Studies (NCSS) states, "the primary purpose of social studies is to help young people develop the ability to make informed and reasoned decisions for the public good as citizens of a culturally diverse, democratic society in an interdependent world." They believe that when students understand the concepts of social studies, the historical events, the functions of government, and the practice of economics they can become independent and informed citizens as they become adults managing their lives in a changing society. The NCSS has designed ten standards to be used to clarify the concepts and core knowledge of this subject area. These standards are organized according to the following themes:

1. culture
2. time, continuity and change
3. people, places and environments
4. individual development and identity
5. individuals, groups, and institutions
6. power, authority, and governance
7. production, distribution, and consumption
8. science, technology, and society
9. global connections
10. civic ideals and practices

The social sciences, part of the general social studies curriculum, include the areas of anthropology, sociology, psychology, economics, political science, global education, environmental education, and current events. Knowledge of these areas helps students understand their world and how they should function within it in the future.

Examinees may find that seeking additional information about history, government, civics, and the social sciences is necessary. They may use the Internet (some web sites are included at the end of this chapter) or seek resources such as books, movies, and school textbooks.

Historical Continuity and Change

Knowledge about significant events and people from the past is an essential component to the curriculum of social science. To gain information and be able to use analysis skills comes from the understanding of cause and effect relationships of historical eras. The periods in history are divided by events and may include: the beginnings of civilization, colonization and settlement, revolution and the new nation, expansion and reform, war and reconstruction, development of the industrial nation, modern states, great depression and war, post war, and contemporary nation. Students will learn about change through their understandings of historical cause and effect events, as this provides a format for logical reasoning and critical thinking that promotes cognitive skills necessary as adults.

In this section of the study guide, a national standard focuses on how history, with its facts and people's opinions, has impacted the lives of citizens. Examinees will learn about the significance of historical documents, artifacts, traditions and places, while also peering into the lives of figures who have made their entry into history books for their accomplishments and influences. This is the first of the four specific areas on the Praxis II exam that pertains to the social sciences.

Most specifically, according to ETS, the Praxis will seek to evaluate whether examinees can

- Demonstrate the ability to use chronological thinking skills and to use and analyze historical data, such as timelines, maps, graphs, and tables.
- Distinguish between fact and opinion with respect to primary and other historical documents.
- Demonstrate an understanding of multiple points of view with respect to primary and other historical documents such as essays, speeches, interviews, or narratives.
- Demonstrate an understanding of the significance of historical artifacts, oral traditions, and historical places.
- Identify and demonstrate an understanding of the impact of individuals, groups, religions, social organizations, and movements on history.
- Identify and demonstrate an understanding of the causes, results, and consequences of social, political, economic, and military events.

Use of Historical Data

When students study history, they learn about people and their past events. This study includes information about governments, civilizations, major events, wars, and accomplishments. History shapes our current world and impacts people's lives. We study it to learn about the past so actions of the present will affect the wise decisions to be made about the future.

Historians and archeologists gather valuable information, items, and oral traditions that they record and document to preserve and interpret history from which people study and learn. Historians must be careful about how they preserve valuable documents and artifacts, and they must be cautious about how they interpret the values, points of view, beliefs, and facts of past lives and periods. Using historical data helps those who live in today's society make changes that influence the world. Change can have a lasting effect, or be reversed by future societies.

Some examples of historical data include the following:

- Religious documents and artifacts like shrines, tablets, scrolls, and tombs.
- Ancient written records, such as writing tablets, books, hieroglyphics, and petroglyphs.
- Architectural structures such as buildings, memorials, statutes, temples, and sculptures.
- Jewelry and tools of daily life, such as bracelets, crowns, goblets, pottery, weapons, masks, costumes, art, pictures, and ornaments.
- Instruments, such as musical, navigational, astronomical, scientific, and mathematical.
- Remains such as animal bones, human skeletons, shells, fossils, or insect carcasses.

Chronology is a critical aspect of outlining historical events and data. Historians and archeologists establish facts, record events and identify artifacts on timelines, charts, tables, graphs and maps. Learning how to read, use and interpret these tools is an essential skill for students, as well as educators. The use of historical resources helps them place items and activities into the proper time periods and then record content using appropriate historical tools.

Timelines provide chronological arrangements of dates, events, and activities in history. They deliver information about how the causes, consequences, developments, and accomplishments influenced history and people in certain time periods. Students must be able to understand the format and use of timelines in applying them to their knowledge of the social sciences.

Graphs and **tables** are used to record statistical and specific historical information. The use of these historical tools necessitates that students have certain skills. These tools generally require that students be able to use critical thinking skills and make interpretations of limited data given.

Maps are used for the study of geography, sociology and anthropology. Maps require that students have the appropriate skills in reading and language to use and interpret the information. Maps help students understand different areas and specific places, acknowledge their place in relation to the world, learn symbols, gain concepts, identify directions, or scales, and to comprehend spatial terms and relationships.

Reference resources consist of materials such as encyclopedias, computer-based programs, almanacs, atlases, gazetteers, dictionaries, statistical abstracts, and data compilations. Students must learn where to find these tools, how to use them efficiently, and to determine the accuracy and reliability of the resources. Once they can decipher fact from opinion, students should gain skills in application and interpretation of the data they seek and record it on historical tools such as graphs, tables, or maps.

Historical Documents

Documents have been collected for centuries to define governments, civilizations and the lives of people for certain periods of time. These are researched and preserved to acknowledge the people and places that have existed prior to the current civilization. There are times when historians must consider whether the document contains facts or statements of opinion.

Primary and secondary sources are used by historians to understand and document the past. A primary source is a written, actual account of the event or activity by those involved in the action, such as agreements, diaries, letters, legal papers, maps, and government documents. It may even include certain evidence or items such as photos, clothing, music, or tools. A secondary source is the study or interpretation of a primary source from a different time. Secondary sources are sources that do not come from first hand knowledge of the event or activity. These may include newspaper accounts, other books, or opinion statements.

Evaluating primary and secondary source documents to gain a historical perspective involves skills in certain areas. To understand that historical information is logically constructed, students must learn to analyze data, interpret facts, and identify opinions. Students must be provided opportunities to study the various sources, and learn how to apply what they know to their lives.

Current event documents contain recent up-to-date information about activities and situations happening around the world at any given time. Local current events reflect the times in which they occur and often students may find a connection with these events. The use of newspapers, radio shows, or television programs reports the news as it happens, but may also embed opinion into the articles or broadcasts. When events happen on a larger world scale, an opportunity emerges for students to use maps, timelines and graphs to decipher and document information. These worldwide current events also make students aware of the customs, and practices of various cultures, and broaden their knowledge about geographic areas.

Documents of essential study for students are those that comprise present day government. Fundamental to the United States government is the agreement that it will serve the people, ensuring individual liberties in a free society. Specific factual documents record and prove the historical movements that created this democratic society. These documents outlined citizen rights and the role of the government in their lives up to present day.

Examples of documents of American democracy include the following:

- **The Mayflower Compact**—In 1620, this document ensured individual liberties for the Pilgrims in the New World away from the rule of the monarch.

- **The Declaration of Independence**—This decree established in 1776, outlined the rights and responsibilities of the people in the American colonies to be free and separate from the rule in Great Britain.

- **The Articles of Confederation**—This document of 1781 was the initial charter of the thirteen colonies, which was replaced in 1789 by the Constitution of the United States.

- **The Preamble**—The introduction to the Constitution that briefly describes the purpose of the government being to protect the rights of the people.
- **The U.S. Constitution**—This 1787 document defined the system of government in the newly established America and contains additional Amendments as they are ratified.
- **The Federalist Papers**—This series of essays written between 1787 and 1788 explained the provisions of the United States' Constitution.
- **The Emancipation Proclamation**—During the Civil War in 1865, President Lincoln freed the slaves through an act and written statement in the Confederate states.
- **The Bill of Rights**—This document contained the first ten Amendments to the U.S. Constitution, which were ratified in 1791.

There have also been numerous documents important to the history of the world that demonstrate various points of view, either by individuals or by groups of individuals. Some of these have been recorded or preserved in speeches, interviews, essays, transcripts, or personal narratives. The speeches and essays are motivational, intriguing, informational, emotional, and persuasive.

Speeches and essays are important to study as they reflect the period of history and capture the impact of events on the people. Although students may not know about or recall the speeches, they are an important component to history instruction. Students must gain an understanding of the period in history during which the account was written or recorded, while also realizing the role of the individual or group providing the perspective. The main skill that is important is the ability to decipher fact from opinion or bias, while understanding the reasons, the point of view, and the motivation behind the piece. Then students may learn to use the information to develop their own personal statement or opinion about the work or the time period.

This list provides a brief overview of some famous speeches and essays of the twentieth century. In presenting this information to students, teachers are encouraged to use printed documents from libraries or the audio-visual clips available on the Internet to study speech delivery and the event.

- **Poor Richard's Almanac**—A publication from 1732-1758 by Benjamin Franklin that provided information about life in the American colonies and left the world with some unique and frequently used famous proverbial sayings.
- **Inaugural Address**—A speech by George Washington in 1789 that concentrated on the new nation's liberties and freedoms in a government instituted of itself.
- **Alexander Pope Essays**—A famous English poet in the 18th century, he wrote satires about the government and high society and his poetry and quotes live on today.
- **Jonathan Swift Essays**—Wrote famous satires on political times and figures (most famous for Gulliver's Travels).
- **The Gettysburg Address**—A speech given by President Lincoln in 1863 is considered one of the most important in history, as it defined the principles of liberty and equality on which the government of the United States was founded.
- **Inaugural Address**—A speech by Franklin D. Roosevelt in 1933 during the Great Depression of the 1930s who stated: *"The only thing we have to fear is fear itself."*
- **Abdication**—A speech by King Edward VIII of England abdicating the throne in 1936 to marry a commoner.
- **What Libraries Mean to the U.S.**—A speech by Eleanor Roosevelt, First Lady in 1936.
- **Blood, Sweat, and Tears**—A speech in 1940 by the British Prime Minister, Sir Winston Churchill, as inspiration to the country prior to the Battle of Britain.
- **Declaration of War**—A speech by Adolph Hitler in 1941 declaring war against the U.S. and supporting the preservation of communism.
- **State of the Union Address**—A speech given by Franklin D. Roosevelt in 1945 about war and renewal.
- **Inaugural Address**—A speech by President John F. Kennedy (1961) to unite the nation and its people, promoting global freedoms and cooperative efforts. He wanted to involve citizens in the workings of the government and is remembered by his remark: *Ask not what your country can do for you, ask what you can do for your country.*

- **One Small Step**—A phrase coined by Neil Armstrong, an astronaut, who landed and then walked on the moon. *"One small step for man, one giant leap for mankind"*.

- **I Have a Dream**—A speech given by Martin Luther King, Jr. at the demonstration of freedom in 1963 at the Lincoln Memorial. It was an event related to the civil rights movement of the 1960's to unify citizens in accepting diversity and eliminating discrimination against African-Americans.

- **International Understanding**—A presentation in 1969, by Indira Ghandi focused on the work of Martin Luther King.

- **Equal Rights for Women**—A speech by Shirley Chisholm in 1969 to promote the rights and acceptance of women in this country.

- **Attainment of Peace**—A speech by Golda Meir in Israel focused on peace in 1970.

Historical Artifacts, Traditions, Places

Throughout history, people have collected artifacts, developed traditions, and designed songs, stories and poems that pertain to their times and their cultures. Those are now used to determine information about the lives these people led and what ideals and values they practiced and believed in. These items help us understand the particular period in history, the issues, the triumphs and accomplishments of the people and the times.

Historical Artifacts

Historians collect, preserve, protect, interpret, and maintain information about original or period objects of historical significance through artifacts that are obtained and secured. An **artifact** is an object produced or shaped by human craft of an archeological, sociological, or historical interest. Artifacts may be placed in large collections that are privately owned or delivered to museums or public collections for others to enjoy the value of the object, learn about the period, or preserve the historical event. Broad general categories that are examples of artifacts include: art paintings or sculptures, jewelry or ornaments, bone or ivory structures, ceramics, pottery or glass ware, textiles or clothing, and tools or weapons.

Oral traditions provide a method for sharing knowledge from one culture to another and across generations without the need for a written system. An oral history is often the only source for some cultures in the world, as their society may not have a form of written language. Therefore, information is passed by word of mouth through stories, songs, prayers, proverbs, chants, poems, and sayings. In modern times, we preserve oral traditions such as events, speeches, and activities through television and radio recordings, movies, or documentaries. The value of oral traditions is in the preservation of the past for future generations.

Oral traditions are significant expressions in the civic history and life of Americans. Anthems and mottos are used today to continue the patriotic celebration of past achievements and the independence of this country. They are representative of the values and beliefs of Americans.

- **The Pledge of Allegiance**—Created by Francis Bellamy, first published in 1892, it is an oath by the people to promise their support. It was amended by Congress in 1954 with approval from President Eisenhower.

- **The Oath of Allegiance**—A naturalization pledge taken by immigrants who want to become citizens.

- **"The Star Spangled Banner"**—In 1814, after a critical battle in the War of 1812, Francis Scott Key created a poem to honor the flag and show respect for patriotism. It became the national anthem in 1931.

- **"America the Beautiful"**—Written by Katharine Bates in 1893, describing a view from Pikes Peak in Colorado, it is now used in many patriotic ceremonies and celebrations.

- **"God Bless America"**—Considered America's unofficial national anthem, written by Irving Berlin, it was first used to honor veterans on November 11, 1938.

- **The Motto of the United States**—Initially, in 1776, it was "E Pluribus Unum" and then officially changed in 1956 to "In God We Trust."

Symbols of the country express the ideals, the values and the history that exist in the country. These are captured in such symbols as the flag, the seals, and other specific items. The U.S. flag with its stars signifies the 50 states and the stripes that represent the first thirteen colonies. The colors also show profound meaning: *red* stands for courage, hardiness and valor, *white* for hope, purity and innocence, and *blue* for vigilance, perseverance and justice. The Great Seal of the United States, the Presidential Seal, the Statue of Liberty, the Liberty Bell, and the eagle are also representative of the deep commitment and patriotism that is present in the country.

Many historical places in America are considered memorials, but they advertise the growth, expansion, freedoms, and liberties that were and are granted through this free society, marking the history of support in the country. Many landmarks are found in the nation's Capitol, Washington, D.C., but some are located in other parts of the country. These include the following:

- **The Washington Monument**—honors the first President of the United States who led the country to independence
- **The Thomas Jefferson Memorial**—stands as a symbol of liberty, inspiration, and reflection of America's ideals
- **The Lincoln Memorial**—honors the 16th President of the United States; it represents that all citizens should be free
- **Mount Rushmore**—honors four outstanding Americans, it stands for the great themes of the United States (independence, expansion, conservation and unification)
- **The Statue of Liberty**—stands as a symbol of freedom, opportunity, democracy and international friendships
- **The Liberty Bell**—symbolizes the proclamation of liberty for all
- **The F.D.R. Memorial**—honors the 32nd President of the United States; it represents an era of devotion in America's history
- **The War Memorials**—WWII Memorial, The Korean Memorial, The Vietnam Vets Memorial: all signify the country's past conflicts and honors the citizens who participated in those wars
- **The U.S. Marine Memorial** (Iwo Jima Memorial)—represents the victory of WWII

Many historical places around the world remain as symbols of the times past. They may be significant of a lost civilization or culture, or represent a global impact.

- **The Great Pyramids**—Built in Egypt, one of the Wonders of the Ancient World, there are three of significance: Giza, Cheops, and Khufu. Taking about 20 years to build, they were completed around 2560 B.C.E. as tombs for the Kings.
- **The Great Sphinx of Giza**—A sphinx is a figure designed in ancient Egypt, and transferred to other cultures. Great statues were built to represent guardians of tombs, figures of religion, and to honor rulers. The Sphinx of Giza, along the Nile River, honors Pharaoh Khafra, around 1400 B.C.E.
- **Stonehenge**—Located in England, this prehistoric monument built around 2500 B.C.E. is steeped in mystery about its construction and purpose.
- **The Hanging Gardens of Babylon**—Built around 1700 B.C.E. for the wife of King Nebuchadnezzar, it is one of the Seven Wonders of the Ancient World.
- **The Great Wall of China**—Built around 200 B.C.E., of over 1400 miles, to protect the dynasty from the hostile Huns and is one of the Seven Wonders of the Ancient World.
- **Machu Picchu**—A battle fort of the Incas in the Andes Mountains of Peru.
- **The Berlin Wall**—Built in 1961 and torn down in 1989, it was a physical barrier between the governments and its people in West and East Germany, separating capitalists from the democratic republic.

Religious and holy sites have a special place in the history of the world, as they signify a certain individual right to practice a selected religion and worship a particular god or group of gods.

- **Tower of Babel**—Established in Babylon in about 500 B.C.E. to help the Jews reach heaven.
- **The Temple of Angkor Wat**—Built for a Hindu god, it later became a Buddhist shrine.
- **The Great Temple of Tenochtitlan**—Created in Mexico in the 1500's it replicated a pyramid and honored the god of the Sun.

- **Taj Mahal**—Completed around 1648 in India, it is a mausoleum to honor Emperor Jahan's wife, Mahal, built of white marble and semi-precious stones.
- **Notre Dame Cathedral**—A Gothic cathedral in Paris, France, it was begun in 1200 and completed around 1345. It was destroyed by riots and wars, and rebuilt in the 1700's, then being renovated several times afterwards.
- **The Kotel (The Western Wall or The Wailing Wall)**—An important Jewish religious site, was built in Old Jerusalem around 19 B.C.E. and was added from the seventh century forward. It remains a place where people may mourn the destruction of the Temple and leave their prayers.

Ancient cities were developed when people began to join together to live and work. Individuals who study ancient cities and cultures can see how their impact influenced the contemporary living situations. Some of those more well-known to the history of the world include the following:

- **Jericho in Jordan**—One of the oldest cities (around 8000 B.C.E.), it was on an important trade route and people raised crops and animals important to life.
- **Catal Huyuk in Turkey**—A city (6000 B.C.E.) known for cattle breeding, various crops, and weapon building, it was built along a fertile river plain.
- **Mesopotamia in current Iraq**—The earliest civilization (5000 B.C.E.) known for crops, irrigation, government, military, wealth, and religion.
- **Mycenae in area of Greece**—Focus of the civilization period from 1600 B.C.E. to 1000 B.C.E. they concentrated on language, beliefs, farming, and trading.
- **Tyre, Sidon, and Carthage along the Mediterranean**—Exported goods to Britain and Africa, trading for other desired items.
- **Caanan in Palestine**—Created the Jewish religion of Judaism, and was in the center of the region's trade routes.
- **Babylon in Middle East**—Excelled in astronomy and mathematics, the people also created a system of measurement and designed maps.
- **Athens and Sparta**—Influenced present day civilizations with the government system and laws.
- **Persepolis in current Iran**—Known for military strength and tactics, as well as spreading culture throughout the world.
- **Byzantium changed to Constantinople and now Istanbul**—Excelled in the arts, designed a legal system, and was a busy port city for traders.
- **Mecca**—A holy city in Saudi Arabia that drew pilgrimages of prayer.

Impact of People, Organizations, and Movements

Prominent people have blanketed history throughout centuries. To define every person's contribution since the beginning of time would take years. Only a few people have been selected for review in this section and they have been chosen based on a cross section of the time period of human existence on earth, as well as the various professions who have contributed to its development.

Humans perform an essential role in the structure of the environment and the transformation of the world. Human interactions have deliberate and planned results in history, as well as unintended repercussions over the entire earth. The movements or events in which they participated may have destroyed features of the earth, consumed major natural resources, or may have diminished populations. Additionally, human activities and participation in significant adventures may have improved the environment, located new resources, or helped the population migrate to more livable areas. Whatever the human contribution, we must analyze its place in the world, knowing that in some way former human existence affected our present day lives.

In this section of the study guide, examinees should study the impact of the people and movements provided. These lists are in no way comprehensive, yet they do illustrate a picture of the overall history of the world and provide a glimpse into the development of the United States. Knowing about the events in the world and the contributions of citizens in timeline order will be one aspect evaluated on the Praxis II exam. Understanding the causes, the affects, and the developments of one movement to the next event is another area assessed on the exam. For further information on people, organizations and movements in the world check textbooks, the library and the Internet for timelines, historical events, important people, and significant places.

Leaders and Prominent Citizens of America

This list provides an overview of the types of people who participated in the expansion and success of America. To avoid any misunderstanding of the time period during which these people contributed to the building of this country, they are listed in alphabetical order by last name.

Susan B. Anthony was a proponent of women's suffrage and alliance.

Clara Barton was a nurse during the Civil War and founder of the American Red Cross.

Andrew Carnegie was a businessman in the 1880's who monopolized the steel industry, including the raw materials and the railway system that moved it, yet donated his wealth to establish libraries in America.

Amelia Earhart was the first woman to make a solo nonstop transatlantic flight in 1932.

Thomas Edison was an extraordinary inventor who changed the way people live, creating the light bulb and other electrical energy formats.

Henry Ford was an industrialist and philanthropist, who was a significant figure in the early car industry.

Benjamin Franklin made major contributions in the areas of politics, inventions and science.

Robert Fulton launched his design of the steamboat in 1807.

Geronimo was the leader of the Apache Indians and feared by both Americans and Mexicans, he later surrendered and was involved in President Roosevelt's victory.

Thomas Jefferson was a lawyer, a farmer, an inventor, an architect, and political leader who wrote the Declaration of Independence. He was governor of Virginia, the first Secretary of State and the third President of the United States.

Martin Luther King, Jr. was a defender of equal protection for all citizens and promoted the Civil Rights period of the 1960s.

Abraham Lincoln was the 16th President of the United States and known for his emancipation of the slaves during the Civil War.

Charles Lindbergh made the first solo nonstop transatlantic flight in 1927 in his airplane called the *Spirit of St. Louis*.

Douglas MacArthur was a respected statesman and general during WWII.

Sandra Day O'Connor was the first woman selected to sit on the United States Supreme Court.

Rosa Parks was a civil-rights freedom fighter in southeast America.

Paul Revere warned the patriots of the British approach in the Revolutionary War and is considered an American hero.

Eleanor Roosevelt was the first lady to President FDR, but was more well-known as a humanitarian.

George Washington was a general and the first president of the United States.

Leaders and Prominent Persons across the World

This list illustrates only a few of the many great people who made an impact in the world. To avoid any misunderstanding of the time period during which these people contributed to the world, they are listed in alphabetical order by most prominent name.

Alexander the Great was conqueror of the largest empire in the ancient world (300 B.C.E.)

Napoleon Bonaparte was a general during the French Revolution and later Emperor of France and King of Italy.

Julius Caesar was a Roman general who ruled the empire in 49 B.C.E.

Charlemagne (Charles the Great) was founder of the Holy Roman Empire (760) and considered the ideal ruler.

Constantine the Great was the first Christian emperor of Rome (Byzantine Empire) in 300 B.C.E.

Leonardo da Vinci was a visionary of the Renaissance period who was also a teacher, an artist, and inventor.

Genghis Khan was ruler of the Persian Empire in the early 1200's and known for his fierce battles and fair rule.

Mahatma Ghandi was a respected political and spiritual leader of the 20th Century.

Kublai Khan was ruler of the Yuan dynasty of a technologically advanced China, and respected for his fair treatment, charity of the sick and hungry, and establishing transportation.

Nikita Khruschev was the leader of the Soviet Union during the Cold War and the Cuban Missile Crisis.

Martin Luther was a German monk who led for religious change that began the Reformation.

Nelson Mandela was the leader in Africa who was imprisoned in 1962 due to his political views and the conflicts there, being released in 1990 when the apartheid ended.

Mohammed was the leader who created the religion of Islam and united the Arab peoples placing the writings of the religion in the Koran.

Sir Issac Newton was a physicist, mathematician, astronomer, alchemist, and theologian. He is the inventor of the reflecting telescope, and prism and defined gravity developing three laws of motion. He is known for his work in mechanics, calculus and optics.

Queen Victoria reigned over the British throne from 1837-1901, helping Britain to become a powerful nation.

Famous World Explorers

Over the period of history, it was the curiosity of people that led to great travels, explorations and migrations for others. Without the bravery and determination of many explorers, lands and resources would have remained "silent." This brief list provides a glimpse of those who suffered and endured to build a nation, join people, utilize lands, and improve the world.

1450–1499 John Cabot—English explorer and navigator who explored the Canadian coastline looking for a northwest passage to Asia.

1451–1506 Christopher Columbus—Italian explorer who voyaged across the Atlantic Ocean in 1492 hoping to find a route to India and then discovered North America.

1454–1512 Amerigo Vespucci—Italian explorer who was first to realize that the Americas were separate from Asia and not part of the East Indies.

1458–1521 Juan Ponce de Leon—Spanish explorer and soldier who discovered the Gulf Stream while searching for the Fountain of Youth in Florida.

1485–1547 Hernan Cortes—Spanish conquistador who wiped out the Aztec Empire and claimed Mexico for Spain.

1491–1557 Jacque Cartier—French explorer who discovered Canada and paved the way for French exploration of North America.

1496–1542 Fernando De Soto—Spanish explorer who explored Florida and the Southeastern United States and discovered the Mississippi River.

1510–1554 Francisco Vasquez de Coronado—Spanish conquistador who explored the American Southwest, killing Native Americans because they would not convert to Christianity.

1521 Ferdinand Magellan—Portugese explorer who attempted to circumnavigate the globe, he was the first to lead an expedition across the Pacific Ocean and cross all of the meridians of the Globe, establishing the International Dateline. As a result of this voyage, a German cartographer made a globe of the world based on the explorer's notes.

1531–1532 Francisco Pizarro—Spanish explorer who traveled to Peru and conquered the Incas.

1552–1618 Sir Walter Raleigh—British explorer, poet, historian, and soldier who established English colonies in the Americas and named the state of Virginia after Queen Elizabeth.

1565–1611 Henry Hudson—English explorer who explored the Arctic Ocean and northeastern North America, credited with founding New York and honored by the naming of The Hudson River, the Hudson Strait and the Hudson Bay.

1577–1580 Francis Drake—English explorer who sailed around the world.

1580–1631 John Smith—English military captain who founded Jamestown, Virginia and explored the Chesapeake Bay and the New England coast.

1681–1741 Vitus Bering—Dutchman who explored Alaska and Siberia and was honored in the naming of The Bering Strait.

1728–1779 Captain James Cook—British explorer and astronomer who led expeditions to the Pacific Ocean, Antarctica, the Arctic and around the world, credited with discovering Hawaii.

1755–1806 Robert Gray—American explorer who circumnavigated the globe and explored the northwestern United States, helping to obtain the Oregon territory.

1734–1820 Daniel Boone—American pioneer, explorer, trapper, and soldier who founded the first United States settlement west of the Appalachian Mountains and explored the Kentucky wilderness.

1774–1809 Merriweather Lewis and 1770-1838 William Clark—American explorers who mapped the American west, traveling through the Louisiana Territory.

1798–1831 Jedediah Smith—American hunter and fur trapper who was first to travel from New York to California through the Rocky Mountains and the Mohave Desert and cross the Great Basin Desert via the Sierra Nevada Mountains and the Great Salt Lake which opened up the expansion of settlers into the American West.

1809–1868 Kit Carson—American explorer, guide, trapper, and soldier who explored the southwest and western United States with John Fremont, destroying the Navajo settlement in Canyon De Chelley and forcing Native Americans on the "long walk."

The Building of a World

The following section provides an overview of the history of the world, the movement and migration patterns of the people, the contributions of various societies, empires and civilizations, and the impact on the growth of nations and world areas.

The study of past people, their cultures and societies demonstrates how individuals have utilized knowledge, natural resources and ingenuity to progress during their period in history. When students trace the beginnings of "man" they can determine how the world has changed, how inventions were necessary and how the past inspired and impacted the future. The use of timelines, the study of governments, an investigation of famous people, determining the contributions to the world and the investigation of geographical areas are some ways to expose students to various civilizations.

Early Civilizations

Early civilizations brought forth to current times some basic achievements that included the wheel, alphabet, mathematics, sciences, art, architecture, religion, and societal practices.

These ancient civilizations include the following:

- **Neolithic Revolution (10,000 B.C.E.)**—Developed agricultural societies, showed a rise in economic, political and social organizations, and were the first to establish settlements.
- **River-Valley Civilization (6000 to 3500 B.C.E.)**—Created agricultural production, built basic tools, and introduced writing, mathematics and politics.
- **Tigris-Euphrates Civilization (3500 B.C.E.)**—Created the earliest form of structured writings, established a political system, improved agricultural practices, introduced astronomical sciences, identified religious beliefs, conducted trade, developed procedures for laws and a standardized legal system.
- **Egyptian Civilization (3000 B.C.E.)**—Used trade along the river, built impressive architectural structures (pyramids and sphinx), produced mathematical achievements, established an effective government, developed a defense system, created a monetary system, and designed transportation systems.
- **Indian and Chinese River Valley Civilization (2500 B.C.E.)**—Prospered in urban civilizations, improved trade, developed well-defined alphabet and artistic forms, maintained and regulated irrigation system, created advanced engineering and architectural technology, developed impressive intellectual establishments, and constructed massive tombs and palaces.
- **Minoan Civilization (2000 B.C.E.)**—Began on the island of Crete as the first major European civilization with a rich culture, promising economy, structured and established society, and the use of wine, grains, and precious metals.
- **Mycenaean Civilization (1600 B.C.E.)**—Developed a society of farmers, traders, and warriors who built cities like forts, and focused on language and belief systems.

Classical Civilizations

These civilizations contributed to the present day organization of trade, key institutions, rules, religions, agriculture, and society.

- **Civilization of China (1029 B.C.E.)**—A significantly influential society that established the model for global trade, developed strong political institutions, created active economies, instituted religions, promoted tax systems, and excelled in technologies.
- **Civilization of Greece and Rome (800 B.C.E.)**—Powerful societies that expanded trading systems, created democracy and city-states, gained territories, excelled in the arts and architecture, taught mathematics, anatomy, and science, developed agricultural and military systems, and promoted the family structure.
- **Civilization of India (600 B.C.E.)**—showed significant advancements in culture and economics, practiced diversity and regionalism, established social classes, utilized a variety of languages, excelled in science and mathematics, and created university programs in religion, medicine and architecture.

Non-European Civilizations

The following civilizations were the most prominent in contributions to present day civilizations.

- **Mayans**—Focused on education in astronomy and mathematics, designed an elaborate written language system, and developed programs that influenced architecture and art.
- **Mongolians**—Unified the code of law, developed a strong military system.
- **Muslim/Islam**—Developed religions, made advances in chemistry, designed high-quality maps, and influenced the arts and sciences.
- **Inca**—Contributed to design of artistic pottery and clothing, developed metallurgy, promoted architecture, designed irrigation, road, and agricultural systems, and organized a supreme military structure.

Expansion of Europe

A shift occurred in civilizations from the Mediterranean to the Atlantic Coast of Europe. Europeans crossed oceans in search of fertile lands to use for agriculture and for international trade. The discovery of the New World (America) was delayed and the establishment and colonization of new lands overseas caused the migration of people. As expansion increased, improvements were made in communication and transportation.

Colonization

The founding of the nation took shape in the last half of the eighteenth century. Prior to that, settlers and colonists were under English rule in Great Britain rather than being an autonomous society.

People in Europe made a pilgrimage from England to the New World for several reasons: to escape religious persecution, to establish business ventures, to reap personal/economic gain, and for political reasons. Unfortunately it was a long, tedious battle to gain individual rights, political, and religious freedoms. During the period, many lives were lost to disease, weather and war.

Important government actions during this period of history included:

- **1765, Stamp Act**—first direct tax placed on the colonies
- **1767, Townshend Act**—placed a tax on essential goods such as paper, glass, tea and so on
- **1773, Tea Act**—tax break given to the East India Tea Company
- **1773, Boston Tea Party**—a protest of the Tea Act by American colonists
- **1774, Intolerable Acts**—four major acts passed-Massachusetts Government Act, Administration of Justice Act, Boston Port Act, and Quartering Act
- **1776, The Declaration of Independence**—adopted by the thirteen colony vote leading to alliance with France, Spain and the Dutch province

Expansion of the Republic

Although a proclamation in 1763 restricted Americans from movement across the Appalachian Mountains, colonists ignored this order and traveled westward. This led to the expansion of the United States and further migration of colonists across North America toward present day California.

Descriptions of Events and Movements in American History

Colonization—Settlers from England moved to America and by 1770 the colonies were economically and politically prepared to be self-sufficient. The people were proficient in fur trading, trapping, fishing and farming. They set high standards of living that surpassed the standards of living in England.

Westward Expansion—The original territorial boundaries of the United States were between Canada to the north, Florida to the south, the Atlantic Ocean in the east, and the Mississippi River in the west. These boundaries were established with Great Britain and defined by the Treaties of November 30, 1782 and September 3, 1783. However, settlers began to move beyond the border in the west, having claimed more land between the colonies and the Mississippi River and the result of this continued movement was full of conflict and uprisings.

Women's Suffrage Movement—A worldwide attempt to allow women the right to vote resulted in years of organized meetings and demonstrations, finally yielding to women gaining the right to vote in other countries and in separate states with the final right to vote in America in 1920.

Agricultural Revolution—Began in the 1700s as a period in history where people looked for better ways to farm and meet the demands of society. New farming practices and machinery were invented during this movement.

Industrial Revolution—Began in Britain in mid-18th century, moving into North America, and transformed society as people moved from the country to work in the factories and industries of the cities. Major contributions in agriculture, manufacturing and transportation impacted the economic and cultural conditions.

The Gold Rush—Colonists and settlers began to move west of the Mississippi in anticipation of great wealth from finding gold and silver in the mountains and streams.

The Roaring Twenties—Occurred after World War I, as people felt it was a time of recovery, but it was a time of unrest and difficulty. Women gained freedoms, but gangsters fought for control.

The Great Depression—As a result of World War I, the economy of European countries faltered and the devastation trickled over to America. People lost their jobs, their homes, their money, and struggled for food and clothing. The Dust Bowl of the Midwest and migration to California brought a crisis to the United States and it affected the entire world.

The Cold War—A non-military conflict (1961–1963) between the United States and the Soviet Union over the influx of communism in Europe.

Civil Rights Movement—A period in history in the second half of the twentieth century, the 1960s, when people attempted to gain rights so they were not discriminated against for their race, gender, religion or skin color in the areas of voting, joining unions or choosing their leaders.

Causes and Consequences of Historical Events

Event	Causes	Consequences and Developments
Colonization	Disputes arose with England over taxation and government control.	• Led to the American-Indian Wars and the American Revolutionary War. • Colonists maintained a strong government resulting in the founding of the United States of America.

Event	Causes	Consequences and Developments
Westward Expansion	Strife occurred when the colonists claimed unoccupied territory between the original colonies and the Mississippi River. Many ignored the government's ban on continuous movement toward the Pacific coast and the migration of people spread.	• New states formed and the Enabling Acts admitted them to the Union. • Exploration continued westward; several annexations expanded the country to the Pacific coast (Louisiana Purchase, the Purchase of Florida, the Annexation of Texas, the acquisition of the Oregon Territory, the Mexican Cession, the Gadsden Purchase, the purchase of Alaska, and the Annexation of Hawaii).
Agricultural Revolution (1700–1850)	As the populations grew, new farming techniques and more crops had to be produced. Farmers could not keep up with the demands of the population.	• Farmers began to seek new ways to deliver crops for produce and manage animals for product use. • The Dutch created pumps powered by windmills to keep the seas low to use the lands and rotated the crop planting. • The plow was improved and the hoe invented. • Laws for land use were passed.
Industrial Revolution (mid-18th century)	Discovery that smelting iron could be done with coal instead of charcoal. The invention of steam engine to pump water from coal mines. Canals and railroads were built to move products from factories to other locations. Towns were established.	• The improved machinery first increased production and could not keep workers busy. • Limited housing and poor working conditions caused people to suffer from diseases, and hunger. • The use of faster machines and better equipment caused more accidents for people at work. • Major developments of machinery, inventions and patents improved society and provided more jobs and increased economic security.
Women's Suffrage Movement (mid-1800s)	The movement of political reform in the 1830's brought the vote to men, but women were not considered. A movement in America began to obtain women's rights around the world.	• By the 1890s, states slowly began to allow women to vote in local elections and other countries passed laws permitting women to vote. • Women wanted more involvement and established suffrage societies, held demonstrations and went to prison. • Not until 1920 were women allowed the right to vote in America.
The Gold Rush (1848–1859)	Discovery of gold in California, Colorado and Nevada encouraged settlers to move west and seek their fortunes.	• Boom towns in the Great Plains and the West sprouted from the thousands of prospectors and families who sought to prosper. • Native Americans were forced to live on reservations and their land was taken.
The Roaring Twenties (The Jazz Age)	Known as the 'fun" times, the government banned alcohol (Prohibition) and gangsters fought for control of the illegal trade.	• People developed new ideas, new music, dances, radio and sound motion pictures. • Women gained more freedoms. • The New York Stock Market crashed resulting in the Great Depression of the 1930's.

(continued)

Event	Causes	Consequences and Developments
The Era of the New Deal (1930s–1940s)	The Great Depression of the 1930's was devastating to the United States economy and its people. People lost their money, homes, and jobs. Dual federalism in which the states manage their affairs and the national government manages foreign affairs began to change. More intervention from the federal government was necessary to bring the country out of the slump.	• President Roosevelt brought forth the *New Deal* of 1933, a system of cooperative federalism, that promoted cooperation of the national, state, and local governments on programs and laws rather than assigning specific functions to each level. • People were given jobs and welfare and labor laws improved conditions. • This type of government continues to this day.
Post WW II (1940's-1950's)	WWII was a European war to combat the encroachment of communism and the U.S. did not get involved until Japan bombed Pearl Harbor. The war took a toll on America, as thousands of men died, and women had to join the work force to keep the country moving. It was a slow recovery, but America became strong.	• The introduction of computers, nuclear fission, and jet propulsion. • Establishment of organizations such as the United Nations, World Bank, World Trade Organization, and International Monetary Fund. • European countries flourished and maintained non-communist government as a result of U.S. involvement.
The Cold War (1961–1970s)	Soviet Union created Communist governments in Eastern Europe, (which had been liberated by the Red Army). This split Europe by an "iron curtain". To prevent the spread of Communism, the U.S. provided financial aid to those countries where the economy had been devastated (The Marshall Plan).	• Berlin Wall built to prevent individuals from escaping from communism. • Establishment of the North Atlantic Treaty Organization (NATO). • Build up of nuclear weapons in the United States and the Soviet Union. • Continued spying in both countries. • Engagement of Cuba in communist affairs.
The Space Race (1950s–1960s)	German scientists developed guided missiles based on technology that could send people into space. The United States and the Soviet Union began competition for the launching of men and women into space.	• Artificial satellites were launched by both superpowers, leading to men and women in space both landing on the moon and orbiting the Earth. • Other countries become involved, world gathers information about space and the planets for many years. • United States and the Soviet Union worked collaboratively on the space project and the International Space Station. • Improvements in computer technology.
Civil Rights Movement (late 1950s–1960s)	Rosa Parks, a black woman refused to give up her seat on a bus to a white man and was arrested. In the south blacks were discriminated against in jobs, health care, transportation, schools, and in the community.	• Marches led by Dr. Martin Luther King, Jr. to inspire people to join together to honor the rights of all people. • 1964 passage of the Civil Rights Act that mandated racial discrimination illegal. • National Organization for Women formed.

Wars of the United States

Wars or conflicts throughout the history of the world occur because of the want for control of land, disagreement over religious beliefs, and the need to preserve a desired government system. It is important to study the historical wars as they provide essential information about the evolution of the people, their governments, economic systems, land areas and uses during that period of history. Wars describe insight about people's struggles and their endurance.

Students should look at the historical period, study the issues present, understand the causes of the war and then determine the results/outcomes both positive and negative. Some conflicts have delivered benefits beyond any expected that have transformed history and people's lives.

Throughout the many years that resulted in the development of the United States and as a country, its citizens continued to fight to protect freedom and their rights. America has been involved in many conflicts and this table indicates some of the major conflicts, as well as the causes and results of such struggles.

Time Period	Name of Conflict	Cause and Results
1587–1890	American-Indian Wars	European settlers and colonists defeated Native American tribes in order to expand ownership of land and it resulted in the placement of Native Americans on land specified for reservations.
1775–1783	American Revolution (The Revolutionary War, or The War of Independence)	A raid on a colonial arms depot by the British began the long involvement that details the struggle of how the United States won independence from the monarch of Great Britain to become an independent democracy. They fought for political and religious freedoms. It became an international conflict when allies from foreign nations (France, Spain and the Dutch Republic) supported the revolutionaries. The Declaration of Independence was signed, as well as the Treaty of Paris, ending the war and recognizing the colonies as the United States of America.
1812–1814	War of 1812	Congress declared war on Great Britain which resulted in increasing national patriotism, uniting the states into one nation, building confidence in the nation's military strength, and brought forth the national anthem; created the Erie Canal to connect the Atlantic Ocean to the Mississippi River.
1846-1848	Mexican-American War	Disputes occurred over the land west of the Mississippi that was ruled by Mexico; settlers wanted it to enrich their new country. Settlers began moving to the recently acquired lands in the West to find places to live. Life was difficult but the government aided these people in 1862 with the passage of the Homestead Act.
1861 to 1865	Civil War	The new nation consisted of states in the North (Union) and the South (Confederacy) with a division of powers. A conflict arose over control of the nation, under dual federalism, and the two factions fought until the succession of the south was squelched, slavery was abolished, the federal government gained great power, uniting the country. Lincoln emancipated the slaves and Amendments 13, 14 and 15 were passed.
1898–1898	Spanish-American War	The United States declared war on Spain after the sinking of the ship in the Havana harbor. This 8 month war ended with the signing of the Treaty of Paris. Spain lost control of its Empire (Philippines, Cuba, Guam and Puerto Rico).

(continued)

Time Period	Name of Conflict	Cause and Results
1914–1918	World War I	A world conflict erupted over the spread of communism that involved Great Britain, France, Russia, Belgium, Italy, Japan, the United States, and other allies who defeated Germany, Austria-Hungary, Turkey, and Bulgaria. Four empires (German Empire, Hapsburg Empire, Turkish Empire, Russian Empire) were overthrown and seven new nations were formed.
1939 to 1945	World War II	A great conflict pertaining to the threat of communism involving Great Britain, France, the Soviet Union, the United States, China, and other allies, defeated Communist Germany, Italy, and Japan. Atomic bombs ended the war after six years of battles and the loss of thousands of lives. Some outcomes of the war: Germany was divided into 4 parts and controlled by the allied powers, geopolitical power shifted away from western and central Europe, United States and Russia became known as superpowers, new technologies appeared and global organizations sprouted.
1950–1953	The Korean War (the forgotten war)	The struggle between communist North Korea aided by China and USSR, and non-communist South Korea aided by the United States, Great Britain, and the United Nations, resulted in the same boundaries between the North and South.
1956–1975	The Vietnam War (longest war and only war the U.S. lost)	A long conflict in which communist North Vietnam supported by China and the Soviet Union tried to overthrow non-communist South Vietnam supported by the United States. It resulted in the take over of South Vietnam and the implementation of a socialist republic where the communist party ruled.
1990–1991	Persian Gulf War (Desert Storm)	The United States led a coalition of allied forces and destroyed much of the Iraqi military forces, which resulted in driving out the Iraqi army from Kuwait.
2003–present	The Iraq War (Iraqi Freedom)	The struggle in which the United States and Great Britain led a coalition of allied forces against Iraq to expel Saddam Hussein and defeat his government and sought to end terrorism.

People, Places, Geographical Regions

There are many factors that change the geography of the world: people, climates, wars, natural disasters, and consumption of resources. Students should study not only current geography concepts and places, but how the geography of the world has evolved. They will better understand the present day situations and what the future may hold.

Following are the five themes of geography study:

- **location**—Defines where something happens
- **place**—Represents the physical and human characteristics of a place
- **interaction of people and environment**—Shows how people adapt, modify, and depend on the environment and how that may cause changes in the environment
- **movement**—Demonstrates how people, goods and ideas move around the globe
- **region**—Defines an area with similar characteristics

One component of geography is the concept of spatial relationships and the organization of people, places and environments that exist in the world. In particular, this includes knowledge about major areas and locations of the world and the specific terms that define examples of spatial organization. This portion of the study guide is directed on how people and places have influence over one another and on how students might use geographic tools to broaden their knowledge base.

This is the second category of the four specific areas on the Praxis II exam that pertains to the social sciences. The Praxis will assess whether examinees can

- Demonstrate an understanding of the interactions between people and places, especially the impact of human activity on the physical environment, the environment's impact on people's lives and culture, and human adaptation to the environment.
- Demonstrate the ability to use basic geographic literacy skills such as maps, graphs, tables, and charts.

The national standard that is related to this section focuses on the theme of "people, places and environments." Knowledge in this area of geography aids students in comprehending the importance and relationships of location about self and others, in developing a geographic perspective so they may interpret current social situations and conditions, in investigating resources and products from around the world, and obtaining general geographic knowledge so they may be involved in the global society. Geography is the study of places that include the physical characteristics, geopolitical information, demographics, and economic information of the world.

Students who study geography within the subject area of social science learn how to organize information about the world in a spatial context. Becoming geographically aware and thinking in **spatial terms** means that students gain the ability to describe and analyze spatial organizations around people and the environments found on the earth's surface. If they acquire a strong foundation of geography they will be better equipped to understand the major concepts, and issues of the world.

Two types of characteristics define a place or region based on physical and human traits. **Physical characteristics** include water systems, animal life, plant life, landforms, and climate. **Human characteristics** consist of values, religious beliefs, language systems, political structures, economic methods, and socioeconomic status. Humans influence the environmental status just as the environment impacts humans' lives.

The Impact of Human Activity on the Physical Environment

Humans play an essential role in the structure and transformation of the environment in which they live. Human interactions have intended and unintended repercussions on earth. These interactions may include deforestation, loss of wildlife habitat, redirection of water, transplantation of vegetation, depletion of the ozone layer, and reduction of air pollution.

For centuries, humans have shown a preference for creating organized groups of people who live and function within settlements as compared to living isolated away from others. This human condition focuses on the economic, communication, transportation, political and cultural systems of an area and impacts the earth in three significant ways: by consuming natural resources and changing natural patterns; by building structures; and by competing for control of lands. The results of these interactions are evident in population growth, increases in urbanization, consumption of natural resources, and the migration of humans.

Both human and natural resources exist in different forms around the world, but they are not evenly distributed. The planet has limited natural resources that are not available on every continent and no one country can produce all of the resources necessary for the world's population or that country's people to survive. Since there is a lack of natural resources, people in other lands must communicate and trade with one other. This promotes the movement of natural resources from one area to another and the **consumption of these natural resources** which ultimately **changes the natural patterns** on the earth. To meet people's demands for natural resources in the world impacts the physical environment.

As humans create organized settlements they have an increased need for economic activity, cultural systems, transportation, and use of resources. To meet their needs, people **build structures** to live in, work in and house their systems. The construction changes the earth's surface and impacts a variety of ecosystems, altering natural resources and land formations.

Conflicts are often the result of disputes regarding the management of natural resources, the acquisition of land, the organization of transportation and migratory routes, or the power over other people. The **competition for control** often results, not only in loss of population, but in the division and the destruction of the earth's surface.

Physical, chemical, and biological cycles, functioning within an ecosystem, form the different environments on earth. When changes occur to one ecosystem, other ecosystems may be positively or negatively affected. The primary change an ecosystem experiences is through the impact of the human factor.

The Environment's Impact on People's Lives and Culture

A phenomenal variety of attributes characterize this planet. These environments affect the human society and also have influences upon themselves. By understanding how physical systems affect the earth, students will begin to understand how the earth serves as a home to plants and animals. In order to understand how the environment impacts people's lives and cultures, students must learn about the earth's lands and systems. Then they may be able to understand how the interactions respectively influence one another. Equally important is the history of **human systems** which can be influenced and shaped by understanding geography.

The information in this section defines some of the components of the environments on earth which aid in understanding the overall value and influence on people and cultures. The **physical features** include such items as climates, landforms, and natural vegetation. The **human features** include their attributes, and their developments-such as cities, towns, agriculture systems, transportation systems, communication systems and industries.

A system is a set of connected parts functioning together. There are two systems that are critical to the Earth: the human systems and the physical systems. **Human systems** are a significant component of the Earth's structure, yet these systems exhibit constant change on the Earth, affecting the ecosystems. Humans migrate, change their population levels by increasing, decreasing, or stabilizing in different places, and they learn different methods of living and adapting that characterize one group of people from the other groups. Human systems develop a network of economic dependency, such as transportation functions, communications, political efforts, and cultural values and practices. Human systems are essentially comprised of population, culture, settlement, and the relationships of those components that involve cooperation, and conflicts. Students must learn about the characteristics, distribution, and migration of human populations on Earth's surface; the patterns of economic interdependence; the functions and patterns of human settlements; and how their conflicts and cooperation efforts affect the Earth.

The three primary ways that humans impact earth are described in more detail in the previous section, *The Impact of Human Activity on the Physical Environment*:

1. consuming natural resources and changing natural patterns
2. building structures
3. competing for control

Physical systems shape the earth's surface and interact with plant and animal life to create, maintain, and change ecosystems that affect the world. The earth's environments as these are critical to all human activity. Physical system conditions include: earthquakes, hurricanes, wind erosion, and weathering.

Four **physical processes** shape and reshape the earth's surface. These are **atmosphere** (air) consisting of climate and meteorology; **lithosphere** (ground and surface) made up of rock formations, plate tectonics and erosion; **hydrosphere** (water) pertaining to the water cycle, water currents and the tides of oceans; and **biosphere** (life) which is focused on ecosystems, habitats and the plant and animal realm.

An **ecosystem** is a key element in the viability of earth as a home. Populations of different plants and animals are called a community. When a community interacts with three components of a physical environment it is called an ecosystem, which is an interwoven infrastructure that produces and consumes energy. Ecosystems can maintain a natural stability and balance when left to function independently. However, the balance of an ecosystem can be significantly changed by natural events, such as flooding or fire. When they are transformed, ecosystems can recover and flourish or diminish and disappear.

Natural disasters are not caused by humans but can have harmful consequences for humans as well as on the environment. Volcanoes, earthquakes, floods, tsunamis, forest fires, tornadoes, insect plaques, hurricanes are unpreventable and unpredictable. The harmful results that natural disasters have on human beings can be lessened through improved construction design, public education, warning systems, and regulations of land usage, which are all adaptations to the environment. Each environment or region differs in its capacity to withstand and sustain use. Environments like ecosystems must have equilibrium and balance between their consumption and production.

The more generalized areas on the planet can be divided into specific regions which are used to organize and identify the overall earth's surface. These regions exude unique and distinct attributes related to both the people who live there and the land forms that are present. **Regions** are cultural groupings of an area that are not dependent upon government or political rule. These are formed by a common history and geography as well as shaped by economics, literature, and folklore. Within each region, there are unique demographics, dialects, language, and attitudes that are based upon its heritage and geography. Six regions comprise the United States of America. Several states are considered a part of each region with special landforms, people, climates and resources. These regions are: New England, Mid-Atlantic, The South, The Midwest, The Southwest, and The West.

Places are also large sections but they are human created areas which are a part of the earth's surface. Each place has a certain bordered area, whether specific or imaginary, and the place has been given meaning according to the humans who live there. A place may be a continent, an island, a country, a state, a territory, a city, a province, a neighborhood, or a village. Each place has a name and a boundary with a specific set of characteristics to help set it apart from other places. Places can change as a result of alterations in human characteristics as well as the physical characteristics and since places are human-generated, people gain a sense of autonomy based on where they live.

A large geographical area of particular plant life and animal life is called a **biome.** A certain biome, specific to a region in the world, is determined by the climate and the geography. There are nine major biomes:

- **Alpine**—Contains weather with snow, high winds, ice and cold
- **Chaparral**—A hot and dry climate where fire and droughts are common
- **Deciduous forest**—Includes the four separate seasons: spring, summer, fall, and winter
- **Desert**—Hot and dry with little rainfall; extreme cold and snow, mostly barren
- **Grasslands**—Tall grass, humid and very wet; short grass, dry and hot summer, with cold winters
- **Rainforest**—Year round warmth and high rainfall levels
- **Savanna**—Two seasons with warm temperatures all year; winter, long and dry and summer, short and wet
- **Taiga or boreal forest** [the largest biome]—Winters are cold and snowy; summers are warm, humid and rainy
- **Tundra** [the coldest and driest biome]—A cold, dark winter with a soggy, warm summer of 24 hour sunshine

Climate is the long term pattern of weather in a specific area on earth and it determines what plants and animals will survive in a region. There are five primary climates:

- **tropical**—high temperatures year round with large amounts of rain
- **dry**—limited rain with huge daily temperature ranges (semi-arid and arid)
- **temperate**—warm and dry summers with cool and wet winters
- **continental**—seasonal temperatures vary widely and overall precipitation is not high; found on the interior of large land masses
- **polar**—extremely cold with permanent ice and tundra present

Culture is described as the total way of life that characterizes a group of people. People across the world are diverse and offer a rich contribution to global unity. They live in cultures throughout the regions of the earth's surface and are often the primary factor in defining an area. People may be categorized in a variety of ways in relation to their characteristics. They are defined by their cultures. It is through the basis of a culture that people make adaptations to the environment and interact with the earth's surface. Cultures are made up of different languages (of which there are thousands spoken in world), a variety of religions (people are characterized by how they worship), economic systems differences, use of technology, how they approach health care and medicine, the agricultural practices, their dress, music, food, arts, sports, and more. When students learn information about the people of the world, they better understand their relationships to the spaces of the world.

The environment impacts people, and people adjust and rely on the environment. Concepts related to cultural changes on the earth pertain to the terms **cultural regions, cultural ecology, cultural landscape, cultural diffusion,** and **cultural interaction**.

Cultural regions, which vary in sizes, are indicated as the part of the earth's surface that have similar cultural aspects, although they have great variety. They may include areas significant to specific religions, languages, or agricultural practices.

Cultural ecology explains the relationships between a culture and the environment. Due to the differences in climate, landforms, and vegetation, people make adaptations regarding food, clothing and shelter. They also make accommodations for the architectural structures and production of goods based on the availability of resources. As people adjust, cultures change and evolve promoting additional cultures.

Cultural landscape is described as the material components of a culture, such as buildings, structures and systems. It includes a population's basic needs of food, clothing and shelter. The cultural landscape helps to define the trends and traditions of a culture.

Cultural diffusion defines the factors related to how a culture spreads across areas of the world, which ultimately changes the geography of a region. This happens over a period of time and includes additional spaces. Examples may include trade, migration and commerce. It is critical to understand that the cultural characteristics of a people or area diffuse as the culture expands. As people migrate they may spread their culture or create new communities that reflect their culture. This is of great significance in today's modern global community.

Cultural interaction depicts the components of various cultures that are interwoven and interrelated with other cultures. Religious beliefs are one of the most powerful and important.

Major Religions of the World

Religion is a world wide practice that is significant in the history of the world. At times, religious beliefs have been the cause of major conflicts and they have impacted how and where people live. Religious beliefs illustrate a number of specific cultures and may define value systems in the people. The major religions by denomination, according to world scholars, and based on the population and the number of practicing followers, include: **Christianity, Islam, Hinduism, Buddhism,** and **Judaism.** These major religions may be categorized into super groups based on their historical origin and the influence they have over the region and its people. These groups include: Abrahamic religions, Middle Eastern (Indian) religions, Far Eastern (Asian) religions, African (Central and West Africa) religions, Tribal religions, and new religions.

Human Adaptation to the Environment

Humans are a critical ingredient to the stabilization of the environment. Humans may destroy or modify the environment which alters the world. Students must study the interactions of humans and the environment and how people adapt to certain areas in order to understand how the world changes. They must also learn how humans utilize the resources of their environment to adapt to the features of the area and promote their survival.

Human survival depends upon the environment. For humans to live in a variety of environments, adaptations must be implemented. However, using the environment to meet human needs modifies nature's balance. Human characteristics, which consist of their values, religious beliefs, language systems, political structures, economic methods, and socioeconomic status, are impacted by the areas in which they live. In specific regions humans must adapt, which is demonstrated in how they use clothing, diet, shelter, transportation, money, social organization, and employment to survive.

Geographic Literacy Skills

The primary goal for the study of geography is to help students realize how the relationships between people and how the combined connections of the people and the land transform lives and impact the world. Through the study of geography, students will analyze the causes, meanings, and influences of the physical and human events that take place on the earth's surface. To use geography, students must be able to apply the content knowledge to the past, present and future in relation to this subject. Geography helps children connect history, culture and economy.

Students must learn about the locations of the world in order to understand the importance of such things as waterways for travel and trade, the emigration and immigration of people, the natural resources, vegetation and climates around the world and how land formations serve to protect people or act as barriers.

Geographic representations are those tools that aid the learner in obtaining information related to geography. These may include maps, globes, graphs, tables, diagrams, aerial photos, and satellite images. These tools deliver valuable information about spatial terms and spatial relationships. Some limitations exist as to the use of these tools. They may not be understood by the students so special lessons on the content and use may be needed. They may also be difficult to access depending on the locations studied.

A **map** is a visual representation of a particular area. Maps can be a mixture of objective knowledge and subjective perceptions. They may depict such abstract features as population density, lines of longitude and latitude, political boundaries, and agricultural products. They are used to analyze the spatial organization of people, places, and the environment on the earth's surface. Maps may show locations of specific places and boundaries between countries or regions and they may show natural land characteristics. A map can depict visible surface features such as rivers, coasts, roads and towns or underground features such as tunnels, subways, and geographical formations. Maps show how information about physical and human features are located, arranged and distributed in relation to one another. When students learn to use maps, they are able to make sense of the world.

Maps require specific literacy skills, both in reading and in language. Students need to be prepared to understand the spatial organization of different areas and maps, be able to locate objects or places in relation to self, and be able to read symbols, scales, directions, legends, and key concepts. Maps are designed by using points, lines, area symbols, and colors. Learners must feel comfortable with the four aspects of maps in order to use them effectively: symbols, scale, directions, and grid.

A limitation to using maps is that they cannot accurately represent a sphere on a flat surface without distortion of the distance, direction, size, and shape of water and land forms. Globes are one way to meet this problem, as they can depict the most precise representation of the earth in size, shape, distance, area, and directions.

Types of Maps

There are many types of maps that show a wide array of information. The type of map chosen depends upon the data and information being displayed and conveyed. Most maps have a compass rose (to show direction) and a key (to explain symbols). The following list defines various types of maps.

- **climate map**—displays weather and typical weather conditions of a region
- **conformal map**—presents land masses and retains proper land shapes but are often distorted
- **equal-area map**—shows land areas with relatively proper sizes; however, distortion can occur
- **fact-book maps**—examines the actual facts of events or activities in certain regions or specific places
- **historical map**—illustrates specific events or population of an area such as trade routes or religions
- **mental map (sketch map)**—demonstrates what a person knows about locations and characteristics of places by construction of a map in the mind
- **physical map**—reveals the features of actual geographical surfaces, like mountains or rivers, and the underlying geological structures, such as rocks or fault lines
- **outline map**—shows some geographic features but does not include others
- **political map**—demonstrates government boundaries and territorial borders for major areas
- **relief map (topographical map)**—exhibits a three dimensional variation of land and water areas
- **thematic map**—demonstrates the location of specific ideas or distributions

Charts, tables, and graphs are tools that offer visual representations of information and can show comparisons and percentages easily and concisely. They contain factual information which allows the opportunity for students to learn how to interpret the content. These tools may be used across subject areas to deliver information, make comparisons, and plot documentation. Students should be taught to identify the substance of the information, decide what interpretations may be assessed and figure out how to use the information.

Common Types of Data Graphs

Data graphs represent a collection of information and are used to show a relationship between changing variables. These graphs are commonly used to organize large amounts of collected information. The types of graphics and charts students may use in the social sciences include spreadsheets, and data regarding nautical astronomical or weather information. There are four main types of data graphs.

- **bar graph**—Uses bars that can be displayed vertically or horizontally, with each bar representing specific data and the value of each is based on the height or length of the bar.
- **line graph (most common) (histograph)**—Uses vertical or horizontal lines to connect plotted data points and shows change or information over a period of time.
- **pie chart (circle) graph**—Has the shape of a circle and displays data in relation to a whole the data is usually represented as a percentage.
- **picture graph (pictograph)**—Pictures or symbols are used to represent numbers of specific items; the value of items is obtained by counting the pictorial representation.

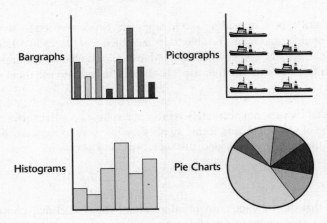

Civics and Government

Standards for civics and government have been established by the National Center for Civics Education proposing that teachers should deliver to students at all levels of education information about the government, the basic ideals of a democratic America, the role of the United States in the world, and the rights and responsibilities of citizens so they become better informed and practice their citizenship responsibilities as adults.

Specifically, it is believed that citizenship education should instruct students on the function and role of government, ways to support a positive and changing society, methods in analyzing social settings, events and conditions, and to help them gain skills to practice value-based decision making and develop personal perspectives to properly participate in civic functions.

In this section of the social science study guide, examinees will review their knowledge and understanding of government systems and the rights and responsibilities of its citizens. This is the third of the four specific areas on the Praxis II exam that pertain to the subject of social sciences. In particular the Praxis exam will assess whether examinees can

- Demonstrate an understanding of the types and function of the various systems of government as well as the major features of the United States' political system.
- Exhibit an understanding of the rights and responsibilities of U.S. citizens based on the establishment of the Constitution.

Systems of Government

For over 5,000 years, formal governments have been in effect around the world, yet the purpose has remained the same for all those periods in history. Governments were established to safeguard individual's liberties, properties, and lives. As people began to work together for this common goal, societies developed and established consistent ways to protect human rights.

The primary function of a government is to establish and enforce the laws or rules. These are essential to prevent conflicts between individuals, and the groups who reside in the same country or land. The government develops procedures to settle conflicts, provide security and manage people.

Depending on the size of a country or state, there may be several levels of government, which might include governments of local, county, district, state, regional, and national origin. Each provide service and order that are critical to the people.

There are also many forms of government, since new governments develop as countries change and borders move. This list explains the most basic guidelines.

- **anarchy**—Rule by no one
- **autocracy**—Rule by one
- **oligarchy**—Rule by minority
- **republic**—Rule by law
- **democracy**—Rule by majority
- **socialism**—Rule by all

The main systems of government used throughout the world include the following:

- **Anarchism**—Form of government that allows people to hold beliefs and attitudes that reject compulsory government such as Isocracy or Tribalism.
- **Authoritarianism**—Form of government that demonstrates strict control where coercion and oppressive measures ensure obedience such as in Communism, Dictatorships and Monarchy.
- **Democracy**—Form of government that gives people certain liberties and freedoms demonstrating power and rule either directly or through representatives such as in Republicanism.

Some specific forms of government are as follows:

- **Communism**—State designs and controls the economy under the power of an authoritarian party and eliminates private ownership of property or individual capital where goods are shared equally by all individuals.
- **Dictatorship**—A single ruler or small group of individuals have absolute power, which is not restricted by a constitution or law, and where citizens have no choice in leadership.
- **Monarchy**—Supreme and absolute power is given to a single monarch who rules over the land for life through hereditary right.
- **Theocracy**—A "deity or god" is ruler and the laws are interpreted by religious clergy.
- **Totalitarian**—Control of all political aspects, economic matters, attitudes, values, and beliefs of the population are subordinate to the state.

The system of government in the United States focuses on the right to life, liberty and the pursuit of happiness. Democracy, where the government has limited powers, promotes equal opportunities, addresses the common good, and seeks truth and justice. This form of government focuses on the people who have the ultimate authority, exercised through elections and representation chosen by the people, with final decisions based on majority rule.

The major features of the government of the United States are defined through the components of the U.S. Constitution that includes a preamble, seven original articles, twenty-seven amendments, and certification of the enactment.

The Preamble is the introduction to the Constitution, and it briefly outlines the overall values and beliefs of the government.

> "We the People of the United States, in Order to form a more perfect Union, establish Justice, ensure *domestic Tranquility*, provide for the common *defense*, promote the general *Welfare*, and secure the Blessings of Liberty to ourselves and our *Posterity*, do *ordain* and establish this Constitution for the United States of America."

The Bill of Rights is the first ten amendments of the Constitution that were ratified in 1791 and describe the rights of citizens and visitors, expressing the freedoms and values of America.

Amendment 1: Freedom of Religion, Press, Expression

Amendment 2: Right to Bear Arms

Amendment 3: Quartering of Soldiers

Amendment 4: Search and Seizure

Amendment 5: Trial and Punishment, Compensation for Takings

Amendment 6: Right to Speedy Trial, Confrontation of Witnesses

Amendment 7: Trial by Jury in Civil Cases

Amendment 8: Cruel and Unusual Punishment

Amendment 9: Construction of Constitution

Amendment 10: Powers of the States and the People

At first, the **Articles of Confederation** (1777–1787) were created to define the freedoms so desired by the people of the New World. They wrote this document outlining the rights and responsibilities which was later known as the Constitution. It was majority ratified and implemented by 1788 and outlined the three branches of government, their powers and the rights of its citizens. The seven articles or principles of the Constitution are as follows:

1. Legislative Power (Popular Sovereignty)
2. Executive Power (Republicanism)
3. Judicial Power (Federalism)
4. States Powers and Limits (Separation of Powers)
5. The Process of Amendments (Checks and Balances)
6. Federal Power (Limited Government)
7. Ratification (Individual Rights)

The Constitution was written by the "founding fathers" to avoid the power of a single figure and to develop a strong centralized government away from Great Britain. The **founding fathers**, delegates to the Constitutional Convention in Philadelphia in 1787, utilizing the concept of separation of powers, created three branches of government, each with their own purpose and responsibilities. These three branches create a system of **checks and balances** that ensure the rights of citizens and appropriate management of the country. These three branches of government are

- **Executive**—This branch guarantees that the laws of the United States are followed. The head of the executive branch is the President of the United States who also commands the military. The President is supported by the Vice President, Cabinet members, Department members and agencies.
- **Legislative**—This branch is comprised of Congress and government agencies. Congress has the power to make laws for the United States and is divided into two parts: House of Representatives and Senate. The Senate allows for two representatives of each state and the House permits representatives from the states based on population, currently with 435 seats.
- **Judicial**—This branch contains the court system, the highest of which is the Supreme Court. Included in the system are the Federal courts. The Courts must ensure that the rules of the Constitution are upheld, so members of the Courts interpret the meaning of laws, and their applications.

After the American Revolution, the original colonies became thirteen independent states and formed a league. This system of cooperation was outlined and established through the Articles of Confederation. However, the national government had limited power and the states held the majority of power. The lack of unity in overall governing left the nation weak, so the Founding Fathers wrote the Constitution to replace the Articles of Confederation. The Constitution was established to divide the power between the federal government and the state governments, defining the responsibilities and creating a federalist system. **Federalism** is the sharing of power between national government and the individual state governments.

Every state has their own Constitution, similar to the U.S. Constitution, but the laws of the individual states cannot conflict with the federal Constitution. Each state, uniquely different from all others, reflects its own history, needs, philosophy, and geography.

Distribution of Power in the United States

The interaction and cooperation of the state, local and national governments is complicated, but it is carefully detailed in the Constitution to maintain a productive and democratic country.

National Government	*State and National Government*	*State Government*
Declares war	Create and enforce laws	Oversees export and import within its boundaries
Maintains foreign relations	Impose taxes	Manages public health and safety
Oversees international, foreign and interstate trade	Borrow money	Ratifies Amendments
Mints money in Treasury		

Citizenship

A main goal of social science studies is to promote citizenship education, so students will learn to make more informed decisions to improve and enhance society. Five elements of citizenship education include: the nature and purpose of government; the forms of government; the United States Constitution; the rights and responsibilities of citizens; and state and local government.

Citizens, as defined by the government, are those people who promise their support and loyalty to the United States and its government. Students should be taught to understand the values, principles, and beliefs of this democratic government, while practicing the positive aspects of becoming a citizen.

Citizenship is described as the way we, as citizens, act and live our lives. Citizenship includes how an individual makes decisions that may affect others and how individuals demonstrate their concern about the community and nation. Teachers should plan activities that help students apply learned citizenship skills to engage in civic activities. Learning about civics helps students understand the rights and responsibilities of people and their relationship towards others and the government.

There are many ways to encourage students to develop proper citizenship in their lives and to enhance the civic education in schools. Some may include encouraging students to participate in service projects for the school or community, visiting local government agencies and speaking with government officials, participating in elections and practicing how to vote, and creating a logo, motto, or rules for a classroom or school. Additionally, teachers may take students on field trips to historical buildings and museums, create specific scenarios where students may practice their skills, and take time to review and debate current issues.

Rights and Responsibilities of Citizens

The founding documents of the United States, the Articles of Confederation and the Constitution, outline the basic rights and responsibilities that were established based on the ideals of the government of democracy. The Constitutional Amendments also outline the various rights of citizens. Together these principles exude the freedoms and protections for our society as they guide and guard individual citizens during their lifetimes. The rights and responsibilities are detailed in the Constitution, but are basically described here.

The **rights** include

- freedom to express yourself
- freedom to worship as you wish
- right to prompt, fair trial by jury
- right to keep and bear arms
- right to vote in elections for public officers
- right to apply for federal employment
- right to run for elected office
- freedom to partake in life, liberty and seek the pursuit of happiness

The **Responsibilities** include

- to support and defend the Constitution against all enemies, foreign and domestic
- to stay informed of the issues affecting your community
- to participate in the democratic process
- to respect and obey federal, state, and local laws
- to respect the rights, beliefs, and opinions of others
- to participate in your local community
- to pay income and other taxes honestly, and on time, to federal ,state, and local authorities
- to serve on a jury when called upon
- to defend the country if the need should arise

Scarcity and Economic Choice

On this Praxis II exam, individuals must demonstrate their knowledge of the economic factors and principles that impact events, nations, and individuals. Examinees must also demonstrate their understanding of how these factors influence diverse cultures, and values, as well as how they affect the geographic features of the world. Economics is a social science described as the study of the production, distribution and consumption of goods and services. This is the final category of the four specific areas on the Praxis II exam that pertains to the social sciences.

National organizations promote economic education and have developed content standards for the instruction of economics in schools. The National Council on Economic Education, the Foundation for Teaching Economics and the National Association of Economic Educators encourage instruction that includes the themes of "production, distribution, and consumption of goods and services" and "global connections" to help students make decisions about resources and usage, as well as how worldwide associations affect societies.

The National Economic Standards suggest 20 standards for grades 4, 8, and 12 and those are summarized on this list.

- Resources are limited, so individuals must make choices.
- Costs and benefits must be analyzed when making economic decisions.
- Economic systems are complex and involve several institutions.
- Economic systems have a specific nature.
- Supply and demand plays a major role in the market.
- Profits, incentives, and prices support the market system.
- Private and public economic sectors are different.
- Employment opportunities are specialized.

- Exchange or money use has various forms.
- Income is determined by market conditions.
- Investment and entrepreneurship are complex topics.
- Government policy affects a market system.

Under this topic of social sciences, students are expected to acquire basic economic concept knowledge and key issues in order to perform economic analysis. Although economic analysis differs in approach from other related subjects, it helps students examine issues and address questions in history, politics, business, and international relations. It aids them in acknowledging facts about the United States, explaining historical events from an economic perspective, comparing economic systems in the world, and making informed decisions. Students will not develop economic reasoning or abstract knowledge for all economic concepts at the same time and they move along the continuum of understanding economic factors from the more complex and the more abstract only as they mature.

Economic Factors and Principles

An economic system refers to a group of institutions and people who manage the production, distribution and consumption of goods, services and resources in the specific society. An economic system is the organization in which a state or nation allocates resources or apportions goods and services to the community. The specific society must follow the set principles and abide by guidelines pertaining to economic resources.

The basic law of economics is that of supply and demand, and individuals must often make choices based on the availability of the resources and their ability to obtain them.

Economic systems have their beginnings in the very earliest periods of civilizations. However, it was not always a monetary system as they are known today. Some civilizations began economic systems based on trade of products, or use of other tokens such as pebbles, beads, or pottery. These systems demonstrate ebbs and flows that reflect on present day economic systems as examples of supply and demand.

Historically, the economy of the United States shows that during the Civil War (1860's) and afterwards, the North was in a boom, as it continued to prosper from the industrial progress of the Industrial Revolution period. The economy in the confederate states of the South declined. In part, the economy of the North improved as the immigrants came to America after the Civil War. They generally settled in the North, since there was more opportunity and it was more well-established. Another reason for the burgeoning of the economy in the North was the creation of a transcontinental railroad system, which moved goods such as food and cattle throughout the North and across to the West. In the South, cotton farmers were not in great demand, and the changes in slave labor affected the plantations.

During the 1870's and 1880's, there was a series of booms and busts to the economy. Farms were destroyed by drought and insects, ranchers had wars over land, and the country was over producing. On the upside, changes in manufacturing, the discovery of oil, and the inventions of steam power and electricity helped improve the economy. Continued manufacturing of saddles, carriages, ready-made clothing, and the lumber and steel industries pushed the economy to a high point. At this time, New York and Chicago became leading cities in the United States.

By the late 1880's stock exchanges sprouted in New York, Chicago, Boston, San Francisco and Philadelphia. Although the first investors in America banked their money on the railroad stock, by this period in history, they moved their investments across country borders and across the oceans to Canada, Japan, Europe, and Mexico. Large companies began to gain monopolies and capitalism started to peak and after much coaxing by certain business people, the government finally stepped in to control the monopolies through regulations. The Sherman Antitrust Act of 1890 followed, which regulated interstate commerce.

Other conflicts of unrest permeated the country during this time. Farmers were concerned about the increased rates for shipping their products on the railway system and the charges for storage of their goods. In 1887, the government passed the Interstate Commerce Act and established the Interstate Commerce Commission (the first regulatory agency) to deliver equal shipping rates to small businesses and farmers across the land. Laborers fought against low wages and tried to establish organized labor groups. The Haymarket Massacre at the Chicago International Harvester plant in 1886 stimulated the thinking of laws for workers in this country. The wealthy citizens increased, the United States was the world's leading industrial power, and the current economic system was on the rise.

The basic economic systems used worldwide include:

- **Autarky economy (closed economy)**—self-sufficient system that limits outside trade, relying on its own resources and products
- **Dual economy**—two systems, local and global, within one country, that occur primarily in under developed countries
- **Gift economy**—believes that goods and services should be distributed without specific reason
- **Market economy**—functions through exchange in the "free market" and is not designed or managed by a central authority, but through privately owned production where the revenue is distributed through the operation of markets
- **Mixed economy**—considered a compromise system, it allows publicly and privately owned companies or businesses to operate concurrently
- **Natural economy**—operates on a trade system rather than a monetary foundation for the exchange of goods and services
- **Open economy**—allows export and import from the global market
- **Planned economy (directed economy)**—designed and managed through a primary authority, whether government intervention or selected group
- **Participatory economy**—guides the production, consumption and allocation of resources through participatory decision making of all its society members
- **Subsistence economy**—the output of services and goods meets the population's consumption of resources which are renewed and reproduced

Common economic formats with government interventions include:

- **anarchism**—no established control or guidelines with voluntary trade
- **capitalism**—property is privately owned and goods are privately produced
- **communism**—common ownership of the means of production
- **industrialism**—uses large industries instead of agriculture or craftsmanship
- **laissez-faire**—promotes private production to maintain freedom, security and personal property rights
- **mercantilism**—depends on capital and an unchangeable world market
- **socialism**—social control of property and income rather than individual control

Economic Effect on Geography, Population, Resources, and Cultures

On a daily basis, individuals are affected by economics. The economy has an effect at the local, state, national, and international levels. The economy is based on those decisions made by individuals who consider the costs and benefits to them personally. Choices may be restricted or affected by laws and regulations. Citizen use of products and services creates competition and promotes the situation of *supply and demand.*

The economy of the United States is based on **competition** and **supply and demand.** This type of economy allows businesses and consumers to decide what should be produced, what employees should be paid, how much products or services should cost, and how much should be provided for the population. The answers to these questions also affect the resources utilized.

The population, the world's diverse cultures, the import and export of goods, and the use of mass communication shape the world. The use of the world's **resources** is of major concern as they affect the geographic state of the earth, they impact the population, and they focus on cultures. There are three types of resources noted: **renewable** (replenish after being used); **non-renewable** (cultivated and used once); and **flow** (used when, where and as they occur).

The interaction of people and the resource allocations follow:

- Location of resources causes population movement and settlement.
- Location of resources causes activity such as employment and use of technology.
- Demand on resources causes economic development.
- Consumption of resources causes social situations such as wealth or poverty.
- Lack of resources causes conflict.

People live in many different parts of the world, using transportation, industrialization, technology, and economic systems to function within the society. They also live in a global community and must function in a global economy. They participate on a larger scale through travel, trade, information flow, and political events. Careful consideration must be made as to how resources are consumed, migration occurs, and economies are built.

The **government role** in the economy and the process impacts in four areas: fiscal policy (taxes), regulation, spending, and monetary policy (credit). Stabilization and growth are the primary concern. The government attempts to guide the economic activities in the country, including the employment rates, prices, and overall growth, by using consumer and producer input. When the government adjusts the fiscal level, manages the supply of money, or controls the credit rates, the economy changes. Spending and taxes are controlled by the President and Congress and that changes the status of the economy in the country, sometimes influencing economies abroad. The government's monetary policy is directed by the nation's central bank, the Federal Reserve Board.

The impact of **technology** illustrates changes in the local and global economies. Technology vastly improved the transportation of products and services via automobiles, trains, boats, and airplanes. Technology affects communication systems and ensures that products and services are distributed on a global scale. The use of computers and the Internet has significant impact on global economies as they are more likely to interact with one another.

International economics is the outcome of economic interactions, practices, and factors between countries. It includes the product development, international trade, and investments. It has influence over labor standards, monetary exchange rates, outsourcing of work, safety issues, worker's income, and resource policies based on supply and demand. Globalization of the economy causes economic conflicts worldwide. The International Monetary Fund (IMF) was established to allocate short-term credit to countries when their economy is out of balance.

Terminology

The subject area of the social sciences provides students with many subtopics of study that includes many new words. The following are some of the additional terms that may be helpful in your study for the Praxis II exam.

affirmative action—policies or programs designed to confront historical injustices that may have been committed against racial/ethnic minorities or other specified groups by making special efforts to provide these groups with access to educational and/or employment opportunities

alien—anyone who is not currently a citizen of the country in which he or she lives

amend—to change the wording or meaning of a motion, bill, constitution, and so on through a formal procedure

budget—the management of current money that requires choices and an analysis of the situation

bureaucracy—the organizations that implement government policies

census—the periodic and official count of the number of persons living in a country

concurrent powers—powers that may be exercised by both the federal government and the state governments, completing such tasks as imposing taxes, borrowing/lending money, and supporting the general welfare

constituent—a person who is represented by an elected official at the local, state or federal level

consumption—the use of resources by citizens and institutions

delegate—a person who acts for or represents others at the local, state or federal level

depression—a long period of financial and industrial decline of the economy

enumerated powers—the powers that are precisely granted to Congress through the Constitution

equal opportunity—an equivalent and unbiased chance for all persons in such areas as education, employment, and political participation

exclusionary rule—the judicial doctrine that is based on the Fourth Amendment and the protection against illegal searches and seizures

fiscal policy—the method in which to regulate the economic activity of the people

foreign policy—the policies of the federal government that are directed to affairs beyond U.S. borders, especially those pertaining to relations with other countries

fundamental rights—the rights that are considered to be the most basic needed and most essential to the people

general welfare—the good of a society as a whole, referring to the *common or public good*

inalienable rights—those rights that are not capable of being taken away or transferred

inflation—the increase in overall prices for products and services in a society

minority rights—the rights of any group that constitutes less than a majority

natural rights—the most basic of human rights demonstrated in The Declaration of Independence as the rights to "Life, Liberty and the pursuit of Happiness"

recession—a period of slow economic growth plagued with high unemployment and minimal spending

revolution—a complete or drastic change of the government and the rules by which government is conducted and may be the first step toward battle engagement

separation of powers—the division of the government's powers among other institutions that must cooperate in the overall decision making

social equality—the absence of the inherited titles of a hierarchical class in the social system

treaty—a formal agreement among nations to develop or restrict the rights and responsibilities, often used to settle a war

unenumerated rights—those rights that were not exactly listed in the Constitution or Bill of Rights, but have been observed and recognized, therefore being protected under the court system

veto—the constitutional power of the president giving him the ability to refuse to sign a bill passed by Congress, which prevents it from becoming a law

Web sites

These web sites may aid examinees in conducting additional study and further research. Examinees may locate standards, a variety of related topics, and extended core knowledge about the subject of social science and citizenship.

Note: At the time of the development of this book, the Internet sites provided here were current, active and accurate. However, due to constant modifications on the Internet, web sites and addresses may change or become obsolete.

www.ncss.org	National Council for Social Studies
www.nationalgeographic.com/education	National Geographic Educator's Resources
www.nationalgeographic.com/resources/ ngo/education/themes.html	
www.sscnet.ucla.edu/nchs/standards/#TOC	The National Center for History in the Schools
www.netstate.com/states/	
www.neh.gov	National Endowment for Humanities
www.civiced.org	Center for Civic Education

www.billofrightsinstitute.org	The Bill of Rights Institute
www.constitutioncenter.org	National Constitution Center
www.apsanet.org	The American Political Science Association
www.crf-usa.org	Constitutional Rights Foundation
www.ned.org	National Endowment for Democracy
www.eduref.org	The Educator's Reference Desk (click Social Studies)
www.ncge.org	National Geography Standards
http://ackerman.eduction.purdue.edu//	The Ackerman Center for Democratic Citizenship
www.youthcitizenship.org	Center for Youth Citizenship
www.civnet.org	CIVITAS and Journal for a Civil Society
www.infoplease.com/	
www.ncee.net	National Council on Economic Education

Science

Introduction

Knowledge about the natural world should be gained through discovery and experiences. In school settings, systematic instruction of the various science topics will help students gain knowledge they need in the life and physical sciences. They will have a better understanding of how to incorporate what they learn in other subject areas, as science is often interrelated with other subject concepts.

The National Science Teachers Association (NSTA) has produced a set of recommended national standards related to science education. Although these are not mandated nor are they found included in required curriculum, many educators seek a copy of this science criteria in order to better address the needs of students and to better prepare students to live in this world. The NSTA believes that "all students, regardless of age, sex, cultural or ethnic background, disabilities, aspirations, or interest and motivation in science should have the opportunity to obtain high levels of scientific literacy."

The principles of these science standards infer that

- Science is for every student.
- Learning science requires an active process.
- Science education should emulate the intellectual and cultural traditions of contemporary science.
- Education reform should include the improvement of science education.

Through these standards, the NSTA created eight suggested student outcomes:

1. unifying concepts and processes in science
2. science as inquiry
3. physical science
4. life science
5. earth and space science
6. science and technology
7. science in personal and social perspectives
8. history and the nature of science

It is according to these outcomes that educators must base their knowledge of science.

Teachers must hold a central understanding of the basic scientific disciplines that include facts, concepts, principles, laws, processes, and methods. The general background knowledge integrated in this section of the examination is comprised of the philosophy, methodology, and role of science in society, the natural processes of the Earth, the biological processes, and the principles of matter and energy. The concepts and procedures of science are essentially unifying and, therefore, may also be found integrated into other content areas.

Many important laws and theories govern science and there are vocabulary and definitions that pertain particularly to the field of science. For example: a **scientific law** is a statement of fact, proven time and time again, while a **scientific theory** is a statement, based on observations, tested and then proven. Educators should be knowledgeable about the laws, theories, and the vocabulary that support the processes and concepts of science.

The primary laws and theories of science are not specifically taught to students in the early elementary grades, however, the general elementary science concepts, instruction, and curriculum are based on these established science guidelines. For example, older students in the upper grades will learn Newton's laws of gravity, while students in the elementary grades will learn the basic concepts about gravity (water flows down stream and hills, or if a ball is thrown up in the air it will return to land, both due to gravitational pull). In this section of the study guide, some of the most prominent laws of science and their descriptions are provided to aid the examinee and educator in understanding and reflecting on the core knowledge that is expected for this examination.

Basic Understanding of Concepts and Processes

For this examination, educators must demonstrate a basic understanding of the primary concepts and processes of science. They must acknowledge their comprehension of the interrelatedness of the science content and show their ability to apply this core knowledge to the integrated fields of education, as some of the concepts and procedures of science are also found in the other content areas, such as mathematics, history, language, and so on.

The science concepts supply students with core knowledge, learned procedures and formulated ideas on how the natural world functions. The National Science Teacher's Association maintains that, "in early grades, (science) instruction should establish the meaning and use of unifying concepts and processes...." These unifying processes include the following components:

- systems, orders, organizations
- evidence, models, explanation
- change, constancy, measurement
- evolution, equilibrium
- form and function

These unifying processes are more thoroughly explained throughout this science content section and some are defined here.

Systems, Orders, and Organization

Being able to think about the whole in terms of all its parts and also about parts as they relate to one another as well as to the whole is an important part of understanding and interpreting the world. Science demonstrates and conveys order and predictability in nature. Learning and comprehending the basic laws, theories and models that explain the world can be accomplished by connecting order and organization to systems. Systems, order, and organization are vital components of the unifying processes of science.

Systems	Purpose	Examples
Small unit of the natural world to investigate Organized group of related parts, objects, components that form a larger whole Have boundaries, input and output, parts and reactions Two Types: • closed (not affected by external forces) • open (can be impacted by external forces)	Keeps track of organisms, energy, mass, events Develops understanding of regularities, commonalities, reactions and equilibrium Extends knowledge of law, theories, and models	machines education organisms transportation numbers galaxy
Order	**Purpose**	**Examples**
Statistically describes the behavior of matter, organisms, events and objects	Develops knowledge of factors influencing matter, organisms, events and objects Promotes improved and increased observations Creates advanced exploratory models	probability four seasons life cycles

Organization	Purpose	Examples
Various types and levels Gathering, grouping and structuring of systems and information	Provides useful ways of thinking about the world Shows interaction of systems Demonstrates hierarchy	Food Pyramid Periodic Table of Elements Organism Classification

Evidence, Models, and Explanation

Students learn to gather evidence as they acquire the processes of science. They come to understand that evidence supports models, and these may be constructed based on the evidence obtained. They must learn the properties and patterns used in constructing the models, why models are useful, and how they differ from the natural world. Models in science provide a concrete, visual representation of something that cannot otherwise been seen. When students confront the evidence, they may develop explanations based on reasonable data (observation), which then translates into scientific ideas.

Most models are based on science objects or processes that are incomprehensibly large or very small (on the nanoscale), so spatial relationships become the most difficult aspect of building the model. Designing and constructing models helps students comprehend the size and use of an object or process in the field of science. Students can investigate and research the object they wish to replicate and they may learn observation, measurement, comparison, and investigative skills.

The following table lists the various types of models.

Type	Definition	Example
Physical	an actual, easy to see model	fish tank to observe animal life
Conceptual	more abstract or replicated from larger example	clay model of a watershed paper mache model of a volcano Styrofoam mobile model of the solar system
Mathematical	one that needs calculation	observing yo-yo energy

Change, Constancy, and Measurement

This portion of the unifying processes helps students observe items in the natural world that remain the same. This is an underlying component of scientific understanding in the world. Students may also observe how change can occur over a period of time, and that this change can be measured in reasonable terms. A constant might be observing chickens laying eggs. This species shows a basic activity that does not change in the next generation. However, a change may occur and a chicken may lay smaller eggs when her nutrition is affected or the weather is such that she is stressed most of the time. Students should ask themselves what they observed during the investigation: Did it remain the same? What changed, and why? The mathematical skills that accompany this process include precision, accuracy, rate, scale, graphing, and measurement.

Evolution and Equilibrium

Under this unifying process, students gain an understanding of evolution, which is defined as how systems change over time. They also learn about the status of equilibrium, which demonstrates how systems attain a steady, balanced state of being as they evolve, helping them survive and adjust to the environment. Systems may be biological, physical, geographical (chemical, physical, biological), or technological. As systems change or react to given forces, a state of equilibrium may occur in opposing directions. Change may also be rapid or occur gradually over time.

Form and Function

This area of unifying processes helps students understand the construction of living and non-living things, as well as the purpose of the individual object's parts and its meaning as a whole object. For example, students may study the human body. They learn about its form, which is the outline of how it is constructed of bones, muscle, tissues, organs, and so on. Then they use that information to understand the body's function, how the parts work separately, and how they interact as an entire organism. Students may also study the ocean. Its form consists of it being a large body of water with various animals and plants. Then they learn about the function of the ocean, how the animals and plants interact with one another, their individual purposes, and how they create this major ecosystem. In this area of form and function, students gain an understanding of how things adapt to the world and why they are important to the environment.

Nature and History of Science

One of the three primary areas of the Fundamental Subjects: Content Knowledge Exam in Science refers to information found in this main topic. Teachers must be able to do the following:

- Demonstrate the ability to gather reliable information about nature and to develop explanations that can account for the information gathered.
- Demonstrate the ability to identify and use the elements of scientific inquiry for problem solving.
- Demonstrate familiarity with the heritage of science such as important scientific events and contributions made by major historical figures.
- Demonstrate understanding of the processes involved in scientific data collection, manipulation, interpretation, and presentation.
- Interpret and draw conclusions from data, including those presented in tables, graphs, maps, and charts.
- Demonstrate the ability to analyze errors in data that are presented.

Gathering Information

Scientists and those who study the world of science need to gather valuable information that may be recorded or documented for research or analysis. As they collect information or data, they must beware of the source that is used as they may contain already processed interpretations, false information, specific points of view, beliefs, or contradictions. Information may be in the form of facts, observations, events, recordings, photographs, journals, diaries, notes, or oral content, or it may be sought through charts, timelines, maps, tables, or graphs. Other sources may include original documents, research studies, or reference materials, such as encyclopedias, statistical abstracts, or computer programs. Gathering and using information requires skills in reading and in critical thinking.

Elements of Scientific Inquiry

Science is the process of obtaining and verifying knowledge. Through this process, we learn **scientific concepts** that produce the learned knowledge. Scientists use the process of **scientific theory** to obtain outcomes:

> Observation-Question-Theory-Experiment-Data-Results-Conclusion

Science is a subject that allows students the opportunity to be curious, to ask questions, to discover information, and to explore possibilities. When students participate in their own method of answer seeking, as the constructivist theory emphasizes, the outcome has more meaning to them. It is highly recommended that the subject of science be *inquiry-based* to promote the basic principles of organization, to support critical thinking skills, to improve scientific reasoning skills, to augment cognitive development, and to enhance the knowledge of science.

Inquiry-based science promotes the following:

- the comprehension of scientific concepts
- an appreciation of the history of scientific knowledge
- an understanding of the nature of science

- an acquisition of the skills needed to become independent thinkers
- the tendency to use skills, abilities and attitudes associated with science

One specific form of inquiry is called **authentic inquiry.** Authentic scientific inquiry allows students to learn science as it is practiced. Students may pose real questions with unknown answers, observe important problems that are often local and meaningful, and socially construct their answers through collaboration, argumentation, and critical evaluation by their peers.

Science inquiry follows a basic format:

- Identify and control of variables.
- Collect data using various instruments.
- Interpret data through reliable and valid reasoning.
- Formulate and test hypotheses.
- Communicate procedures, methods, results, interpretations.

Twelve Processes of Science

A **process** is a systematic chain of actions, directed toward a conclusion, that usually follows a set of steps to clarify the concepts. The processes of science are the fundamental building blocks of the subject.

1. **Observation**—Use of the five senses to focus on the world and watch the movement within it.
2. **Classification**—Utilize commonalities of objects to logically group items.
3. **Communication**—Share findings, outcomes, and results with others.
4. **Measurement**—Use appropriate tools and equipment.
5. **Prediction**—Use of prior knowledge and experience to determine occurrences.
6. **Inference**—Use of prior knowledge and experience to state the reasons for an occurrence and provide a supporting statement.
7. **Variable identification/control**—Determine factors and stabilize all but one.
8. **Formulation of hypothesis**—Develop an assumption based on variables.
9. **Interpretation of data**—Use of collected information and constructing charts, graphs, or narration to deliver reasonable results.
10. **Define operations**—Apply mathematical equations and principles to issue.
11. **Experimentation**—Use of prior knowledge and a hypothesis to attempt different solutions.
12. **Constructing models**—Identify the need for a model and create an accurate and appropriate sample.

Scientific Events, Contributions, and Historical Figures

Science is a field of the known and the unknown. Science covers many different areas and might be categorized according to the century, the type of science, or the kind of activity. The field of science is managed and studied by people who come from many different areas who are risk takers and idea makers. Students learn science information that has been researched and studied by people in these fields.

Categories of science include scientists such as

astronaut	chemist	geologist	paleontologist
astronomer	ecologist	geneticist	pharmacist
astrophysicist	entomologist	inventor	physician
biochemist	environmentalist	meteorologist	physicist
biologist	herpetologist	oceanographer	researcher
botanist	hydrologist	ornithologist	zoologist

Events

In the field of science, an event may be considered something that happens that is noted throughout a country, continent or the world. It may affect many people and various areas of their lives. These events may be thought of in terms of historical activities that promote science and future discovery. These are often celebratory events as they are exciting and have value in scientific discovery. Some examples include the following:

- Space exploration, which includes launching satellites and probes
- Space shuttle travel and space station work
- Landing on the moon
- Observing significant changes in supernovas, galaxies, comets, asteroids, planets
- Archeological discoveries of tombs, skeletons, and fossils
- Nobel Prize acknowledgements for research, discovery, and invention
- Explorations for lost treasures (Titanic or the Pyramids)
- Explorations of environments or animals (giant squid, Komodo dragon, rainforest)
- Dust Bowl of 1936, the hottest and driest summer recorded in Midwest U.S.

Contributions

A contribution is considered something that has influence or an impact on the future. It may be a discovery or an event that changes, for example, how processes work, or how medical treatment is administered. A contribution often affects many people and countries, as the result is shared and its influence permeates the world. Examples include the following:

- Preventative treatments for diseases such as Penicillin, AIDS, diabetes
- Computer science program advancements
- Discovery of a new species and its affect on the environment
- Outlining the causes, aspects, and needs for addressing global warming
- Creation of scientific laws, which guide an area in the field

Historical Figures

The individuals who are famous in the field of science may have participated in an event, made a major contribution, or implemented a discovery. All of them play a role in how the field of science unfolds and changes. Each of these people has changed a part of our society through their scientific work and there are thousands missing from this list. This is not an exhaustive list and further information on the historical figures in science may be found on the Internet, in the library, or in science texts.

Year	Figure	Discovery
1284	Salvino D'Armate	Invented eyeglasses
1499-1530	Nicolaus Copernicus	Determined Earth was not the center of the universe and the planets orbited the sun; explained the seasons and Earth's rotation on its axis
1500's	Leonardo da Vinci	Invented the hygrometer (measure moisture in the air) and invented the anemometer (measure wind speed)
1593	Galileo Galilei	Invented thermoscope, which became known as the thermometer
1598	Galileo Galilei	Discovered all objects fall at the same rate and studied the orbits of the planets
1608	Hans Lippershey	Patented the telescope

Year	Figure	Discovery
1610	Galileo Galilei	Used a refracting telescope to see the parts of the moon, Jupiter (discovered moons), and Venus
1644	Evangelista Torricelli	Created mercury barometer to measure atmospheric pressure
1666	Sir Isaac Newton	Discovered the principles of gravity and invented a reflecting telescope
1667	Robert Hooke	Redesigned the anemometer
1668	Robert Boyle	Discovered relationship between volume and pressure of gas
1670's	Anton van Leewwenhoek	Invented the microscope
1714	Daniel Fahrenheit	Created a scale to measure temperature
1750	Benjamin Franklin	Discovered lightning and static electricity
1774	Joseph Priestley	Discovered oxygen
1778	James Watt	Invented the steam engine
1794	Eli Whitney	Invented the cotton gin
1802	John Dalton	Defined relative humidity
1829	Gustave-Gaspard Coriolis	Defined *kinetic energy*
1835	Charles Darwin	Discovered the principles of species evolution
1835	Gaspard Coriolis	Determined the mechanical energy of a waterwheel
1837	Samuel Morse	Invented the telegraph and code
1839	Charles Goodyear	Invented vulcanized rubber
1848	Lord Kelvin	Created the scale for measuring thermodynamics
1851	Isaac Singer	Designed a practical sewing machine
1853	William Rankine	Defined *potential energy*
1858	Louis Pasteur	Discovered the existence of microbes and pasteurization
1865	Gregor Mendel	Discovered the principles of genetics
1869	Dimitri Mendelyeev	Created the periodic chart
1869	John Hyatt	Formulated celluloid plastics
1875	Alexander Graham Bell	Invention of the telephone
1878	Karl Benz	Invented gasoline powered automobile and internal combustion engine
1879	Thomas Edison	Invented the light bulb
1881	Pierre Curie	Invented the electrometer to measure electric currents
1894	Guglielmo Marconi	Invented the radio
1895	Wilhelm Roentgen	Discovered the X-ray
1896	Henri Becquerel	Discovered radioactivity

(continued)

Year	Figure	Discovery
1896	Svante Arrhenius	Calculated the effect of carbon dioxide on the climate (the potential theory of global warming)
1898	Madame Marie Curie	Discovered radium
1905	The Wright Brothers	Designed the motorized airplane
1909	Sir Gilbert Walker	Figured out the global climate pattern systems
1916	Albert Einstein	Developed the theory of relativity
1917	Florence Sabin	Discovered the origin of blood
1921	George Washington Carver	Identified 300 products made from peanuts
1925	Igor Sikorsky	Developed the helicopter
1928	Philo Farnsworth	Invented the first working electronic television system
1928	Alexander Fleming	Discovered penicillin
1929	Edwin Hubble	Determined light in space was proportional to the distance and led to the Big Bang Theory
1941	Konrad Zuse	Invented the first functional program controlled computer

A Time Table of World Discoveries and Developments through the Ages

A study of the historical periods in science with a comparison to the events in history reveals the characteristics and needs of the people and the state of the society in those times. It may also be ascertained how particular discoveries and inventions led to others in later years. This chart reveals the discoveries or developments that occurred from the beginning of one period to the beginning of the next.

Time Period	Discovery or Development
3000 BCE*	Levers and ramps created, glass made, hemp crops grown, masonry and stone used in building, wheeled vehicles invented, seed drills created, silver used for ornamentation
2000 BCE	Cotton grown as crop, horse drawn vehicles used, masonry used for dams, copper ore smelted, silver sheet metal work used
1500 BCE	Rice and maize crops grown, simple pulleys used, iron usage developed, alphabet created, vellum and script utilized
500 BCE	Magnetic compass invented, complex pulleys and cranes created, tin mining ensued, crossbows used
1 CE*	Steel made, use of brass determined, tea grown, silk imported, paper manufactured, waterwheels designed, crank developed
500 CE	Paper manufacture refined and spread, paddleboats, ships and sails utilized, mechanical clocks created, caustic alkalis discovered
1000 CE	Magnetic compass created, watermills and windmills used, explosives invented, dyes and pigments used
1500 CE	Spring clocks developed, coinage used, handheld firearms created, navigation tools designed (first navigation of the globe), anemometer invented
1600 CE	Telescope invented, crop rotation system designed, gunpowder used in mining, pendulum clock created, blister steel used

Time Period	Discovery or Development
1700 CE	Iron smelted, fire engine designed, atmospheric experiments conducted, iron rail used, smallpox inoculation discovered, lightning conductor designed, marine chronometer utilized
1800 CE	Food canning and preservation created, steamship and steam locomotive invented, cotton gin invented, power loom invented, photography developed, mine safety designed, gas and oil lighting used, harvest machines invented, principle of thermodynamics created, electric battery designed, balloon flight implemented, threshing machine created, telegraph invented
1850 CE	Internal combustion designed, typewriter created, oil wells used, phonograph invented, electric power stations established, pasteurization discovered, antiseptics developed, telephone invented, radio waves discovered, compressed air machines designed
1900 CE	Electric cooker developed, cinema established, motorized car invented, radioactivity discovered, submarine designed, diesel engine designed, x-rays discovered, torpedo designed, geothermal energy used, radio signals used, "aeroplane" flight implemented, helicopter designed, escalator designed, electrocardiograph invented, aerial bomb created, atomic structure discovered, stainless steel used
1920 CE	Aircraft carrier designed, sound films invented, liquid fuel rocket used, airlines formed, insulin discovered, iron lung designed
1930 CE	Neutrons discovered, television implemented, concrete roads used, radar established, crystal clocks invented, synthetic rubber invented
1940 CE	Jet fighters implemented, natural gas discovered, nuclear fission discovered, xerography designed, magnetic mines used, nuclear reactors designed, electronic computer invented, atomic bomb invented
1950 CE	Polio vaccine discovered, microwave ovens designed, nuclear power station established, transistors used, color television designed, stereo designed
1960 CE	Pacemaker designed, lunar lander used, weather satellite established, manned space flight occurred, laser used, weather Doppler invented
1970 CE	Email implemented, supersonic airliners used, space station established, synthetic organs designed
1980 CE	Fiber optics used, personal computer developed, space shuttle implemented, comet probe designed
1990 CE	Genome project underway, worldwide web implemented, smart bombs created, Mars rover sent
2000 CE	Sheep cloned, brainwaves studied, space studies and flights increased, smart materials developed

BCE refers to "before the current era" or "before the common era" and CE refers to the "current era" or the "common era." (This era began when the calendar system was employed.)

Discoveries by decades can help us follow the patterns of science. Recognizing the period in history and the category of science reflects on the people of the time and the subjects that were of interest and products needed.

Data Collection, Interpretation, and Analysis

Data is a collection of information or facts, through an observation, an experiment, or an experience. It is gathered as it is presented without any trace of interruption or alteration to the information and provides an outline to gain further knowledge about a subject. It may include numbers, words, ideas, and measurements. Data acquisition is the process of collecting the physical properties of an object or subject to be examined.

Various types of data are used in science: raw data, which is a basic collection of facts, numbers, or images that may be converted or processed by a human or a computer; and experimental data, which is that information generated through a scientific investigation of observation and documentation. Scientists manage the data in files, notebooks, databases, and spreadsheets.

Often scientists protect their work by storing their data and recording methods as an archive, and this data may then be shared with other scientists, used for confirmation of an outcome or for later studies. Archiving is more easily accomplished with new technologies and quicker access through computer links.

Data analysis is another aspect of managing scientific information. This is the process of collecting, modeling and transforming the data into usable information. This allows for decisions to be made, predictions to be forecasted, conclusions to be drawn, and outcomes to be supported. There are many different methods that scientists employ to analyze data and place it in a reputable and organized state. It depends on whether the data consists of statistics, long wordy descriptions, or observational notes. As they proceed with analysis, however, they should ask about the quality of the data, the quality of the measurement, whether the data focused on the study, and what the characteristics of the data sample reflect.

Scientists learn to use a variety of data and so should students who study science. These types may include timelines, charts, graphs, tables, maps, reference resources, or current events documents. It is critical that students understand the format of these various sources and use critical thinking skills to make interpretations of the data from the source. Even considering whether the source is reliable is a learned skill and necessary in the study of science.

Following are the sources of data and a description of their importance:

- **Current event documents** will include the up-to-date information about events and perhaps natural phenomena occurring around the world. Students will need to understand how to decipher the factual information from the opinions when using this type of "news" and use it to best suit the scientific needs.
- **Graphs or tables** are necessary for recording statistical information. The data is provided and used on a limited basis, so students need to understand how to summarize, interpret and plot data of this type.
- **Maps** may be helpful in the study of geology, astronomy, ecology, oceanography, and the environment. It is necessary to possess adequate reading skills and understand how to use maps.
- **Reference resources** include encyclopedias, computer programs, Internet, atlases, dictionaries, and statistical abstracts. Students must know how to access these sources and how to use them for accuracy and reliability. They should also learn how to record the data given.
- **Timelines** are a chronological arrangement of dates, events, phenomena, or activities pertaining to science. Students must learn the format and use the data appropriately.

When faced with possible data errors, scientists often try to "clean up" the data. They will address items that appear to be erroneous or suspect and then inspect and correct the information. However they should never dismiss or destroy any data entries and must preserve the original data. Careful scrutiny is necessary when making adjustments to data, as data is a valuable resource in the field of science. Students should learn proper data maintenance and usage.

Basic Principles and Fundamentals of Science

The second of the three primary areas of the Fundamental Subjects: Content Knowledge Exam in Science refers to information found in this main topic. Teachers must be able to

- Demonstrate the ability to use basic principles of science to explain natural phenomena and events.
- Demonstrate understanding of the importance of energy relationships and transformations in both living and non-living contexts.
- Demonstrate understanding of the structure and properties of matter and the forces that act upon it.
- Demonstrate understanding of the diversity and characteristics of living organism and their interactions with the environment and each other.
- Demonstrate understanding of the processes that have led to changes in the dominant organisms at various times and in various places.
- Demonstrate understanding of Earth as a part of the universe and a body with specific features and processes.

Natural Phenomena and Events

The function and structure of the natural world provide occasions to observe and explain unpredictable events that intrigue people around the world. Some of these occurrences have no explanation, while others motivate scientists to study the information, gather data, and reach conclusions about their unique existence.

Natural phenomena occur in the natural world but are not produced by humans. These may include geological, meteorological and astronomical events and activities and the existence of these phenomena may seriously affect human and animal life on the planet. Although many of the natural events are harmless and provide incredible opportunities for observation, others are dangerous and may even be deadly. These natural phenomena may change the course of history and science as they produce a memorable and significant impact on the people, the landscape, and the symbiosis of the two.

Throughout history, as far back as it may be recorded, natural phenomena has been documented and studied. When reviewing the many phenomena that have been recorded, one might surmise a certain pattern of their occurrences in the natural world (repeated hurricanes, dust storms, volcanic eruptions, and so on). Some of these events are still considered *famous* to this day due to the critical impact imposed on the people and/or the environments of the world.

The list provides a glance at the types of natural phenomena and events that have occurred or repeatedly happened in the natural world.

volcanic eruptions (Mt. Vesuvius, Mount St. Helens, Krakatoa)	northern lights (Aurora Borealis)	meteors, meteor showers (Meteor Crater-AZ)
tornadoes (Tri-State Tornado, Super Tornado Outbreak)	unusual storms (Rain of Fish)	droughts/floods (Johnstown, PA Flood, The Dust Bowl-drought)
hurricanes (New Orleans)	comets (Halley's Comet)	waterspouts
supernovas	polar lights	moonrises
lightning (Catatumbo)	rainbows (Fire Rainbow)	tidal waves (Pororoca)
tsunamis (Indonesia)	summer snows	colored rains
sun halos	balls of lightning	sea floods
gale winds	solar eclipses	earthquakes

The primary purpose for students to study the occurrence of natural phenomena is two-fold. First, they will gain insight into the study of science as an unfolding subject, using authentic inquiry to learn science as it is practiced or as it occurs. Secondly, they will be better able to understand how to apply scientific principles to draw conclusions about these events.

When a natural phenomenon occurs, like a tsunami, students are able to "watch" scientists in action as they figure out the reasons for such a devastating event. Teachers should point out the use of observation as scientists watch the specific event unfold or as they return to view the origination of the event (storm, earthquake, volcano). Teachers should describe how scientists confront the evidence that is present (20 foot tsunami), how scientists develop an explanation(s) based on the reasonableness of the data collected, and how they finally draw conclusions and evaluate their findings. Students may "work" in their classrooms performing similar tasks as the current event unfolds, depending on their age and their stage in the acquisition of core science knowledge and concepts.

Energy Relationships and Transformations

The area of physical science is the study of the tangible or material world. Scientists focus on facts, concepts, principles, theories, and models to deliver the information related to this study of science. The science of matter and energy and how it affects many processes in our daily lives is called physics (building structures, body functions, using tools and implementing machines, light, sound, and movement). Although elementary students do not study a course in physics or learn the laws that pertain to energy and matter, they do learn basic concepts about the events in the physical world. Educators need information about the laws and theories in order to understand these concepts well enough to teach them.

The sub topics of physical science include the following:

- structures and properties of objects, materials, matter
- motion and force
- light, heat, electricity, magnetism
- energy (transfer, consumption, production)

Energy cannot be created or destroyed, but it can change. It changes based on the force that is imposed upon it. James Joule developed the laws that pertain to energy in the natural world, based on the theory of thermodynamics.

> **First Law of Thermodynamics:** There is always as much energy after something happens as there was before it happened.
>
> **Second Law of Thermodynamics:** Everything directs itself toward the lowest energy state with the most equal distribution of resources. There are three principles:
>
> > Heat moves from a hot to cold body.
> >
> > Heat cannot be converted completely into other forms of energy.
> >
> > Systems become more disorganized over a period of time.

Rudolf Clausius developed the concept of entropy, affecting thermodynamics, which he defined as the way that natural events generally proceed toward states of greater disorder and usually increase in disorder if left uninterrupted.

Energy is necessary to do *work*. **Work** is defined as the process of an object being moved over a distance in response to some force being applied. Energy may be transferred from one object to another and an object can have energy without moving. **Power** is defined as the rate or measure of the time work can be done. *(power = work/time)*.

The equation used to determine equivalents of the work being completed is $w = fd$ or work = force × distance.

Force is the pressure or change applied to an object and includes gravity, electricity, and magnets. This may all be measured in pounds or Newtons. There is no one formula to find force. But force can be found using F = ma (Force = mass × acceleration) or F = w/d (Force = work ÷ distance).

Speed is how far something travels in a specified time and is measured by miles and hours or meters per second. You can determine the speed of an object by the formula: $s = d/t$ or speed equals distance divided by the time.

To measure force, work, and speed, use the length and time factors. **Length** is the distance between two points and is measured by inches, feet, miles, centimeters, meters, kilometers, and light years. You can measure **time** by seconds, minutes, hours, days, years and centuries.

There are two primary types of energy important for elementary students:

1. **Potential energy (not moving)**—This is the energy that could possibly do the work if it was released or a force was imposed on the object. Example: A jack-in-the-box has a coiled spring which is compressed inside the box. This coiled spring is waiting to explode and therefore has potential energy.

2. **Kinetic energy (moving)**—This is the energy that does the work or is the energy that is occurring. Example: When the jack-in-the-box is opened the coiled spring is freed and the jack leaps out from the force of the spring. The spring now has kinetic energy.

One energy form can be changed into another energy form, depending on the force applied; however, the total energy will remain the same. Some of the other types of energy are defined in this portion of the study guide and include: radiant energy, thermal energy, sound energy, light energy, electromagnetic energy, elastic energy, magnetic energy, and gravitational energy.

The scientific laws that govern this portion of science evolved from the basic laws of conservation, as well as the work of Einstein, Newton, Ohm, and Faraday. Although developed hundreds of years ago and taught to older students, these laws aid elementary educators in understanding the concepts and relationships that pertain to energy, mass, and matter. Certain laws are defined here.

Following are the **Conservation Laws,** the fundamental laws of all science:

Conservation of Mass/Matter—Matter can neither be created nor destroyed, but it can be rearranged. The sum of the matter and the energy in the universe remains the same.

Conservation of Energy—Energy remains constant in a system and cannot be recreated, but it can change forms.

Conservation of Momentum—Total momentum remains the same unless acted upon by an outside force demonstrated by the equation: $p = mv$ (momentum equals the mass of the object times the velocity of the object)

Charge Conservation—Electric charge can neither be created nor destroyed but is always conserved.

Following are **Einstein's Laws:**

Mass-Energy Equivalence—When a body has a mass, it has a certain energy even if it is not moving. Based on this concept, Einstein designed a formula to demonstrate the relationship between energy and matter, and it was discovered that particles of matter can go fast enough to increase in mass.

$E=mc^2$

E is the amount of energy. m is the given mass.

c is the speed of light (300,000 km/s).

General Relativity—Gravitational attraction between masses is the result of the nearby masses. Gravity has waves.

Following are **Newton's Laws:**

First Law: Law of Inertia—An object will remain at rest or in motion unless acted upon by an outside force.

Second Law: Law of Acceleration (*considered the most important law in Physics*)—An object will move in the direction of the force applied to it. The object's acceleration is proportional to the force applied to it and inversely proportional to the mass of the object. $F = ma$ (*Force equals mass times acceleration*).

Third Law: Law of Reciprocal Actions—For every action there is an opposite and equal reaction.

General Law of Gravitation—Describes the gravitational attraction between two masses; gravitational force between two objects is equal to the gravitational constant times the product of the two masses divided by the distance between them squared. The formula: $F = G(m_1 m_2 \div r^2)$

Fourier's Law (Law of Heat Conduction)—The transfer of heat moves through matter from higher temperatures to lower temperatures in order to equalize differences.

Following are **Electromagnetic Laws:**

Ohm's Law—Measures the voltage and current in electrical circuits, stating that the current going through a conductor is equal to the voltage divided by the resistor. The formula is written as *I=V/R (I represents the current in amperes, V represents volts of potential difference, and R represents the resistance.)*

Faraday's Law of Induction—Explains the way that voltage can be generated as any change in the magnetic environment of a coil of wire will cause voltage to be produced. Represented by *EMF (electromotive force).*

The Law of Simple Machines—The force put into the machine (effort force) times the distance the effort moves equals the output force from the machine (resistance) times the distance the resistance moves. The formula is EF × ED = RF × RD. (EF is the effort force, ED is the distance the effort is applied, RF is the resisting force, and RD is the distance required to move the object.)

Structure and Properties of Matter

The universe is comprised of things made from energy and matter. These materials found on the Earth include elements, compounds, and mixtures. **Matter,** which cannot be created or destroyed, can be converted into another form without losing its mass. Matter takes up space, and increased matter has increased weight. The weight depends on how strong the gravitational pull is on the object. **Mass** is the amount of matter and on earth it is measured by weight (pound, gram, kilogram).

An atom is the basic component of all matter. **Energy,** which cannot be created or destroyed, can be separated into several categories that relate to physical science at the elementary level. These forms of energy can be changed into another form without the loss of any energy. They include **heat, sound, light, magnetic, mechanical, electrical, chemical,** and **nuclear.**

In 1808, John Dalton thought that all matter was composed of atoms, but it took until the twentieth century to prove the atomic theory. Niels Bohr, in the 1920s, discovered the structure of the atom with all the component parts and developed the Bohr diagram to illustrate the atom. He discovered the value of electrons in chemical bonding. An **atom** is so minute that it can not be divided any further. Atoms can interact with one another causing a chemical reaction and forming a compound (H_2O). Molecules are a group of two or more atoms that are held together by very strong bonds. Molecules can be formed by the same atomic element (O_2) or different atomic elements (H_2O). An atom is the basis for the study of *chemistry*. An atom has a nucleus comprised of protons (positive charged particles) and neutrons (particles with no charge) and seven shells full of orbiting electrons (particles with a negative charge). The atomic mass is based on the total number of protons and neutrons. The atomic number is determined by the number of protons found within the nucleus and is also equal to the number of electrons found orbiting the atom.

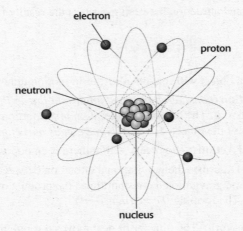

The components of an atom are as follow:

    Nucleus—The center of the atom, it contains neutrons and protons and has a positive charge (+).

    Proton—Located in the nucleus, it has a positive (+) charge and is symbolized by '*p*', combined with the number of neutrons being the atomic weight.

    Electron—Located in the shells that orbit an atom's nucleus, it has a negative (–) charge and is symbolized by '*e.*'

    Neutron—Located in the nucleus, it has no charge, and the symbol is '*n.*'

Chemistry

Chemistry is the branch of natural sciences that examines the properties, composition, stages, structure, and reactions (atomic and molecular) of matter and how matter can change. Chemists are people who study chemicals, compounds, elements, and chemical reactions in order to perform such tasks as design formulas or create medicines.

Elements are the very basic stage of matter that cannot be further separated into a different kind of matter by chemical reaction. Most elements were discovered and named by the 1800s. Dimitri Mendeleev discovered the properties of the elements as they are repeated at periodic intervals or cycles and he then placed them on the Periodic Chart. Some of the most common elements that may be referenced at the elementary level are as follows:

H = Hydrogen	O = Oxygen	He = Helium
C = Carbon	Cu = Copper	Ag = Silver
Au = Gold	Ni = Nickel	Sn = Tin
Fe = Iron	Al = Aluminum	N = Nitrogen
S = Sulfur	I = Iodine	K = Potassium
Ca = Calcium	Na = Sodium	Mg = Magnesium

Chemical Compounds

A chemical compound is a set of molecules that consists of two or more atoms of different elements that are linked together but can be split apart into simpler substances. It is the chemical bonding of two or more elements in which the new substance has different chemical and physical properties to form their individual parts.

Common compounds at the elementary level include the following:

H_2O = water

$NaCL$ = table salt

CO_2 = carbon dioxide

Fe_2O_3 = rust (iron oxide)

CO = carbon monoxide

$NaHCO_3$ = baking soda

SiO_2 = sand or glass

$C_{12}H_{22}O_{11}$ = sugar (sucrose)

Chemical reactions either give away or absorb heat as they occur. Matter does not increase or decrease in a chemical reaction and energy is not lost or gained. Some types of chemical reactions include the following:

- Oxidation
- Photosynthesis
- Light from the sun
- Human food consumption
- The joining of an acid and base

The three **states of matter** are described in this table.

State	Definition of Type of Matter	Example	Graphic Representation
Gas	Weak molecular forces No shape, color or volume Can expand infinitely to match the shape that holds it	air hydrogen helium	**Gas** Shape of container Volume of container

(continued)

State	Definition of Type of Matter	Example	Graphic Representation
Liquid	Molecular forces weaker than a solid Fixed volume Takes on the shape of the container	milk water apple juice	**Liquid** Shape of container Free surface Fixed volume
Solid	Strong molecular forces Fixed shape and volume Holds shape	wood ice rock	**Solid** Holds shape Fixed volume

The state of matter changes by adding or removing energy. Matter can move from one state to another state as temperature and pressure are applied. There are two forms of energy that can change a state of matter: heat (expands it) and cold (contracts it). However, ice is the exception, because it expands as it cools due to the molecules of water rearranging into a crystalline matrix which occupies more volume as a solid than as a liquid.

$$\text{Solid} \xrightarrow[\text{Increase energy}]{\text{Decrease pressure}} \text{Liquid} \xrightarrow[\text{Increase energy}]{\text{Decrease pressure}} \text{Gas}$$

Matter is measured in volume, weight, and length. There are specific measurement units with which one needs to be familiar. Measurement is a process (method) in science used to describe length, distance, volume or capacity, mass, and temperature. **Volume** is the space occupied by mass. **Density** is the mass per unit of volume. **Length** is the distance between two points. **Mass** is the amount of material in something. **Weight** is the pull of gravity on something and the amount depends on the strength of gravity.

Measurement Units			
Distance	**Volume**	**Mass**	**Temperature**
inches (in) feet (ft) yards (yds) miles (mi) league meters (cm, mm, Km)	ounces (oz) cup (c) quart (qt) gallon (gal) liter (mL, cL, KL)	pounds (lbs) grams (mg, cg, Kg)	Fahrenheit (F) Celsius (C) Kelvin (K)

Length

Standard or Conventional Measure	Metric Measure
12 inches (in) = 1 foot (ft)	100 centimeters (cm) = 1 meter (m)
3 feet = 1 yard (yd)	1,000 mm = 1 meter (m)
5,280 feet = 1 mile (mi)	1,000 m = 1 kilometer (km)
3 miles = 1 league	2.54 cm = 1 in.

Volume

Standard or Conventional Measure	Metric Measure
8 ounces (oz) = 1 cup (c)	1 liter (L) = 1,000 milliliter (ml)
4 cups = 1 quart (qt)	1 ml = 1 cubic centimeter (cc)
4 qts = 1 gallon (gal)	

Metric Prefixes Chart

Milli	Centi	Deci	Unit	Deca	Hecto	Kilo
1/1000	1/100	1/10	1	10 times	100 times	1000 times
.001	.01	.1				

Mechanical Energy

Mechanical energy refers to that action or power created by use of machines. They may be complex or simple machines. A **simple machine** is a tool with only a few or no moving parts that does *work*. There are six types of simple machines.

Machine	Purpose	Illustration
Lever	Magnifies force, increases speed or changes directions and is used to lift things Three types of levers follow: • 1st class (fulcrum in the middle or between the effort and the load). For example, scissors and seesaw. • 2nd class (fulcrum is at one end, so the load is between the fulcrum and the effort). For example, stapler, wheelbarrow. • 3rd class (fulcrum at the end, and the effort is between the fulcrum and the load) . For example, tweezers, fishing rod.	

Machine	Purpose	Illustration
Wedge	Magnifies force; used to push things apart or secure things together.	Wedge
Incline Plane	Magnifies force and distance increases; used to help move things up and down; reduces the force needed.	Inclined plane
Pulley	Reduces force needed to move an object, but increases the distance; moves things up and down and changes the direction of force.	Pulley
Wheel and Axel	Increases speed; facilitates motion, and movement of objects.	Wheel & Axle
Screw	Magnifies force by increasing distance.	Screw

Force

Force is that which can cause acceleration of an object with mass. Forces that cause changes in the motion or state of objects are gravity, friction, air resistance, inertia, pushing, pulling, and throwing. Some of the terms are defined here.

- **Gravity**—The acceleration of objects toward the center of the Earth
- **Inertia**—The state of an object remaining at rest or in motion
- **Friction**—The force between any two objects that comes into contact with one another and cannot be eliminated

Heat Energy

Heat energy may be produced in many ways, all of which cause an increase in the motion of particles of a substance. It is this motion of the particles that causes the heat. The hotter an object is or becomes, the faster the motion of particles and the cooler an object is, the slower the motion of particles. Heat energy is measured through calories, ergs, and joules.

Most solids, liquids, and gases expand when they are heated due to the increase in the motion of particles and contract when cooled due to the decreased motion of particles. For example, a balloon that is filled with air will increase in pressure as it is heated and it expands. When it is left to cool or is exposed to cold air, it will contract and eventually shrivel up as the particles become slower and slower.

Following are types of heat movement:

- **Conduction**—The transfer of heat energy by moving particles that make other particles move. The heat moves from warmer areas to cooler areas along materials that absorb or conduct the heat, such as metal.
- **Convection**—The transfer of heat through the collision of molecules that occurs only in liquids and gases as they circulate.
- **Radiation**—The transfer of heat by means of waves in an empty space as in the form of infrared radiation, occurring only in gases.

Following are terms related to heat energy:

- **Diffusion**—The movement of particles from a high concentration to an area of low concentration. Diffusion occurs when the concentrations in all areas is the same and is called **a state of equilibrium.**
- **Friction**—The rubbing of one object against another that produces a form of heat energy.
- **Melting (heat of fusion)**—When a solid reaches a point where its particles move so rapidly that they escape their boundaries, they begin to move more freely becoming a liquid.
- **Vaporization/Evaporation**—When the particles in a liquid are heated to such a temperature that they become uncontainable within liquid boundaries, they escape into a gas.

Sound Energy

Sound is present in things with mass and has energy in vibration form. Sound travels due to the collision of molecules and the speed of sound depends upon the space between the molecules. Sound travels the quickest through solids and the slowest through a gas. It travels at 0.3 kilometers per second, or 1,000 feet per second, or 700 miles per hour.

Sound waves, the longitudinal movements in which the compressions and rare fractions travel spherically outward from the source, are made of matter and have wavelengths. **Wavelengths** are the distance between two successive compressions or two successive rare fractions. **Sound** is measured by its frequency.

Following are rules of sound:

1. The more rapid the vibration, the higher the pitch of the sound.
2. Sound travels through solids, liquids, and gases at different rates of speed.
3. Objects produce sound by causing a series of compressions and rare fractions (wave) of molecules.

The three characteristics of sound are as follow:

Characteristic	Definition	Cause
Pitch	how high or low the sound; the frequency of sound	rate of vibration
Amplitude	loudness or volume of the sound wave	force used to create the sound (the greater the force, the louder the sound)
Resonance	quality the original sound makes; a distinctive timbre	source of the sound

Light Energy

Sunlight is the most basic form of energy for living things. There are two forms of light: visible and electromagnetic radiation. Light passes through anything that is transparent or translucent. Light travels in waves with each color having a specific wavelength. It travels at 3,000,000 kilometers per second or 186,000 miles per second.

Christian Huygens discovered that light is a set of waves, and Sir Isaac Newton discovered that light is a set of tiny particles (photons). Newton also discovered white light, which is a mix of all light colors together by using a prism.

The universal rule of reflecting surfaces is that the angle of incidence equals the angle of reflection, which means that a rough surface scatters light and a smooth surface bounces light equally.

Some colors of light have more energy than other colors as they vibrate faster and have a shorter wavelength. Red has the least energy of the visible light as it has the longest waves and the lowest frequency. Blue has the most energy of the visible light as it has the shortest waves and the higher frequency. Visible light is that described by colors, which are found in the rainbow (red, orange, yellow, green, blue, indigo, and violet). The light spectrum shows the colors of visible and nonvisible light according to the amount of energy from less to more energy and low to high frequency. White light reflects wavelengths and absorbs no light. Black light shows the absence of light and color, as it absorbs all colors of light.

Colors in the visible light spectrum appear in bold:

radiowaves   infrared   **red   orange   yellow   green   blue   indigo   violet**   *ultraviolet*   x-rays

Following are the laws of light:

- **Newton**—Colored light when mixed together produces white light.
- **Young**—Light is a wave, and the length of the wave determines the color.
- **Einstein**—Light travels at a constant speed.

Following are the rules of light:

1. Travels in rays, which are straight lines outward from the source.
2. Travels at different rates depending on the density of the object: the denser the medium, the slower light travels.
3. Travels in transverse ways.
4. Is an electromagnetic wave created by causing electrons to move rapidly and emit energy.

Terms used in science when referencing light are as follows:

- **Transverse wave**—A series of crests and troughs
- **Wavelength**—Distance between the crest or the distance between the troughs
- **Reflection**—Caused by light rays bouncing off a surface
- **Refraction**—Change in direction or bending of the light rays as they pass through various materials

Magnetic Energy

Basically, magnetic energy and electrical energy are the same. Since they are so interrelated, we often hear the term **electromagnetic energy.** This was first established in 1820 by Hans Oersted. Metals that have magnetic power often contain iron. When magnets are individually used, they have specific properties. There are two poles, which are labeled North and South. Similar poles repel (N-N, S-S) one another, and opposite poles attract (N-S, S-N) one another.

Electrical Energy

Electricity was invented based on the principles of electromagnetic laws created by Ohm and Faraday. They were determined to find ways to measure and generate electrical currents through mathematical formulas. Their discoveries changed the world and led to numerous major inventions: telegraph, telephone, lights, computers, audio and visual recordings, and so on.

The laws are defined in a previous section of this guide, "Energy Relationships and Transformations." Essentially students should learn the following:

- Static electricity is a result of the accumulation of electric charges.
- Like charges repel one another (+ +, − −).
- Opposite charges attract one another (+ −, − +).
- Electricity flows through conductor as current.

The formulas of electrical energy include

watts = volts × amps

volts = amps × ohms

amps = volts/ohms

ohms = volts/amps

Terms relative to electrical energy are as follows:

- **Amperage**—The amount of electricity that flows through a conductor.
- **Amp**—The unit of quantity of electron flow.
- **Circuit**—A path that electrons flow through called an electric current.
- **Conductor**—A material that allows an electric current to flow through it, such as metals.
- **Electric current**—It contains electrical energy and a conductor.
- **Insulators**—Any material that does not allow electric current to flow through it, such as rubber or plastic.
- **Ohm**—The unit of resistance to electron flow.
- **Resistance**—It causes electron flow to do the work, decreasing the flow of amperage in a circuit.
- **Voltage**—The force that causes electrons to flow; the amount of force of the current.
- **Volt**—The unit of measurement of the force for electron flow.
- **Watt**—The measurement unit of electric power.

Following are the two types of circuits:

- **Parallel**—Each resistance is attached to the main circuit with its own connection, and if one is disconnected the others will still work.
- **Series**—The resistances are connected to one another, one following another. If one resistance is disconnected, the circuit fails to work.

Chemical Energy

Chemical energy is the outcome of a material found on Earth interacting with another material (elements, compounds, or mixtures). An **element** is a simple form of matter and everything in the universe is made up of some type of element. There are 92 known elements naturally found in the world and another 21 known elements that are manmade (all radioactive). A **compound** is the result of a chemical reaction between two or more elements. A **mixture** is the combination of two or more elements without a chemical reaction.

Nuclear Energy

Nuclear energy is a powerful form of energy in the world. It can disrupt life and destroy countries, or it may be used to promote life and sustain countries. Two types of nuclear reactions are known:

- **Fission**—The nuclei of atoms are disintegrated (for example, nuclear reactors or atomic bomb).
- **Fusion**—Two or more nuclei are smashed together with increased force to form a different kind of nucleus (for example, the sun or hydrogen bomb).

In the creation of nuclear energy, the nucleus of the atom forms a different kind of element producing increased energy. This change or disintegration of the nucleus represents the half life of the substance. Radioactivity is a form of nuclear energy, which can be used in the field of medicine, creating electricity or powering generators.

Diversity and Characteristics of Living Organisms

The domain of life science examines the existence of organisms. It encompasses the following:

- Characteristics of organisms, behavior and regulation, diversity and adaptation
- Life cycles, reproduction, heredity
- Structure and function in living systems
- Organisms and environments, populations and ecosystems

Millions of species exist, and there are newly identified organisms each year. Through the years, the development of organisms has been studied by scientists around the world. One scientist who is credited with the specific study of the origin of the species is Charles Darwin. His laws for evolution and the order of species have been debated and followed for many years.

Darwin's Laws

- **Natural Selection**—Individual organisms with favorable traits are more likely to survive and reproduce.
- **Evolution**—The world is in a constant state of change.
- **Common Descent**—Every group of living organisms on Earth descended from a common ancestor.
- **Multiplication of Species**—Species split into or produce other species depending on geographical locations.
- **Gradualism**—Changes occur through the slow gradual change of population, not through fast sudden production of new beings.

Organization of Living Things

The organization of living things is studied as a ladder or a pyramid within the traditional Linnean classification system. Living things are categorized according to kingdoms, consistent with the shared physical characteristics:

Kingdom, Phylum, Class, Order, Family, Genus, Species

Carolus Linnaeus was a botanist who designed the system of binomial nomenclature used for naming various species. Each species is given a two-part Latin name, formed by affixing a specific label to the genus name. The genus name is capitalized and then both the genus name and specific label are italicized.

For example, common dog is *Canis familiaris*.

The five kingdoms of the Linnaen system are as follows:

- **Monera**—Single-celled organism without nuclei (bacteria)
- **Protista**—Single-celled organism with nuclei (algae, protozoans)

- **Fungi**—Single-celled and multi-celled organisms (mold, yeast, lichen)
- **Plantae**—Multi-cellular plant organisms (moss, fern, flowering)
- **Animalia**—Multi-cellular animals (10–21 phyla)

Each **kingdom** may be broken down into smaller categories named phyla. A **phylum** contains organisms that are genetically related through common ancestry. Each phylum is then broken down into separate classes. A **class** is a more specific breakdown of organisms in which the group shares a common attribute, characteristic or trait. A class is further divided into orders. **Order** then specifically divides the class into smaller shared characteristics and splits into smaller units called **family** in which organisms have multiple traits in common. Family is broken into **genus** where the organisms show many more specific common attributes. The last division is into **species** in which organisms can interbreed and produce offspring that can propagate the species.

Example of the classification of a **Human:**

Kingdom: Animalia

Phylum: Chordata (animals with backbones)

Class: Mammalia (with hair, female makes milk)

Order: Primate (apes and monkeys)

Family: Hominadae (great apes and humans)

Genus: *Homo* (humans)

Species: *Homo sapiens*

Example of the classification of a **giraffe:**

Kingdom: Animalia

Phylum: Chordata (animals with backbones)

Class: Mammalia (with hair, female makes milk)

Order: Artiodactyla

Family: Giraffidae

Genus: *Giraffa*

Species: *Giraffa camelopardalis*

Living systems include the plants and animals that inhabit the Earth. Living organisms have certain characteristics:

- made of protoplasm
- organized into cells
- use energy
- capable of growth
- have definite life spans
- reproduce, give rise to similar organisms
- affected by the environment
- adapt to the environment
- respond to the environment

A **cell** is the foundational unit that provides the structure and function of life. All living things are made of cells. This is a description of a living organism:

A group of similar cells becomes **tissue.**

A group of tissues working together becomes **organs.**

A group of organs working together becomes a **system.**

A group of systems becomes an **organism.**

Three functions of a cell exist in a living organism:

> To produce proteins and other materials for building new cells
>
> To manufacture energy as a source to sustain life
>
> To reproduce offspring to ensure the survival of the species

Parts of a Cell—Animal and Plant

Cell membrane	Form and structure permits inward passage of needed items, outward passage of waste
Nucleus	Control center of cell; "the brain" that contains DNA and nucleolus
Cytoplasm	All materials outside of the nucleus; gel-like filling
Endoplasmic reticulum (ER)	Transport canals that travel from the nucleus to cytoplasm; may be either rough (with ribosomes) or smooth (without ribosomes)
Ribosomes	Manufactures proteins
Mitochondria	Release energy to cell through chemical reactions; power plant
Lysosome	Hold enzymes to breakdown molecules and other substances
Golgi apparatus	Packages the proteins and transports them through the cell and packages waste for removal from cell
Vacuoles	Store food, water, and minerals

In addition to those parts listed in the previous chart, plant cells also include the following:

Cell wall	Made of cellulose to provide rigid structure for plant
Chloroplasts	Plastids that contain chlorophyll, which allows the plant to make its own food when combined with sunlight, minerals, carbon dioxide, and water (photosynthesis)
Plastids	Provide color, storage, chemical factories

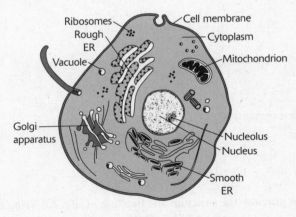

Animal Cell

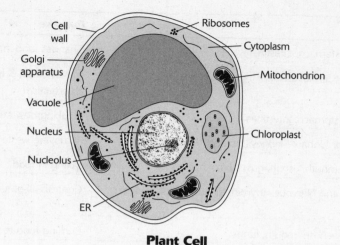

Plant Cell

Structure and Function of Plants and Animals

For plants to survive as a species, they must have systems that support the cells necessary for growth, reproduction, and interaction within the environment.

Form-Structure	Function-Description/Purpose
Roots	The anchor—absorbs water and minerals
Stem	The transport—takes nutrients to the leaves
Leaves	The builder—manufactures food for the plant
Flower	Sexual organs—reproduction site of the plant
Fruit	The ripened ovaries of flowers

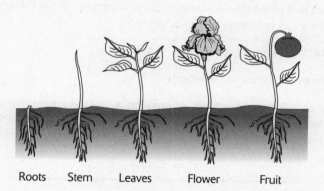

Roots   Stem   Leaves   Flower   Fruit

Flowers are the reproductive organs of plants. Insects and birds are attracted to the petals and help transport and disperse pollen for cross-fertilization. The stamen, male reproductive organ, manufactures the pollen. The pistil, female reproductive organ, has multiple parts: a **stigma,** which is the sticky top that captures pollen; **styles** that transport the pollen to the ovary; **ovary**, which makes the ovules. When pollen joins the ovule, fertilized seeds are the outcome.

For **animals** to function and survive as a species, they must grow, reproduce, and interact within the environment. Animals have systems that must support each of their individual cells to carry out their purpose. There are eight basic life functions of animals.

Function	System	Purpose
Assimilation	Digestive—stomach, intestinal walls	Changes food into useful substances
Circulation	Circulatory/Cardiovascular—blood vessels, arteries, heart	Moves blood & lymphatic fluid to all parts of an organism
Digestion	Digestive—stomach, intestines	Breaking down of food
Excretion	Excretory or Urinary—kidneys, spleen, liver, colon	Removing waste products
Ingestion	Digestive—mouth, esophagus, stomach, intestines	Taking in food
Regulation	Endocrine and Nervous—thyroid, glands, lymph system, hormones	Controls all other life processes
Respiration	Respiratory—nose, mouth, lungs	Burning food to make energy
Reproduction	Reproductive and Nervous—male/female sex organs and hormones	Making more of the same kind of species

Changes in Dominant Organisms

Reproduction is the system of living organisms that ensures the survival of the species. Reproduction is carried on in different ways among Earth's living species, but essentially it is the joining of two parent organisms to produce an offspring.

There are two different methods of reproduction:

1. **Asexual**—A cell creates two identical pairs of chromosomes, splits, and forms nuclei around the chromosomes. The cells divide by a process called **mitosis.** New cells are created using only one "parent" such as in algae, bacteria, sponges, mold, and fungi.

2. **Sexual**—Requires the union of a male gamete (a reproductive cell) and female gamete. **Meiosis** is the process that produces gametes. Each gamete has half of the chromosomes needed for reproduction. When the two gametes combine, they each donate half of the chromosomes to the new nucleus. When combined, the egg is fertilized with a full chromosome count such as in humans and most animals.

The stages of an embryo in most organisms is as follows:

egg → zygote → embryo → fetus → newborn

DNA or deoxyribonucleic acid carries the code of protein production, or instructions, for growth, reproduction, and other life activities. **Chromosomes** are made of genes that are comprised of strands of DNA. Chromosomes come in pairs with a gene for each trait on each part of the pair. Traits can be dominant or recessive. Humans have 23 pairs of chromosomes.

DD	Dominant trait appears in organism.
DR	Dominant trait appears in organism, but organism carries recessive trait and can pass it on to its young.
RR	Recessive trait appears in organism.

Following are examples of traits:

D traits—Brown eyes, curly hair, ability to curl tongue

R traits—Blue eyes, straight hair, cannot curl tongue

Gregor Mendel was considered the father of genetics, and in 1865, based on a study of pea plants, he created a table that showed the reproduction of two parents and the possible genetics of the offspring based on the recessive and dominant genes.

For example, if a female carried one dominant gene for brown eyes, and one recessive gene for blue eyes, it would be recorded as Bb. If the male carried one dominant gene for brown eyes, and one recessive gene for blue eyes, it would be recorded as Bb. Thus, this pair of parents would have the ability to have three offspring with brown eyes and one with blue eyes as illustrated. In other words, a 75 percent chance of having a brown eyed child and a 25 percent chance of having a blue-eyed child.

	B	b
B	BB	Bb
b	bB	bb

Biological evolution is a scientific process in which inherited traits of organisms change from one generation to the next. In general, most offspring show a genetic similarity to their parents, however abnormalities can sometimes occur during reproduction. Abnormal or mutant genes happen when mistakes in DNA duplication occur which may result in a non-fertilized egg. Yet sometimes, a mutation does allow for fertilization and it makes the offspring more able to prosper or have a better chance of reproduction than offspring without the mutation. When this happens, eventually, the majority of the species will possess the mutation.

There are two primary beliefs by people that pertain to biological evolution.

1. **Natural Selection**—This is the process in which organisms produce and pass on the traits that are most helpful or necessary for the survival of the organism or species. It shows how organisms with favorable traits survive and reproduce so they become better adapted to survive in the environment while the organisms with less favorable adaptations or traits die out.

   Camouflage brown lizards living in the desert are more apt to survive than if they were black.

   An Arctic fox with white fur is more likely to survive the Arctic climate and predators than a fox with black or brown fur.

2. **Adaptations**—This is the process whereby the greatest changes in a species occur after the successive, small, and random changes in traits have been present. Through natural selection, the best traits for the specific environment are kept or propagated forth.

   The beak shape of a seed-eating bird versus the beak shape of a raptor who eats meat.

   A koala bear has paws that are adapted for life in a tree (have a large gap between their first and second fingers to allow a vice-like grip upon trees).

The basic principle of ecological evolution is the theory of **Survival of the Fittest.** This means that the organism that is best adapted to an environment will generally produce the most offspring and the offspring that possess the more favorable traits will survive and reproduce.

The nature versus nurture debate exists in relation to human development. Genes are a natural part of the origin of a species (nature) and learning is based on the environment and the upbringing (nurture). There also exist the differences in the behaviors that are exhibited by organisms: learned and instinctive. Learned behavior is gained through conditioning, imitation, and reasoning while instinctive behavior relies on the passing on of the genes.

The Earth

The study of the Earth is important for students, as the changes on the Earth are a reflection of human behavior and the impact that humans have on their environment. This study is called Earth Science and students can examine the Earth as well as study space and the universe. This area of science includes:

- Properties and structure of Earth systems
- Earth's history
- Earth within the solar system
- Objects in space
- Changes in Earth and space

The laws that describe the function of the Earth and the planets were developed by the German astronomer Johannes Kepler in the early 1600s. Although Aristotle, Ptolemy, and Brahe worked in the fields of astronomy and physics to design a certain set of theories about the planets, Kepler challenged those which changed the fields of astronomy and physics. Some of Kepler's work confirms the theories and observations of the earlier Copernicus. After Kepler established his theories and laws, a century later, Isaac Newton used his laws of motion and universal gravitation to deduce Kepler's Laws. In the modern century, Kepler's laws are still used to calculate the paths of satellites and surmise the orbits of other bodies (asteroids, planets, and so on) around the sun. These laws follow.

Kepler's Laws (Planetary Motion)

- **Kepler's First Law: Law of Ellipse**—*The orbit of every planet is an ellipse with the sun at a focus.* This means that the revolutionary path of the planets around the sun is in an elliptical shape with the sun at the center.

- **Kepler's Second Law: Law of Equal Area**—*A line joining a planet and the sun sweeps out equal areas during equal intervals of time.* The speed of the planets is constantly changing and a planet moves the fastest when it is near the sun and slowest when it is farther away. This law also confirms the conservation of momentum.

- **Kepler's Third Law: Law of Harmony**—*The square of the orbital period of a planet is directly proportional to the third power of the semi-major axis of its orbit.* This law compares the orbital period and the radius of the orbit of a planet to the other planets, providing an accurate description of the time and the distance for the planets to orbit around the sun.

Newton's Laws are further described under the section "Matter and Force."

The Earth within the Universe

Scientists believe that the universe originated approximately 20 billion years ago due to a catastrophic explosion that spread outward in all directions from the epicenter. The galaxies then formed into galactic clusters. The **Milky Way Galaxy**, where Earth is located, includes everything that is seen in the sky with the naked eye.

The **solar system** consists of the sun and all the bodies that revolve around the sun. There are a set of (eight or nine) **planets** that include Mercury, Venus, Earth, Mars, Jupiter, Saturn, Uranus, Neptune, and Pluto (which is currently under debate as the ninth planet). Each planet revolves around the sun at varying speeds in an elliptical orbit. Each planet has its own moon(s) that revolves around the planet in a gravitational path.

The Earth orbits the sun every 365 days, which is the basis for our calendar. Its orbit is an elliptical shape and when the Earth is closest to the sun it is on a perihelion path and when it is farthest from the sun, it is called an aphelion path. Based on the path of the Earth around the sun and the various points along the orbit, scientists have developed four periods of rotation.

Period	Date	Description
Autumnal equinox	September 22 (Northern Hemisphere)	The first day of fall
		Days and nights same length
	March 20 (Southern Hemisphere)	Oceans warmest and tropical storms and hurricanes form
Summer solstice	June 21 (Northern Hemisphere)	The first day of summer
	December 21 (Southern Hemisphere)	The longest day

Period	Date	Description
Winter solstice	December 21 (Northern Hemisphere) June 21 (Southern Hemisphere)	The first day of winter The shortest day
Vernal equinox	March 20 (Northern Hemisphere) September 22 (Southern Hemisphere)	The first day of spring Days and nights are equal length

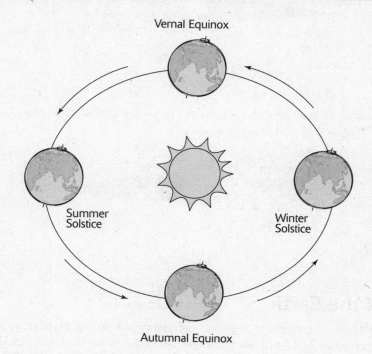

Following are terms related to the study of the universe:

- **Asteroids**—Thousands of small rocky bodies that appear between Mars and Jupiter
- **Comet**—A celestial body that revolves around the sun and possesses a nucleus and a tail that always points away from the sun due to the solar wind
- **Constellations**—A type of boundary system astronomers use for organizing the night sky according to 88 constellational regions
- **Meteoroid**—A stony or metallic particle (meteor) in space that revolves around the sun
- **Meteor**—A small body of matter that travels through space and becomes a meteorite when it lands on Earth

Earth's Moon

The Earth has one moon that takes one (lunar) month to revolve (28 days) around the Earth. The moon does not emit its own light but rather reflects light from the sun. The moon rotates on an axis similar to Earth, at exactly the same speed. Therefore, the same side of the moon is seen at all times from Earth. The **moon phases** are caused by the position of the moon relative to the sun. The moon exhibits five different phases during its rotation around the Earth.

Additionally, the moon plays a key role in an occasional natural phenomenon that may be seen from Earth, called an **eclipse**. There are two types of eclipses.

During a **lunar eclipse** the moon is blocked by the Earth's shadow in the following pattern: sun—Earth—moon.

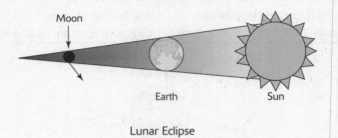

Lunar Eclipse

Solar eclipse: The moon casts a shadow upon the Earth in the following pattern. sun—moon—Earth.

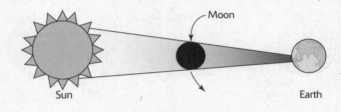

Solar Eclipse

The History of the Earth

The Earth has an amazing history with periods of growth and beauty and periods of darkness and destruction. Scientists estimate that the Earth emerged about 4.5 billions years ago. They have traced back to a period of 700 million years ago when they believe there was one major continent or land mass called Rodinia. Then at about 280 million years ago, this **supercontinent** changed and was called Pangaea, which scientists believe was the beginning of much animal and plant life. It is thought that a mighty force or impact against the Earth split these land forms, which eventually moved them into their current locations. It was during the Mesozoic Era, 180 million years ago, that Pangaea drifted apart and began to form the Earth's seven continents of present day.

Currently, it is estimated that the Earth travels at a speed around the sun of 66,000 mph.

About 97 percent of the Earth's water is ocean with 71 percent of the Earth's surface being ocean. The Earth's tectonic plates move about 2–5 cm per year, sometimes causing earthquakes and other natural phenomena.

Geology is the study of the history of the Earth, its life forms, and the rocks. Geological historians investigate how the Earth and its life-forms have developed over time.

Two geologic principles exist:

> **The Principle of Uniformitarianism**—The scientific laws that govern the Earth today are the same laws that existed since the beginning of time ("the present is the key to the past").
>
> **The Law of Superposition**—The oldest rocks and events are found at the bottom of Earth's formations, and the youngest are found at the top of Earth's formations (the past is on the bottom).

An **eon** is an indefinite or very long period of time. Eons explain the age of the universe and the age of the Earth. According to geologists, there were two major eons in the development of the Earth as we know it:

Precambian Eon—The period of the formation of Earth (4.6 billion years ago) to the rise of life-forms (similar to present day life forms)

Phanerozoic Eon—The period of the remaining time of development, to present day (about 4,600 million years to present).

Geologic Time Scale of Phanerozoic Eon

Geologic time is a long period of time that shows a sequence of events that occurred during the development and in the history of the Earth.

Era	Age (Million years)	Life Forms	Geologic and Plant Life Forms
Cenozoic	66 million years ago to present time	Hominids and modern man, primates, horses, mastodons, whales, alligators, saber-toothed tigers	Rocky Mountains, the Alps, the Cascade Mountains, the Ice Age (a reoccurring period of time when sheets of ice cover areas of continents)
Mesozoic	245–144 million years ago	Mammals, birds, dinosaurs	The Sierra Nevada Mountains, the Atlantic Ocean, flowering plants, grasses, cereals
Paleozoic	570–286 million years ago	Trillobites, reptiles, amphibians, sharks, fish, shelled animals, insects	The Appalachian Mountains, Pangaea, the Ice Age (a reoccurring period of time when sheets of ice cover areas of continents), Laursia, Gondwana Trees, land plants, sea plants, seed ferns and plants, mosses, spores

There is some scientific information about a possible fourth era in the Phanerozoic Eon that emerged very early in the Earth's birth around 4600–700 million years ago, called the **Proterozoic** or Archean Era. During this period, scientists suspect that some invertebrates may have emerged and the oldest rocks might have been meteorites.

Structure of the Earth

The Earth is comprised of many complex systems. These systems include the various components and layers of the Earth, both on the surface and above the Earth. There are four principle components that create this intricate system.

- **Atmosphere** (Air)
- **Lithosphere** (Land)
- **Hydrosphere** (Water)
- **Biosphere** (Life)

There is a fifth layer known as the cryosphere, the frozen part of the Earth's surface, including the polar ice caps, continental ice sheets, glaciers, sea ice, and permafrost.

During the 1890s, scientist Leon Bort identified that the Atmosphere consisted of at least two layers. It is estimated that the Atmosphere of Earth contains 21 percent oxygen and 78 percent nitrogen, along with some amounts of carbon dioxide and gases such as argon and hydrogen. Presently, scientists have discovered these five layers:

- **Exosphere** (from 300–600 miles to 6,000 miles)
- **Thermosphere** (Includes Ionosphere) (265,000–285,000 feet to 400+ miles)

- **Mesosphere** (160,000 feet to about 285,000)
- **Stratosphere** (23,000–60,000 to about 160,000 feet)
- **Troposphere** (23,000 to 60,000 feet)

The layers of the Earth are composed of four concentric spheres.

Layer	Thickness	Structure	Placement
Crust	5-30 miles thick	not fixed, a mosaic of moving plates	outer shell
Mantle	1,800 miles thick	plasticity (ability of solid to flow), has circulating currents, which cause the plates to move	second layer moving inward
Outer Core	1,300 miles thick	viscous liquid, the Earth's magnetic field originates here	third layer moving inward
Inner Core	800 miles to the center of the earth	a solid, possibly made of iron metal	center of the Earth

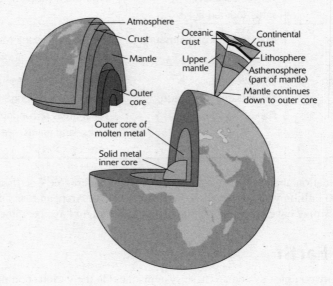

The Earth's Plates

Scientists have discovered (1960s) that the Earth's surface is a group of interconnected plates of rock (plate tectonics). The outermost layer of the Earth, lithosphere, is comprised of seven rigid plates. The plates vary in size and thickness and continually drift and shift. Plates are located under continents (continental plates) and beneath the oceans (oceanic plates). These plates move at different rates and speeds, sometimes crashing together or pulling apart. This activity caused by the plates account for the appearance of mountains, volcanoes, and earthquakes.

There are three types of plate boundary movements:

- **Divergent**—The separating or pulling apart of two or more plates, resulting in rifts and the formation of new crust (most commonly called sea-floor spreading).
- **Convergent**—The collision or crashing together of two or more plates resulting in the rise of mountains, earthquakes, and volcanoes.
- **Transform fault**—The rubbing together of two or more plates resulting in earthquakes and the recycling of the Earth's crust.

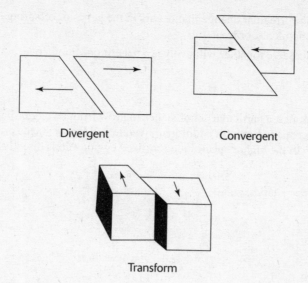

Divergent   Convergent

Transform

Processes of the Earth Systems

Ecology is the study of the interaction of organisms within their environment and with one another. The environment in which a group of organisms exist as a community that includes such necessities as air, land, and water is called a **biosphere.** This community of living things existing within a non-living environment, promoting energy flow, incorporating the Earth's processes, and recycling of minerals is called an **ecosystem**.

Numerous organisms inhabit the Earth, and they must adapt to one another and function in diverse environments (ecosystems). The Earth systems then interact with and upon each other to deliver balance within the various ecosystems.

There are three key characteristics for obtaining a balanced ecosystem:

- Constant source of energy (sun-solar energy).
- Energy is converted to glucose (needed by all living things).
- Organic nutrients and matter are recycled successfully.

Ecosystem balance depends upon species interactions. Some conditions that may change the balance of an ecosystem includes

- Supply of energy changes.
- Food cycle is interrupted.
- Organic matter and nutrients increase or decrease.
- Natural disasters occur (floods, earthquakes, drought).
- Natural phenomena appear (tsunami).
- Human contributions invade (air pollution, radiation, deforestation).

An example of the Earth systems that are interdependent are plants (biosphere) pull water (hydrosphere) from the ground and nutrients from the soil (lithosphere) and then release oxygen and water vapor into the air (atmosphere) for animals to use.

- **Extinction**—When an entire species "dies out" or disappears due to extreme changes in the environment or the inability to adapt to change quickly.
- **Instinct**—An inherited gene that sets natural behavior patterns of a species and remains the same even if the situation changes. Examples include hibernation, reproduction, and migration.

- **Mutation**—An accidental or irregular change that occurs in the genes of offspring that may be due to an influence of the environment, chemicals, or toxins.
- **Symbiosis**—The species that live together will evolve to benefit one another.

Life Cycle

Every living organism moves through a particular set of stages to grow from an egg or larva stage into an adult, entering the final stage. Some of the lower species exhibit additional juvenile and larvae stages prior to developing into adults (for example, frog, salamander). In the higher species the fertilized egg develops directly into the adult (for example, dog, human).

1. Come into being (sometimes a larvae state)
2. Grow
3. Metamorphase
4. Mature
5. Reproduce
6. Die

Some of the processes of the Earth systems that are also present on the planet and affect life include the heat cycle, food chain cycle, weather/climate cycle, the water cycle, the oxygen cycle, and the phosphorus cycle (rocks).

Heat Cycle

Heat influences the Earth more than any other process. Two sources of heat exist:

- **Solar Heat** (energy from the sun)—The sun hits the surface of Earth at varying angles, which causes major climates to be present in certain areas, as well as influencing the type of life forms that exist in those various regions. Solar heat also affects the Earth's weather, which affects the vegetation and conditions like erosion.
- **Radioactive Heat** (at the Earth's core)—The activity within the Earth creates the structures on the Earth. The radioactive heat is responsible for the movement of the plates, causing most volcanoes, earthquakes, and so on. This generates mountains, valleys, ocean basins, and most other land forms.

Food Chain Cycle

This Earth system exists to provide balance within an ecosystem. It demonstrates a set pattern of how organisms in a **community** use the next lower organism in the sequence for food. It creates a system of predators, as animals eat other animals to survive, but this also balances the population in an ecosystem. It is the primary way the ecosystem can transmit and disperse energy.

An example of a food chain in a field ecosystem:

plant   →   grasshopper   →   field mouse   →   snake   →   hawk

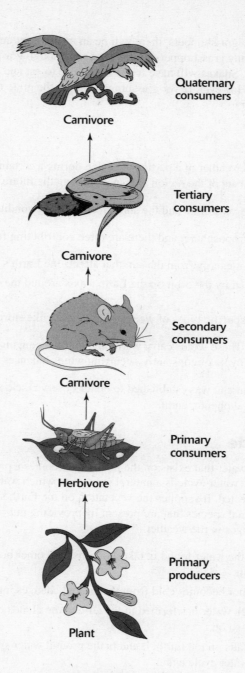

Quaternary
consumers

Carnivore

Tertiary
consumers

Carnivore

Secondary
consumers

Carnivore

Primary
consumers

Herbivore

Primary
producers

Plant

A terrestrial food chain

Within the food chain, there are producers (plants, algae, plankton) that provide food and energy for consumers (herbivores like insects or carnivores such as mammals, reptiles, amphibians, and birds). There are also decomposers which breakdown the consumers once they have died (bacteria and fungi). The consumers can be separated further into primary, secondary, tertiary, and quaternary consumers. Each level of the food chain increases in the amount of energy needed, so that the top of the food chain is the consumer needing the highest amount of energy. This breakdown of energy requires large amounts of energy on the lower levels of the chain in order to meet the needs of the top consumers. (For example, there must be more plants than grasshoppers in order to provide the energy needed to sustain the grasshoppers.) This interdependence between all species helps maintain the balance (equilibrium) between plants and animals, producers and consumers within communities. Without this balance of life, the system will fail and be forced to reset itself.

For example, when there are too many grasshoppers, there will be an insufficient amount of grass for all of them to eat, which will lead to the starvation of many grasshoppers. If there are not enough grasshoppers, then the field mice population will shrink also from starvation. Snakes will have fewer field mice to eat and may die of starvation, which will also impact the survival of the hawk. However, fewer grasshoppers allow the grass to flourish and multiply, resetting the cycle of food within the community.

Weather/Climate Cycle

Climate is the average or accumulated weather of a particular region during a certain period of time and can include unusual and extreme conditions. The climate of the region aids in predicting the future climate patterns of that same region.

Weather is the variation of the climate, as storms and the sun affect the daily conditions.

The weather cycle occurs first in the troposphere, and there are three contributing factors:

- Solar radiation, which is the heat energy from the sun that affects the Earth's surface.
- Earth movement, which is caused by the orbit on the Earth's axis around the sun creating conditions such as the seasons.
- Water cycle, which creates the specific types of weather conditions, like storms, cloud cover, and so on.

Winds circulate air around the Earth. These winds carry warm air from the equator to the poles and also cold air from the poles in opposite directions. This cycle of constantly occurring winds balances the Earth's temperature.

In 1890, the United States Weather Bureau was established to better observe the conditions around the world, as well as to predict changes and research natural phenomenon.

Water (Hydrologic) Cycle

Because there is a limited supply of water that exists on the planet, it becomes a precious resource and very important to the process of the water cycle. The water cycle is a natural process in which water evaporates (and transpiration), condensates, precipitates, and is collected. It supplies the vegetation on the Earth's surface to promote growth. It also contributes to the survival of the animal species that are present by providing nutrients and hydration. It is also the Earth system that contributes to changes in the weather.

- **Evaporation**—The Sun heats the water found in lakes, oceans, and other bodies of water so they become steam or vapor, which goes into the air.
- **Condensation**—The water vapor becomes cold from the air and changes into a liquid, which forms the clouds.
- **Precipitation**—When too much water has formed in the air and the clouds become heavier, the water falls to the ground as hail, snow, rain, and so on.
- **Collection**—When the water falls on the Earth, it enters the ground water system or returns to the oceans, lakes, and streams, which starts the water cycle again.

The water cycle includes cloud formation which results in different combinations of weather across the Earth's surface. There are many kinds of clouds formations that include: cirrus, stratus, nimbus, and cumulus.

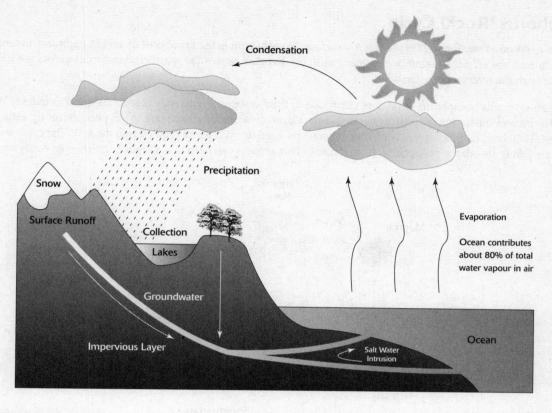

Oxygen Cycle

Almost every living organism needs oxygen for survival. Oxygen supports the body's cells by providing much needed energy. Plant life begins the oxygen cycle as they use energy from sunlight to convert carbon dioxide and water into oxygen via photosynthesis. The plants expel oxygen which animal life needs for survival. Animals breathe in the oxygen and break it down into energy via respiration. This process eliminates carbon dioxide into the air, which the plants then use again.

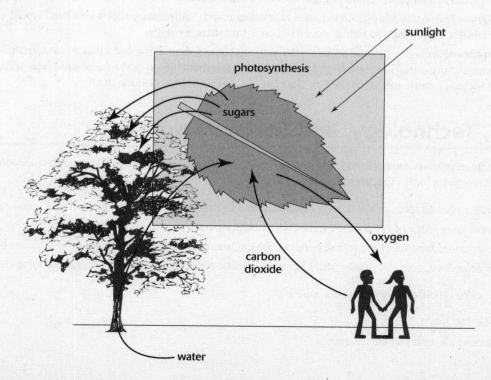

Phosphorus (Rock) Cycle

Rocks are exposed to weathering on the Earth's surface. **Weathering** is the process of changing natural structures, such as rocks through the effects of wind, water, ice, and so on. **Erosion** moves the weathered materials across the Earth's surface through the rivers and by the wind.

Every organism needs phosphorus to process chemicals in their systems. Plants may absorb phosphorus quickly through the soil. Herbivores obtain phosphorus by eating plants. Carnivores, such as humans, can get phosphorus by eating the herbivores. Then both herbivores and carnivores excrete phosphorus as a waste product into the soil. The cycle will begin again as the plants absorb the phosphorus from the soil. This process can help to maintain or balance an ecosystem.

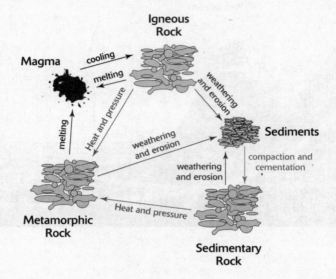

Rocks develop from the mantle of the Earth, except for limestone. The three types of rocks are as follows:

- **Igneous**—Forms when magma cools. Magma that cools and solidifies under the Earth's surface is called intrusive igneous rock. Magma that erupts as lava, cooling and solidifying outside or on the Earth's surface is called extrusive igneous rock. Examples include granite, obsidian, basalt, quartz, or pumice.
- **Sedimentary**—Forms when layers of sediments are compressed. Sedimentary rocks are often layered and cemented with minerals. Examples include sandstone, chalk, coal, limestone, or shale.
- **Metamorphic**—Forms through the transformation of igneous, sedimentary, and other metamorphic rocks through heat and pressure. The rock does not melt but is changed underground by immense heat and pressure. Examples include marble (once limestone), slate (mica), gneiss, schist, or quartzite.

Science, Technology, and Social Perspective

The third of the three primary areas of the Fundamental Subjects: Content Knowledge Exam in Science refers to information found in this main topic. Teachers must be able to

- Demonstrate understanding of the impact of science and technology on the environment and human affairs.
- Demonstrate knowledge of the societal issues with health awareness and medical advances.
- Demonstrate understanding of the social, political, ethical, and economic issues arising from science and technology.
- Demonstrate understanding of relationships between societal demands and scientific and technological enterprises.

This study of science specifically covers these topics:

- Personal health
- Populations, resources, and environments

- Natural hazards, local challenges, risks, and benefits
- Science and technology, technological design, artificial versus natural designs

Environment and Human Affairs

Science produces products such as jet engines, medical advances, communication systems, computers, draught resistant crops, renewal resources, and so on. Humans need products to advance their daily lives, but sometimes the demand outweighs the need. Scientists have been forecasting for centuries about the decline of the planet if humans did not address the needs of the environment. We know that the planet has gone through many changes in its lifetime, with atypical weather patterns and changes in the natural world, but now we face the destruction and decline of the planet due to overuse.

Humans must take a critical look at the use of natural resources, so they may devise a plan that incorporates care of the natural world. A **natural resource** is a material found on the planet that occurs in a natural state, but has economic value, such as timber, water, mineral deposits, oil, coal, and land.

For example, The Amazon Rainforest contains about one-third of the planet's land species, which adds to the balance of the world's ecosystem. However, deforestation adds about 500 million tons of carbon dioxide to the atmosphere each year. The rainforest has existed for tens of millions of years supporting life and regenerating the Earth. But, it is estimated that within this century or in the next 50 years, this fragile rainforest could be greatly damaged, almost beyond repair, or completely destroyed. This will have a major impact on the ecosystems of the world.

Global warming is a hugely debated subject in science and throughout the world. There is belief that the temperatures of the Earth are beginning to increase, and even a minor change of 1–4 degrees could cause catastrophic disasters. There does not seem to be any one answer to the question of what is causing the global warming, but several theories emerge. Some scientists believe it is only one reason, while others think there is a combination of ideas. Some of these ideas include ozone layer destruction, increased gamma rays from space, a change in the planet's position in the solar system rotation, more heat from the sun caused by debris hitting it, and the effects of moving through a different part of the Milky Way that has increased dust and debris.

Scientists have warned about the major greenhouse effect, being caused by dangerous toxins in the air. They believe it creates pollution and affects the ozone layer, which cannot then protect the Earth from gamma rays and other radiation of the sun or from the solar system.

For example, sulfur dioxide is a by-product of the burning of coal or oil, the smelting of metals, the making of paper, volcanic eruptions, and other industrial processes. Sulfur dioxide affects the air we breathe and the toxins that are added to the environment. In the atmosphere, it has the following effect:

sulfur dioxide $\rightarrow$ sulfuric acid $\rightarrow$ acid rain $\rightarrow$ toxin in air and on crops

Other major contributors to the greenhouse effect include the following:

CO_2-major greenhouse gas	CO-carbon monoxide	combustion of fossil fuels
nitrogen oxide	ozone effects	methane gas
gasoline	aerosols	chlorofluorocarbons

Health Issues and Medical Advances

The field of medicine was once practiced by observation and superstition. Practitioners were not required to have specific training, but an ability to read and try new treatments. Over the years, this field became a more exact science. With advances in technology, scientific research and training, the field of medicine has improved. It has only been recently (this century) that the machinery, equipment, instruments, and technology have been able to further advance the practices around the world.

The field of medicine has been directly affected by the innovations and discoveries made in science. Researchers and physicians consistently work on new methods and treatments to address medical issues around the world. As societies transform and the world changes, health issues evolve. The medical advances of the twentieth century have made great progress toward sustaining life and providing extended quality of life periods.

Some of the earliest contributions to science included the following:

16th century	Identified details of the human anatomy (Vesalius)
	Formed clinical symptoms of diseases (Sydenham)
	Defined medicinal properties of plants (Fuchs and Gerard)
17th century	Identified blood circulation and purpose of the heart (Harvey—1628)
18th century	Promoted the development of immunizations (Jenner)
	Discovered oxygen and respiration
19th century	Implemented use of anesthesia
	Used techniques with antiseptics
	Developed chemotherapy and other treatments
	Designed asepsis techniques
	Created germ theory
	Developed pre- and post-sterile operation procedures (Lister—1865)
	Implemented use of x-rays (Rontgen—1895)
	Invented electrocardiography (Waller—1887)
	Developed sphygmomanometer for blood pressure (Riva-Rocci—1896)
20th century	Identified significance of vitamins
	Discovered the four blood group types
	Implemented major organ transplants

Health education is an important topic under a science curriculum. The primary goal is for students to attain and maintain a healthy lifestyle. The curriculum should focus on the following:

- Instruct behaviors that ensure proper health, reducing at-risk behaviors
- Instill skills to use the behaviors or establish conditions in personal lives
- Teach attitudes, values, and knowledge of the behaviors and conditions
- Provide opportunities to practice and acquire the skills

Health Awareness

Certainly the issues in the field of medicine change on a regular basis. They are affected by the needs of the people, and the society that in turn drives the resolution and promotes discovery, inventions, or innovations. Some of the present day issues are as follows:

water supply	environment	enough trained personnel	biological warfare
waste disposal	immunizations	diseases	food sources and safety
moral decisions about life	health care costs	antibiotic rejections	air and water pollution
sufficient supply of energy	aged populations	disasters	biodiversity
space and ocean exploration	medications	climate change	bioterrorism
	treatments	organ transplants	globalization
	equipment	biohazards	
	facilities		

Medical Advances

We live in a time of significance and rapid change. We have available to us the most advanced medical techniques and procedures of human history, with new advances being established almost daily. Science plays an enormous role in the field of medicine and health. Researchers continue to address the health issues of the world by imposing scientific principles and processes to their studies with tremendous results.

This list provides a look at the medical advances that have changed our world during the twentieth century.

1900s	Electrocardiograph refined
1920s	Insulin, electroencephalograph, penicillin, cardiac catheter
1940s	Artificial kidney, fluoridation
1950s	Heart lung machine, kidney transplants, pacemaker, external defibrillator
1960s	Contraceptives, present day CPR techniques
1970s	Synthetic organs, CAT scanner, MRI scanner

Social, Political, Ethical, and Economic Issues

This area of science aids students in obtaining an understanding so they may act upon personal, social, ethical, political, and economic issues. These perspectives promote, encourage, teach, and allow individuals to develop decision-making skills. They also learn how science is intertwined with technology.

Societal beliefs and human values are connected to science, discoveries, and inventions as they focus on money, morals and laws. Research projects require funding, are at times politically motivated, and may bring up topics that are morally debatable. Students must learn in their overall study of science how to connect to their world, the greater society, and how science is impacted by the world's views and perspectives.

Societal Demands and Technology Issues

Society places great demands on the environment. Scientists believe that some of the environmental problems began as early as the Industrial Revolution, as this began a serious period of air pollution. Students must be taught through their science curriculum that society should only make the demands of the environment that can be replaced, corrected, or renewed.

Technology advances affect all areas of life and change the quality of people's lives. Technology touches on architecture, communications, medicine, transportation, research, environment, food production, housing, and so on. Technology should be a strong component of a science education program. It is one of the specific disciplines of science and can be utilized to enhance student knowledge about science.

Technology encompasses the media (films, vidoes, audiorecordings), 3-D hard copies (charts, displays, models, manipuatives), electronic tools (calculators, lab equipment), and computers (databases, distance learning opprotunities, software). Information is easily accessible, and areas of science may be reachable throughout the world via technology. Reasons for using technology in science education:

- Computers are available and used throughout the world.
- Students are comfortable with electronic equipment and media.
- Information is readily available, and new information is constantly obtainable.
- Electronic equipment provides opportunities for investigation and research.
- Students' learning needs may be addressed.
- Technology is a vehicle of science that scientists use.

Technology and science are in sync. Technology is defined as the means by which humans control or modify their environment. Technology has helped humans adapt to their world and environment, creating more sophisticated methods to meet their needs; metal tools instead of stone tools, cars for transportation rather than horses, email for communication rather than telegraphs, and so on. Science forges new opportunities to improve in the area of technology and face the needs of the twenty-first century: global computer networks, telecommunication systems, more powerful satellites.

Terminology

The subject of science offers many opportunities for improved and increased vocabulary exposure. The acquisition of science terms, both in physical and life sciences, many of which are applicable to other areas of study and life, enrich the student's core knowledge of this basic topic. The following list of terms, although not exhaustive, provides additional words that perhaps were not defined or mentioned in this content area. Remember that each grade level, preschool to eighth grade, has specific terms most suitable for instruction due to the specific science topics covered in those age groups.

adaptation—an inherited manner of an organism that improves its chance of survival

amphibian—animals that are members of the cold-blooded vertebrates categorized by having aquatic gill-breathing larval stage followed by terrestrial lung-breathing adult stage (typically)

conservation—management of natural resources; preservation and protection of an environment

constellation—a pattern formed by a set of stars

consumer—an organism that receives energy by devouring other organisms

classification—a category or grouping of organisms based on similarities and differences

endangered—the threat of extinction of a species

extinct—the absence of a certain plant or animal species

fossil—prehistoric remnants or residue of a plant or an animal found in a rock or in petrified form

friction—the resistance one object or surface experiences when going against or over another

germinate—the process of sprouting a plant from a seed

habitat—an environment that is home to a specific species

hibernation—a state of rest for an animal during the winter season; a dormant period

instinct—a natural response by an organism to adapting to the environment

invertebrate—any of the group of animals that do not have a spinal column

mammal—animals that are members of the warm-blooded vertebrates distinguished by possessing hair or fur, giving live birth, and the secretion of milk by females to nourish the young.

nutrients—an ingredient or substance that provides nourishment

osmosis—the diffusion through a semi-permeable membrane

prism—a transparent material so designed that may disperse a beam of light

propagation—to reproduce through sexual means

protist—a group of unicellular or non-cellular organisms such as bacteria

reclamation—to repair or alter from an undesirable state

reptile—animals that are members of the cold-blooded vertebrates categorized by having dry, scaly skin and laying soft-shelled eggs on land (typically)

senses—a specialized function of animals (sight, hearing, smell, taste, touch) used to engaged surroundings

solution—a liquid mixture in which a minor ingredient (solute) is uniformly distributed within the major ingredient (solvent)

symbiosis—the cohabitation of two unlike organisms who find mutual benefit from living together

vertebrate—any of the group of animals that have a spinal column

Web sites

The following web sites are provided for additional study and research. Examinees may want to review national science standards, reflect on the various specific topics in science education, study some of the units and lessons, and consider the strategies and methods of science education for the elementary level found on these sites.

Note: At the time of the development of this book, the Internet sites provided here were current, active, and accurate. However, due to constant modifications on the Internet, web sites and addresses may change or become obsolete.

http://www.map.edu/readingroom/books/nses/	National Science Education Standards
http://www.wcer.wisc.edu	National Institute for Science Education (NISE)
www.sciencenetlinks.com/	Science NetLinks
www.nsta.org/	The National Science Teachers Association (NSTA)
www.science-teachers.com/	The Science Teachers
www.nsf.gov/	The National Science Foundation (NSF)

PRACTICE EXAMINATIONS WITH ANSWER EXPLANATIONS

Answer Sheet for Practice Exam 1

(Remove This Sheet and Use It to Mark Your Answers)

Language Arts

1 Ⓐ Ⓑ Ⓒ Ⓓ
2 Ⓐ Ⓑ Ⓒ Ⓓ
3 Ⓐ Ⓑ Ⓒ Ⓓ
4 Ⓐ Ⓑ Ⓒ Ⓓ
5 Ⓐ Ⓑ Ⓒ Ⓓ
6 Ⓐ Ⓑ Ⓒ Ⓓ
7 Ⓐ Ⓑ Ⓒ Ⓓ
8 Ⓐ Ⓑ Ⓒ Ⓓ
9 Ⓐ Ⓑ Ⓒ Ⓓ
10 Ⓐ Ⓑ Ⓒ Ⓓ
11 Ⓐ Ⓑ Ⓒ Ⓓ
12 Ⓐ Ⓑ Ⓒ Ⓓ
13 Ⓐ Ⓑ Ⓒ Ⓓ
14 Ⓐ Ⓑ Ⓒ Ⓓ
15 Ⓐ Ⓑ Ⓒ Ⓓ
16 Ⓐ Ⓑ Ⓒ Ⓓ
17 Ⓐ Ⓑ Ⓒ Ⓓ
18 Ⓐ Ⓑ Ⓒ Ⓓ
19 Ⓐ Ⓑ Ⓒ Ⓓ
20 Ⓐ Ⓑ Ⓒ Ⓓ
21 Ⓐ Ⓑ Ⓒ Ⓓ
22 Ⓐ Ⓑ Ⓒ Ⓓ
23 Ⓐ Ⓑ Ⓒ Ⓓ
24 Ⓐ Ⓑ Ⓒ Ⓓ
25 Ⓐ Ⓑ Ⓒ Ⓓ

Math

1 Ⓐ Ⓑ Ⓒ Ⓓ
2 Ⓐ Ⓑ Ⓒ Ⓓ
3 Ⓐ Ⓑ Ⓒ Ⓓ
4 Ⓐ Ⓑ Ⓒ Ⓓ
5 Ⓐ Ⓑ Ⓒ Ⓓ
6 Ⓐ Ⓑ Ⓒ Ⓓ
7 Ⓐ Ⓑ Ⓒ Ⓓ
8 Ⓐ Ⓑ Ⓒ Ⓓ
9 Ⓐ Ⓑ Ⓒ Ⓓ
10 Ⓐ Ⓑ Ⓒ Ⓓ
11 Ⓐ Ⓑ Ⓒ Ⓓ
12 Ⓐ Ⓑ Ⓒ Ⓓ
13 Ⓐ Ⓑ Ⓒ Ⓓ
14 Ⓐ Ⓑ Ⓒ Ⓓ
15 Ⓐ Ⓑ Ⓒ Ⓓ
16 Ⓐ Ⓑ Ⓒ Ⓓ
17 Ⓐ Ⓑ Ⓒ Ⓓ
18 Ⓐ Ⓑ Ⓒ Ⓓ
19 Ⓐ Ⓑ Ⓒ Ⓓ
20 Ⓐ Ⓑ Ⓒ Ⓓ
21 Ⓐ Ⓑ Ⓒ Ⓓ
22 Ⓐ Ⓑ Ⓒ Ⓓ
23 Ⓐ Ⓑ Ⓒ Ⓓ
24 Ⓐ Ⓑ Ⓒ Ⓓ
25 Ⓐ Ⓑ Ⓒ Ⓓ

Social Studies

1 Ⓐ Ⓑ Ⓒ Ⓓ
2 Ⓐ Ⓑ Ⓒ Ⓓ
3 Ⓐ Ⓑ Ⓒ Ⓓ
4 Ⓐ Ⓑ Ⓒ Ⓓ
5 Ⓐ Ⓑ Ⓒ Ⓓ
6 Ⓐ Ⓑ Ⓒ Ⓓ
7 Ⓐ Ⓑ Ⓒ Ⓓ
8 Ⓐ Ⓑ Ⓒ Ⓓ
9 Ⓐ Ⓑ Ⓒ Ⓓ
10 Ⓐ Ⓑ Ⓒ Ⓓ
11 Ⓐ Ⓑ Ⓒ Ⓓ
12 Ⓐ Ⓑ Ⓒ Ⓓ
13 Ⓐ Ⓑ Ⓒ Ⓓ
14 Ⓐ Ⓑ Ⓒ Ⓓ
15 Ⓐ Ⓑ Ⓒ Ⓓ
16 Ⓐ Ⓑ Ⓒ Ⓓ
17 Ⓐ Ⓑ Ⓒ Ⓓ
18 Ⓐ Ⓑ Ⓒ Ⓓ
19 Ⓐ Ⓑ Ⓒ Ⓓ
20 Ⓐ Ⓑ Ⓒ Ⓓ
21 Ⓐ Ⓑ Ⓒ Ⓓ
22 Ⓐ Ⓑ Ⓒ Ⓓ
23 Ⓐ Ⓑ Ⓒ Ⓓ
24 Ⓐ Ⓑ Ⓒ Ⓓ
25 Ⓐ Ⓑ Ⓒ Ⓓ

Science

1 Ⓐ Ⓑ Ⓒ Ⓓ
2 Ⓐ Ⓑ Ⓒ Ⓓ
3 Ⓐ Ⓑ Ⓒ Ⓓ
4 Ⓐ Ⓑ Ⓒ Ⓓ
5 Ⓐ Ⓑ Ⓒ Ⓓ
6 Ⓐ Ⓑ Ⓒ Ⓓ
7 Ⓐ Ⓑ Ⓒ Ⓓ
8 Ⓐ Ⓑ Ⓒ Ⓓ
9 Ⓐ Ⓑ Ⓒ Ⓓ
10 Ⓐ Ⓑ Ⓒ Ⓓ
11 Ⓐ Ⓑ Ⓒ Ⓓ
12 Ⓐ Ⓑ Ⓒ Ⓓ
13 Ⓐ Ⓑ Ⓒ Ⓓ
14 Ⓐ Ⓑ Ⓒ Ⓓ
15 Ⓐ Ⓑ Ⓒ Ⓓ
16 Ⓐ Ⓑ Ⓒ Ⓓ
17 Ⓐ Ⓑ Ⓒ Ⓓ
18 Ⓐ Ⓑ Ⓒ Ⓓ
19 Ⓐ Ⓑ Ⓒ Ⓓ
20 Ⓐ Ⓑ Ⓒ Ⓓ
21 Ⓐ Ⓑ Ⓒ Ⓓ
22 Ⓐ Ⓑ Ⓒ Ⓓ
23 Ⓐ Ⓑ Ⓒ Ⓓ
24 Ⓐ Ⓑ Ⓒ Ⓓ
25 Ⓐ Ⓑ Ⓒ Ⓓ

Language Arts

Directions: Read the following multiple-choice questions and select the most appropriate answer. Mark the answer sheet accordingly.

1. The following is an example of a warning label from *Red Bite Insect Repellant*.

   > Contents flammable under pressure.
   > If ingested do not induce vomiting.
   > For normal use, spray lightly, and keep away from eyes, nose and mouth.
   > Do not use near flame or fire.
   > Do not puncture or incinerate.
   > Do not store near foods.

   What is the most critical reading skill that should be taught in order for an individual to use this product appropriately?

   A. vocabulary
   B. negative meanings
   C. use of words in context
   D. meanings of new words

2. Which of the following is an example of an oxymoron (contradiction of words)?

   A. tea bag
   B. jumbo shrimp
   C. extra medium
   D. hamburger bun

3. If a teacher asked his 5th grade students to compose a story about their own lives, he would be asking the students to write

   A. biographies
   B. realistic fiction
   C. personal legends
   D. autobiographies

4. One method of enhancing students' skills in learning to decipher meanings from words in context is to instruct them on the use of

   A. fictional text
   B. word analysis
   C. word imagery
   D. hypothesis text

5. Which of the following is most effective according to the research for addressing improved vocabulary skills in reading?

   A. Students should be allowed study time when given new words to learn.
   B. Students must memorize new words, meanings, and spelling to improve.
   C. Students should be provided vocabulary instruction in every subject area.
   D. Students should be given weekly spelling tests and sentence writing of new words.

6. High-frequency words are important for reading success, and these are defined as those words that

   A. are most easily spelled by the majority of students
   B. are most basic in reading passages, used often on a regular basis
   C. are primarily the words that are specific to the subject area being taught
   D. are words that are most irregular and rare, specific to time periods and genre

GO ON TO THE NEXT PAGE

7. Which of the following is the BEST selection when considering the importance of text-to-world connections for students in their reading?

    A. They will understand more about the current events and historical situations.

    B. They must be able to search for information about other cultures and traditions.

    C. They need to be aware of and analyze the issues that are similar in a present day world.

    D. They will be better prepared to function in society after they have graduated from school.

8. The following sentence is an example of which type of figurative language?

The winter winds wound through the wetlands and weeping willows.

    A. idiom

    B. simile

    C. alliteration

    D. consonants

9. A primary purpose for teaching reading to students is for them to understand that reading provides an aspect of

    A. growth

    B. pleasure

    C. experience

    D. contemplation

10. The omniscient point of view is when the story is told by

    A. a narrator whose knowledge is contained to knowing all inner thoughts and feelings of one character

    B. a narrator who is detached from the story and tells about the actions and dialogue of characters

    C. a narrator who is directly involved in the story and action and may or may not be trusted

    D. a narrator who knows everything about every character including all inner thoughts and feelings

11. An interview is an example of which kind of source?

    A. primary

    B. secondary

    C. observational

    D. written

12. Justin, an avid bird watcher, was on a trip in a tropical region. He expected to see the unusual and rare woodpecker reported in the national newsletter. He quietly and carefully moved through the dense growth of the island, emerging in an opening to see the stunning bird.

In the underlined sentence, the word *quietly* is used as

    A. an adverb

    B. a participle

    C. an adjective

    D. a preposition

13. Look at the following words, which are some of the most commonly misspelled words in the English language.

Which word is spelled incorrectly?

    A. liaison

    B. judgement

    C. maneuver

    D. occurrence

14. Which of the answers states which word should be used to coordinate the subject-verb agreement in the following sentence?

Neither Bryce nor Louise _____ supposed to be in the ocean when the red flag is up on the beach.

    A. The verb *is* should be used as the subject is singular (neither).

    B. The verb *are* should be used as the subject is plural (two people).

    C. The verb *is* should be used as the nouns show singularity (ocean, flag, beach).

    D. The verb *are* should be used as the people, Bryce and Louise, show a compound subject.

Read the written passage and answer questions 15–17 about the content of the story.

Mabel, a purebred Boxer, was a rambunctious and inquisitive animal. From the time of her birth, she excitedly approached anything that came her way, whether it was greeting people, devouring food, pushing a beetle, or destroying a cardboard box. Her excitement often engulfed others who entered her space. Young children would gaily play with her, and a passersby could hear glorious giggling glittering the air. Mabel was gentle and often searched for a friend to cuddle, like a sleepy toddler seeking his mother, in order to find and give comfort. She would softly nuzzle at one's neck and rest contentedly for long periods. One could count on Mabel to bring a joyful feeling to an otherwise dismal day.

15. Which sentence is an example of alliteration?

   A. 2
   B. 4
   C. 6
   D. 7

16. The following phrase, *like a sleepy toddler seeking his mother,* is an example of which of the following?

   A. simile
   B. metaphor
   C. alliteration
   D. personification

17. In sentence 6, "She would softly nuzzle at one's neck and rest comfortably for long periods," the pronoun *she* refers to

   A. Mabel
   B. the mother
   C. the toddler
   D. any of the three

Read this poem created by a sixth-grade student and answer questions 18–20.

Alone

The playhouse stood so stately
Out in the old backyard
The children hadn't played there lately
It was now a child's discard.
What fun they had in the playhouse
Such a short time ago
And now it stands quiet as a mouse
Just standing there alone.

18. What does the author mean by the passage "and now it stands quiet as a mouse?"

   A. When the children play in the house, they do not make much noise.
   B. The playhouse is deserted, and no sound comes from its use anymore.
   C. The mice are very quiet in the playhouse when the children are playing.
   D. No one uses the playhouse anymore except the mice who now live there.

19. Why has the author chosen a playhouse as the main character for this poem?

   A. She probably had a playhouse when she was little and misses it.
   B. She wants the reader to compare the image of a child's real house to that of the playhouse.
   C. She wants readers to make a connection with a common object from childhood that is no longer used as an adult.
   D. She probably did not want to use the idea of a toy because toys can be passed from generation to generation but playhouses get torn down.

20. What meaning is the author trying to convey to the readers?

   A. The playhouse is falling down.
   B. The playhouse is infested with mice.
   C. The children are alone in the playhouse.
   D. The children are grown and have lost interest in the playhouse.

GO ON TO THE NEXT PAGE

21. Read the following sentence and choose the answer that best depicts the grammar-related corrections that should be made.

The executive board of the Paris children's museum met for two hours yesterday to decide on the bylaws, goals, budget, exhibits and employees; however they decided that the meeting should continue next week with the presence of the Mayor.

A. The Executive Board of the Paris Children's Museum met for two hours yesterday to decide on the bylaws, goals, budget, exhibits, and employees; however, they decided that the meeting should continue next week with the presence of the mayor.

B. The executive board of the Paris children's museum met for two hours, yesterday, to decide on the bylaws, goals, budget, exhibits and employees, however; they decided that the meeting should continue next week with the presence of the mayor.

C. The Executive board of the Paris (children's) Museum met for two hours yesterday, to decide on the bylaws, goals, budget, exhibits and employees; however; they decided that the meeting should continue next week with the presence of the Mayor.

D. The Executive Board of the Paris children's museum met for two hours, yesterday to decide on the bylaws, goals, budget, exhibits and employees: however, they decided that the meeting should continue next week with the presence of the mayor.

22. The speech therapist in a second grade classroom is reading a story to the children. The purpose for his involvement in the reading period is to assess which children are using age appropriate articulation of their vocabulary. As an activity, he asks each child to repeat certain words in the story and records their _____ of the words.

Which of the following is the correct spelling for the missing word?

A. pronunciation
B. pronouncition
C. prononceation
D. pronounciasion

23. Children often have problems learning figurative language, such as idioms or idiomatic expressions. They generally think in more concrete terms and have a hard time extracting the meaning of such phrases in passages, unless they are taught the meanings through direct instruction. Read the following sentence with an idiomatic expression and choose the meaning from the answers given.

Jillian's grandmother was teaching her how to make vegetable soup, and she knew she would be in hot water if she did not pay attention.

A. Jillian would be in trouble if she did not listen.
B. Jillian needed to understand how much water to use.
C. The grandmother was comparing the vegetables and water.
D. The grandmother was explaining important instructions to Jillian.

Use the following passage to answer questions 24–25.

The southwestern cheeseburger at the Burger Hut was the single worst excuse for a meal I have ever had. The meal was lacking in not only taste, but color and texture as well. It seems that the chef got his degree at The Back Alley Culinary Institute. It would have been better had I scraped the two-day-old road kill off my driveway and fried it up, slapped it on a bun, and thrown a slice of cheese on top.

24. What line is an example of hyperbole (over exaggeration to make a point)?

A. 1
B. 2
C. 3
D. 4

25. Which word BEST describes the author's voice?

A. emotional
B. opinionated
C. factual
D. sorrowful

Math

Directions: Read the following multiple-choice questions and select the most appropriate answer. Mark the answer sheet accordingly.

1. Find the average of 50%, 0.25, and $5\frac{1}{4}$.

   A. 3
   B. 2
   C. $5\frac{1}{4}$
   D. $2\frac{1}{2}$

2. Lauren's soccer team has 8 girls who weigh 105, 115, 130, 125, x, 142, 122, and 128 pounds. If the average weight of these players is 122.25 pounds, what is the value of the missing value?

   A. 110 lbs
   B. 125 lbs
   C. 111 lbs
   D. 106 lbs

3. Find the average of a, $6a$, $2a$, $9a$, and $7a$.

   A. $5a$
   B. 5
   C. $5a^2$
   D. $\frac{1}{5}$

4. Dr. Suketu drove for 5 hours at 80 miles per hour and for 3 hours at 75 miles per hour on his way to a pathology conference in California. What was his average rate, in miles per hour, for the entire trip? (Round the answer to the nearest whole number)

   A. 79 mph
   B. 80 mph
   C. 78 mph
   D. 75 mph

5. If 4 bottles of organic, farm-fresh orange juice cost $18, how much would 10 bottles cost?

   A. $36
   B. $72
   C. $180
   D. $45

6. If b boys can eat c hotdogs in one hour, how many hotdogs can n boys eat in the same amount of time?

   A. $b*n*c$
   B. $\frac{c}{(b*n)}$
   C. $\frac{(n*c)}{b}$
   D. $\frac{(c*b)}{n}$

7. Write $4\frac{1}{2}\%$ as a decimal.

   A. 4.5
   B. 0.45
   C. 0.045
   D. 4.05

8. During a huge blow-out sale at The Rider Shack, Kahoon found a surf board for 30% off the original price of $659.59. What is the sale price of the board Kahoon found?

   A. $641.17
   B. $461.71
   C. $617.41
   D. $461.72

GO ON TO THE NEXT PAGE

Use the diagram to answer questions 9–10. (not to scale)

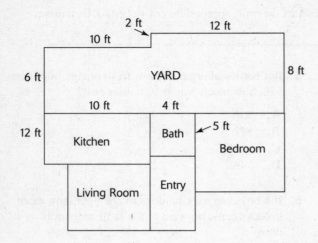

9. Alec wants to retile part of his house. If each square foot of tile costs $6.20, how much money will it cost Alec to tile his bathroom and kitchen?

   A. $384.40

   B. $868

   C. $686

   D. $22.58

10. Alec also wants to fence in his backyard. Each section of fencing covers 3 ft, and no partial sections are sold. How many sections of fencing will Alec need to purchase for his yard?

   A. 13

   B. 12

   C. 8

   D. 7

11. Jeanine teaches a class of 26 college students. Each class is 55 minutes long, and each student must present a final project lasting 5–6 minutes. What is the minimum amount of class days that Jeanine needs to allocate to presentations?

   A. 2

   B. 3

   C. 4

   D. 5

12. Kelly can edit one page of a textbook in 3 minutes. She has a 282 page book to edit. Which equation shows how to solve for the amount of time Kelly will spend on this book?

   A. $x = \dfrac{282}{3}$

   B. $x = \dfrac{3}{282}$

   C. $x = (282)(3)$

   D. $x = 282 + 3$

13. 692 feet is equivalent to how many inches?

   A. 0.017 inches

   B. 8,304 inches

   C. $57\dfrac{2}{3}$ inches

   D. 6,920 inches

14. Place the following set of values in numerical order from least to greatest.

$$\frac{1}{8}, 0.25, 90\%, 15.6, 4\frac{1}{2}$$

   A. $15.6, \ 4\dfrac{1}{2}, 90\%, 0.25, \dfrac{1}{8}$

   B. $0.25, \dfrac{1}{8}, \ 4\dfrac{1}{2}, 15.6, 90\%$

   C. $\dfrac{1}{8}, 90\%, 0.25, \ 4\dfrac{1}{2}, 15.6$

   D. $\dfrac{1}{8}, 0.25, 90\%, \ 4\dfrac{1}{2}, 15.6$

15. Solve for x: $2x + 3y - 9z = 243$.

   A. $2x = 243 + 9z - 3y$

   B. $x = 124.5$

   C. $x = (243 + 9z - 3y) \div 2$

   D. $x = (243 - 9z + 3y) \div 2$

16. John is on a bird counting expedition. He has been assigned to a specific county to evaluate. If his county is shaped like a parallelogram measuring 120 miles long by 75 miles wide, how many miles must John cover during his expedition to cover the entire area he was assigned? ($Area_{par} = b \cdot h$ or $l \cdot w$)

   A. 390 square miles

   B. 195 square miles

   C. 4,500 square miles

   D. 9,000 square miles

Record Wind Chills in Omaha, NE

Month	Record Temperature (degrees in Fahrenheit)
January	−31
February	−25
March	−10
April	5
May	50
June	78
July	90
August	85
September	70
October	30
November	10
December	−15

17. The monthly record wind chills are listed in the preceding table. What is the range of wind chills based upon this chart?

   A. 59
   B. 121
   C. 116
   D. 85

18. If Chip has a batting average of 0.342, which of the given fractions is closest to his average?

   A. $\dfrac{1}{2}$

   B. $\dfrac{1}{4}$

   C. $\dfrac{1}{3}$

   D. $\dfrac{2}{5}$

19. Which equation represents the statement "4 times a number increased by 2 and distributed equally 3 times?"

   A. $(4x - 2) \div 3$
   B. $(4x + 2) * 3$
   C. $(4 + x + 2) * 3$
   D. $(4x + 2) \div 3$

20. Haley bakes 15 lemon scones with icing, 9 with poppy seeds on top, and 24 cranberry scones. What percentage of the scones do not have icing? (Round to the nearest whole percentage.)

   A. 69%
   B. 68%
   C. 31%
   D. 32%

Use the following pie graph to answer questions 21–23.

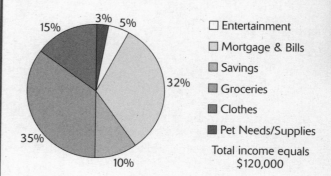

21. How much money has the Schedlin family budgeted for entertainment?

   A. $60,000
   B. $6,000
   C. $500
   D. $50,000

22. If this pattern of budgeting continues for the next 5 years at the same total income rate, how much money will the Schedlin family have saved?

   A. $60,000
   B. $12,000
   C. $6,000
   D. $1200

23. If the Schedlin family increases their yearly income by $15,000, how much of that raise will go toward the mortgage and bills?

   A. $32,000
   B. $38,400
   C. $43,200
   D. $4,800

GO ON TO THE NEXT PAGE

24. Solve the following equation:

$$\left(\frac{4}{5}+123.8\right)+7^2*89\%.$$

    A. 172.710

    B. 137.06

    C. 168.21

    D. 123.354

25. What is the mean of 328, 347, 442, 298, 400, 323, 287, 315?

    A. 1,370

    B. 342.5

    C. 134.8

    D. 442

Social Sciences

Directions: Read the following multiple-choice questions and select the most appropriate answer. Mark the answer sheet accordingly.

1. The original motto of the United States, *E Pluribus Unum*, created in 1776 is translated as

   A. in God we trust
   B. out of many, one
   C. in courage there is strength
   D. united we stand, divided we fall

2. The colors of the flag of the United States represent different values that are evident in this country. What does the white color stands for?

   A. hope, purity, and innocence
   B. courage, hardiness, and valor
   C. peace, cooperation, and tranquility
   D. vigilance, perseverance, and justice

3. What do both Abraham Lincoln and George Washington have in common?

   A. Both are found on Mount Rushmore and on U.S. currency.
   B. Both were Revolutionary generals and signed the Declaration.
   C. Both were re-elected to a third term and buried in Washington D.C.
   D. Both were assassinated while in office and honored with monuments.

4. Mount Rushmore is a sculpted landmark of four great presidents that represents the four themes they pursued for this nation during their leadership. These themes include

   A. life, liberty, unification, and the pursuit of happiness
   B. independence, expansion, conservation, and unification
   C. liberty, expansion, the pursuit of happiness, and patriotism
   D. freedom, independence, perseverance, and communication

5. Which Amendment to the U.S. Constitution, ratified in 1920, allowed women the right to vote?

   A. the 14th Amendment
   B. the 19th Amendment
   C. the 21st Amendment
   D. the 24th Amendment

6. The elementary student council meets to decide how the school should participate in the community festival. Which of the following forms of political systems is represented by this example?

   A. direct democracy
   B. individual monarchy
   C. constitutional monarchy
   D. representative democracy

7. The First Amendment to the U.S. Constitution guarantees to all its citizens the

   A. freedom to vote
   B. right to fair trial
   C. right to bear arms
   D. freedom of expression

8. The settlers in the original colonies moved westward in a mass exodus due to the discovery of

   A. the large rivers
   B. rifles and weapons
   C. the covered wagon
   D. the approach of diseases

GO ON TO THE NEXT PAGE

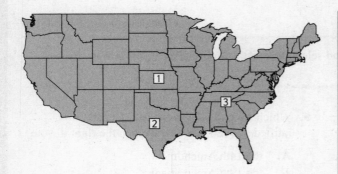

Use this map of the United States to answer the next three questions.

9. Which of the following states is indicated by the number 1?

   A. Iowa
   B. Illinois
   C. Kansas
   D. Missouri

10. Which of the four major rivers is located in the area at the number 2?

    A. Ohio
    B. Colorado
    C. Rio Grande
    D. Mississippi

11. Which of these four main topographical regions describes number 3?

    A. Great Plains
    B. Rocky Mountains
    C. Central Lowlands
    D. Appalachian Mountains

12. If you were preparing a timeline, indicate the placement of the following wars in order of the period in which they occurred, beginning with the earliest war.

    1. Civil War
    2. Korean War
    3. Persian Gulf War
    4. American-Indian War
    5. American Revolution

    A. 4, 5, 1, 2, 3
    B. 3, 4, 1, 5, 2
    C. 1, 5, 4, 3, 2
    D. 5, 1, 3, 2, 4

13. Which of the following contributions was a direct result of World War II?

    A. The United Way
    B. The United Nations
    C. The Head Start Program
    D. The American Red Cross

14. These two world leaders, John F. Kennedy and Nikita Khruschev, were in power during which of the following historical events?

    A. World War II
    B. The Cold War
    C. The Great Depression
    D. The Civil Rights Movement

15. What is the number of Senate seats in Congress based upon?

    A. two seats per state
    B. one seat per district
    C. five seats per region
    D. a percentage of the census

16. A system of checks and balances has been established in the U.S. government. If the U.S. Supreme Court rejects a law that Congress has passed, this is an example of the _____ branch checking the _____ branch.

    A. executive, judicial
    B. legislative, judicial
    C. judicial, legislative
    D. legislative, executive

17. The _____ Mountain range is considered the most valuable in the world due to the mineral resources of gold, silver, copper, tin, iron, and platinum found in it.

    A. Urals
    B. Andes
    C. Himalayas
    D. Appalachian

18. How does the Gulf Stream impact the people in Britain?

    A. improves the trade route
    B. produces warmer climate
    C. exchanges ocean water for sea water
    D. moves storms onto the island quicker

Using the following map, answer question 19.

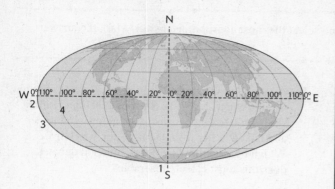

19. Using this map of the world, identify what the numbers represent on it by selecting the correct answer. (1, 2, 3, 4)

  A. prime meridian, equator, line of latitude, line of longitude

  B. international date line, continental divide, prime meridian, equator

  C. prime meridian, line of latitude, line of longitude, continental divide

  D. line of latitude, line of longitude, international date line, continental divide

20. How did the Tigris-Euphrates Civilization influence present-day society in the area of law?

  A. It established a standard legal system.

  B. It developed a system of checks and balances.

  C. It created professions, such as lawyers and judges.

  D. It designed university programs that taught people the laws.

21. What was the most influential contribution of the ancient Greek city of Athens to modern times?

  A. religion of Judaism

  B. system of agriculture

  C. government of democracy

  D. rrchitecture of skyscrapers

22. In 1989, the Berlin Wall was demolished as a result of

  A. the nuclear explosion at a plant

  B. the new power established in Europe

  C. the war's destruction of the foundation

  D. the collapse of communism in East Germany

23. Which of the following was most affected in the North by the development of the transcontinental railroad of the 1860s?

  A. the economy

  B. the population

  C. food processing

  D. crop stabilization

24. A tribe in Africa has established an economic system in which they use their bead work to trade for fruits and vegetables with a nearby tribe. This is an example of which type of economy?

  A. natural economy

  B. market economy

  C. planned economy

  D. autarky economy

25. People from Mexico immigrate into the southwestern United States and become citizens. They work, raise families, and encourage their relatives to join them in their new town. Over a few years, many more people join them, and together they begin to share their traditions and customs again. They introduce some of their culture to the people in the U.S. town. This is an example of

  A. cultural ecology

  B. cultural diffusion

  C. cultural interaction

  D. cultural development

GO ON TO THE NEXT PAGE

Science

Directions: Read the following multiple-choice questions and select the most appropriate answer. Mark the answer sheet accordingly.

1. A second grade student found a rock near the creek. She was fascinated by the sunlight on it, but when she held it up she could not see through it. She remembered that a(n) _____ object cannot allow light to pass through it.

   A. opaque
   B. obsidian
   C. translucent
   D. transparent

2. Which of the following happened between the invention of the telephone in 1875 and the invention of the motorized airplane in 1905?

   A. the discovery of genetics
   B. the discovery of penicillin
   C. the invention of the light bulb
   D. the invention of the steam engine

3. When two species live together in harmony and make changes to their own species to benefit one another, it is called

   A. instincts
   B. mutation
   C. symbiosis
   D. conditioning

4. Charles Darwin established "laws" in science that have been over time, highly debated. However, he has pointed out specific information about the population of the species we see in the world. One of his laws states that changes in a species occur through a slow process of the population, and not through any sudden production of new beings. To which of the following of Darwin's laws does this refer?

   A. Gradualism
   B. Multiplication
   C. Natural Selection
   D. Common Descent

5. A second grade student is in need of glasses as she squints when she reads. She has excellent reading skills for her age, because her parents read to her and talked to her from the time she was born. Which of the following developmental debates does this most closely resemble?

   A. nature versus nurture
   B. genetics versus education
   C. imitation versus reasoning
   D. instinct versus conditioning

6. Which scientist is best known for his theory about how species develop new traits to adapt to the environment which will ensure the survival of that species?

   A. Louis Pasteur
   B. Madame Curie
   C. Gregor Mendel
   D. Charles Darwin

7. Many species around the world have behaviors specific to them. All behaviors may be further defined and described according to the type of behavior it is. Which of the following is an example of an instinctive behavior?

   A. A dog will sit when given a command or a treat.
   B. A bird begins to fly by repeatedly observing a parent.
   C. Humans wear heavier clothing for protection in cold weather.
   D. Bears enter into extended sleep patterns during winter months.

8. Which part of the visible light spectrum produces the most energy?

   A. red light
   B. violet light
   C. infrared light
   D. ultraviolet light

Consider the following timeline.

Darwin	Roentgen	Curie	Sabin	Fleming
Theory of evolution	Discovery of x-ray	Discovery of radium	Discovery of origin of blood	Discovery of penicillin
↓	↓	↓	↓	↓
1	2	3	4	5

9. Where does the theory of relativity, discovered by Einstein, belong on this timeline?

    A. between 1 and 2
    B. between 2 and 3
    C. between 3 and 4
    D. between 4 and 5

10. When water is subjected to increased temperature that reaches 212 degrees Fahrenheit or more, it achieves the state of a

    A. gas
    B. solid
    C. liquid
    D. matter

11. A family who is camping notices lightning in the distance and a few moments later hears thunder. What reason does the father give to the children for the difference between seeing the lightning and hearing the thunder from this particular storm?

    A. Light travels faster than sound.
    B. Sound travels faster than light.
    C. Lightning must strike to create a sound.
    D. Thunder produces the lightning when it rains.

12. The human eye can perceive color due to the way the given object reflects the light it receives. Based on this theory, which of the following is true? A person sees a banana as yellow

    A. due to the low frequency of the yellow light.
    B. due to the high frequency of the yellow light.
    C. because a banana reflects all the colors of the spectrum except yellow.
    D. because a banana absorbs all the colors of the spectrum except yellow.

13. When the days and nights are the same length due to the rotation of the Earth around the sun, which period of rotation is being described?

    A. phase
    B. eclipse
    C. solstice
    D. equinox

14. A third grade student found a glob of stones and mud near the creek that he wanted to show his teacher. He was excited that there might be an animal living inside the glob that was stuck together. Because the mud had dried it was very hard. The teacher suggested he use a _____ to pry it apart, as this simple tool would magnify the force and push the glob apart.

    A. lever
    B. plane
    C. pulley
    D. wedge

15. How long does it take for the Earth to make a complete spin on its axis?

    A. 24 hours
    B. 365 days
    C. 12 months
    D. 180 degrees

GO ON TO THE NEXT PAGE

16. Sound is measured by frequency, which are the cycles of the sound wave. The units of measure are called Hertz (Hz). Which of the following shows the greatest frequency or highest Hertz?

A. 1
B. 2
C. 3
D. 4

17. A living organism possesses a group of systems that function pertinent to its life. Which basic life function can ensure the survival of a species?

A. digestion
B. respiration
C. assimilation
D. reproduction

18. In a science experiment, a student tries to set up a circuit using a battery connected to a light bulb with a rubber band. The student tries several times, but the bulb will not light up. What is the reason for this?

A. The rubber band is a convection mechanism.
B. The rubber band must be wet to move the circuit.
C. The rubber band must be stretched to carry a current.
D. The rubber band acts as an insulator and not a conductor.

19. A sky diver traveling in an airplane sits in the open doorway ready to jump. Which of the following best describes the form of energy this skydiver has in this situation?

A. kinetic energy
B. potential energy
C. equivalent energy
D. transferred energy

20. Ecosystems are present around the world and vary depending on the plant and animal life and the climate. Which of the following does an ecosystem's balance depend on the most?

A. food resources
B. climate constancy
C. plant reproduction
D. species interactions

21. The ground begins to shake and pictures crash off the walls of Jack's house. He runs outside and sees the street moving in a wave-like motion. The city emergency sirens begin sounding. Jack is witnessing which natural phenomenon?

A. There is the possibility of an emerging volcano.
B. The rubbing of the tectonic plates is recycling the Earth's crust.
C. There has been a collision of the tectonic plates forcing the ground upward.
D. A river of magma has begun to form under the surface.

22. In the stage of a developing embryo of a human being, where would the zygote stage appear?

A. after the egg
B. before the fetus
C. after the embryo
D. before the newborn

23. Each plant or animal cell has a special set of parts, each having a specific purpose in the function of the cell. Which of the following parts of a cell is considered the control center that contains the DNA?

   A. nucleus

   B. ribosomes

   C. cytoplasm

   D. mitochondria

24. Health education is one component of a science curriculum. Students should learn more about health issues in the world, and medical advances that affect their lives. The primary purpose of instructing students in the area of health is to

   A. promote healthy personal behaviors

   B. instill the desire to work in the field of health

   C. learn to perform CPR and first aid techniques

   D. study the past and compare the advances of the future

25. A second grade class is preparing to conduct an experiment on household plants. The teacher asks them to divide the plants into those that flower, those with seeds, those that are fruits and those that are vegetables before placing them in the dye prepared solutions. Which of the scientific processes is the educator reinforcing with the students?

   A. inference

   B. prediction

   C. observation

   D. classification

IF YOU FINISH BEFORE TIME IS CALLED, CHECK YOUR WORK ON THIS SECTION ONLY. DO NOT WORK ON ANY OTHER SECTION IN THE TEST.

Answer Key

Language Arts

1. C
2. B
3. D
4. B
5. C
6. B
7. C
8. C
9. B
10. D
11. A
12. A
13. B

14. A
15. B
16. A
17. A
18. B
19. C
20. D
21. A
22. A
23. A
24. D
25. B

Math

1. B
2. C
3. A
4. C
5. D
6. C
7. C
8. B
9. B
10. A
11. B
12. C
13. B

14. D
15. C
16. D
17. B
18. C
19. D
20. A
21. B
22. A
23. D
24. C
25. B

Social Sciences

1. B
2. A
3. A
4. B
5. B
6. D
7. D
8. A
9. C
10. C
11. D
12. A
13. B

14. B
15. A
16. C
17. B
18. B
19. A
20. A
21. C
22. D
23. A
24. A
25. B

Science

1. A
2. C
3. C
4. A
5. A
6. D
7. D
8. B
9. C
10. A
11. A
12. D
13. D

14. D
15. A
16. C
17. D
18. D
19. B
20. D
21. B
22. A
23. A
24. A
25. D

Answer Explanations

Language Arts

1. **C.** Students may learn new vocabulary and understand the isolated meanings of words, but in order to fully comprehend the meanings of these warnings, students need to possess the reading skill that enables them to understand the use and meaning of words in context. A student may understand the word *vomiting,* but do they understand the meaning of *inducing vomiting* or *not inducing vomiting*? They may know the meaning of the word *store* as a place to shop, but do they know another meaning as a verb?

2. **B.** An oxymoron is defined as a pair of words that are combined to portray a meaning when the words independently have the opposite meanings. Examples include small fortune, working holiday, and sweet tart. Therefore, the best choice in this question is jumbo shrimp.

3. **D.** Each student would be writing an autobiography as it is a written documentation about the author's own life, while a biography is about another person's life.

4. **B.** Word analysis is a method used to help students learn how to access the meaning of words in context. They are taught how to break down words into the basic root word and identify the prefixes or suffixes that may add a different meaning to the word.

5. **C.** The research on ways to effectively enhance students' abilities in vocabulary acquisition and usage focus on the need to expose students to new words throughout their day at school. Each subject area teacher should provide adequate time to learning new words that are associated to the subject area and these may cross disciplines. It is evident that students graduating from high school are currently in *word deficit,* as they are not provided direct instruction in the various subject areas on a regularly basis.

6. **B.** High-frequency words are also called *basic words,* as they are used regularly in all genres and are found in writing, reading, as well as conversing. These words are perhaps the easier words to learn for young children as they occur so much that the repetition of seeing and hearing them instill acquisition of skills. They may include words like *and, but, the, am, as,* and so on.

7. **C.** Students need to be aware of and analyze the issues that are similar in a present day world. By choosing reading selections that have a text-to-world connection, teachers may assist students in learning the skills to attack these types of literature and to be able to analyze the issues, relating them to the current world situations.

8. **C.** It is an example of alliteration, which is the use of repeated beginning sounds. In stories or poetry, this develops the mood, creates melodic language, and helps the reader focus on important words, sometimes pointing out similarities and differences.

9. **B.** Students should learn that they may read for pleasure. It is one of the essential life skills.

10. **D.** Omniscient point of view allows the reader to know all that is going on both externally and internally with all characters. *Limited omniscient* point of view is when a narrator knows everything about only one character (major or minor). The reader must draw conclusions about other characters through this one point of view and setting and dialogue to get the complete picture and meaning of the story. The *objective* point of view is when the narrator is a detached observer and tells only the dialogue and actions so that the reader must infer all inner thoughts and feelings. *First person* point of view is when the narrator is directly involved in the story and may or may not be a reliable source for the reader.

11. **A.** An interview is a questionnaire used to help gather opinions and preferences first hand. A *primary* source is when resources/research is gathered from an original source in order to give the reader direct, first hand knowledge.

12. **A.** The word *quietly* is used as an adverb, as it modifies or describes the verb. In this example, the word *quietly* demonstrates more specifically how Justin moved. He moved *quietly* as opposed to *quickly, smoothly,* or *clumsily.*

13. **B.** The word judgment does not include the 'e' in the correct spelling. When the word judge is combined with the suffix -ment, the silent 'e' is dropped. The spelling judgement is incorrect.

14. A. In the sentence the proper subject-verb agreement requires the use of the verb *is*. When two singular subjects are connected by *either/or* or *neither/nor,* the sentence requires the use of a singular verb according to the subject-verb agreement rules.

15. B. The sentence that demonstrates alliteration is sentence 4. Alliteration is a literary technique in which words begin with the same sounds, primarily consonants, but may also rhyme or use vowel sounds to get across the emotion. The use of alliteration provides the reader with interest and change in the flow of a piece. In this sentence *glorious giggling glittering the air* demonstrates alliteration. Another example is the tongue twister *Peter Piper picked a peck of pickled peppers.*

16. A. A simile is a figure of speech that compares two unlike items by using the words *like* or *as*. In this story, Mabel is compared to a toddler, when the author refers to her gentle and cuddly nature and how she seeks comfort.

17. A. The pronoun *she* refers to the primary subject or noun in the previous sentence, which is the dog, Mabel. Pronouns are used to refer back to the previous or nearest noun. In this example, since the *she* is in a separate sentence, it would not refer back to mother or the toddler, as they are contained in a dependent clause. This sentence refers back to the previous sentence in which Mabel is the subject.

18. B. It appears that the author is pointing out the loneliness of the playhouse. It seems that children no longer play in the house, and it has become deserted. There is no evidence in this poem that mice live in the playhouse; however this passage is the use of figurative language comparing the status of the playhouse to the quietness of a mouse.

19. C. The author wanted to use a common symbol of childhood so that readers could make a connection to the poem and feel the sadness that comes with the leaving behind of childhood.

20. D. According to the author, the playhouse had been a place for the children to play, but it seems time has passed. Apparently, the children have not been in the playhouse for a while, and now it stands alone in the yard.

21. A. This is the corrected version of the sentence, adding the appropriate capitalization and commas. The words Executive Board, and Paris Children's Museum should be capitalized as they refer to a particular board and specific museum. A comma is needed after the word *exhibits* as this is part of a list. A comma is necessary after the word *however* as a semicolon was used to join the two independent clauses together with one of the conjunctive adverbs: however, moreover, therefore, consequently, otherwise, and nevertheless. The word *mayor* is only capitalized if it refers to a particular person, such as Mayor Johnson.

22. A. The correct spelling of the word is *pronunciation*, although a phonetic speller would have difficulty deciphering the sounds in this word.

23. A. The idiomatic expression used in the sentence is "(in) hot water." The literal meaning is a heightened temperature for the specified liquid (water). However, the figurative meaning is to be "in trouble." In this sentence, it means that Jillian knew she would be in trouble if she did not pay attention to her grandmother.

24. D. The author forcing his point home by stating "It would have been better had I scraped the two-day-old road kill off my driveway and fried it up, slapped it on a bun, and thrown a slice of cheese on top." This clearly would not be a better meal to eat, but he is making an overstatement about the awfulness of the cheeseburger he ate.

25. B. The author is stating his opinion about the meal he had at The Burger Hut. He does not provide any factual evidence but instead simply states his feelings and viewpoint upon the cheeseburger.

Math

1. B. To solve for the mean (average) of these numbers, first convert all to decimals. When the decimals are added together, divide by 3 (the number of numerals in the set).

$$50\% = 0.5 \qquad 5\frac{1}{4} = 5.25$$

$$(.5 + 0.25 + 5.25) \div 3$$

$$6 \div 3 = 2$$

2. C. The average is given (122.25) along with 7 of the weights. Let x represent the missing weight and calculate using the equation of averages. There are 8 total weights that must be added and then divided by 8 to achieve the average of 122.25.

$(105 + 115 + 130 + 125 + 142 + 122 + 128 + x) \div 8 = 122.25$

$(867 + x) \div 8 = 122.25$

$(867 + x) \div 8 * 8 = 122.25 * 8$

$867 + x = 978$

$x = 111$ lbs.

3. A. To solve for the average, add up all the numerals (this includes the variables). When this is done, divide by the number of values in the set. The variable a remains part of the answer, because it has not been divided out.

$a + 6a + 2a + 9a + 7a = 25a$

$25a \div 5 = 5a$

4. C. This problem requires you to find the average. Dr. Suketu drives 5 hours at 80 mph and 3 hours at 75 mph, which totals 8 hours of driving. To find the average speed at which he traveled, add up the five 80 mph hours and three 75 mph hours and then divide by 8 hours: $[(5 * 80) + (3 * 75)] \div 8 = 78$ mph.

5. D. The problem is best solved using a proportion. Let x represent the unknown cost.

$\dfrac{4}{18} = \dfrac{10}{x}$ (Cross multiply.)

$4 * x = 18 * 10$

$4x = 180$ (Eliminate the coefficient using division.)

$x = \$45$

6. C. This answer requires only the use of variables and the knowledge of how to write a proportion. Remember to keep the same units in the numerator on each ratio. Let x represent the unknown value.

$\dfrac{b}{c} = \dfrac{n}{x}$ (Cross multiply.)

$bx = nc$ (Isolate the variable by using division to eliminate the coefficient.)

$x = \dfrac{(n * c)}{b}$

7. C. To change a percent to a decimal, you must divide the decimal by 100, which requires knowledge of place value. When you divide 4.5 by 100, simply move the decimal point two places to the left. (This question does not ask you to write 4½% in decimal form, so 4.5% is incorrect.)

$4\dfrac{1}{2}\% = \dfrac{4.5}{100} = 0.045$

8. B. There are two ways in which to solve this problem.

The first is to set-up a proportion:

$\dfrac{x}{659.59} = \dfrac{30}{100}$ (Cross multiply.)

$100x = 19787.70$ (Eliminate the coefficient by using division.)

$x = 197.88$ (When dealing with money, round to the hundredths place.)

Now subtract this value from the original price to obtain the sale price.

The second method is to multiply the percent in decimal form by the original price.

$0.30 * 659.59$

197.88

Now subtract this value from the original price to obtain the sale price. ($659.59 – $197.88 = $461.71)

9. B. To solve, first recognize what the problem is asking for. This problem requires the calculation of area to be retiled. Determine total area to be tiles and then calculate the total cost.

$A_{kit} = 10 \text{ ft} \times 12 \text{ ft} = 120 \text{ ft}^2$

$A_{bath} = 4 \text{ ft} \times 5 \text{ ft} = 20 \text{ ft}^2$

$A_{total} = 120 \text{ ft}^2 + 20 \text{ ft}^2 = 140 \text{ ft}^2$

Total cost = $140 \times \$6.20$.

It will cost Alec $868 to retile.

10. A. This problem requires you to calculate the perimeter of the yard to be fenced and then divide by the amount each section covers. (Perimeter is the distance around and found by adding up all sides of a shape).

$P_{yard} = 6 + 10 + 2 + 12 + 8$

$P_{yard} = 38 \text{ ft}$

$38 \text{ ft} \div 3 \text{ ft} = 12.66666666$ (Divide the perimeter of the yard by the length of each sections.)

Since there are no partial sections sold, the answer must be rounded up, yielding 13.

11. B. This problem requires you to assume that each student presents for the full 6 minutes in order to find the total minutes possible used on presentations. Multiply the number of students by the minutes used by each to get the total time spent on presentations ($26 \times 6 = 156$ minutes). Divide the total possible minutes by the number of minutes per class to get the number of full classes needed for presentations ($156 \div 55 = 2.836$). Jeanine must allow 3 class days to ensure that all students have ample time to present their projects.

12. C. To solve the problem, you need to set up a proportion and then simplify to solve for the variable, which represents the total time spent.

$\dfrac{1 \text{ page}}{3 \text{ min}} = \dfrac{282 \text{ pages}}{x \text{ min}}$

Once simplified, $x = (282)(3)$

13. B. Set up a proportion to solve the conversion $\left(\dfrac{1 \text{ ft}}{12 \text{ in}} = \dfrac{692 \text{ ft}}{x \text{ in}} \right)$. Because 12 inches equals one foot, and you have 692 feet, the product of 12 times 692 will be the answer (8,304in).

14. D. Convert all numbers to decimals in order to more easily compare the values. Look at the values and place from smallest to largest. Remember to include 0.25 which is already in decimal form.

$\dfrac{1}{8} = 0.125$ (Divide the numerator by the denominator.)

$90\% = 0.9$

$4\dfrac{1}{2} = 4.5$

$15.6 = 15.6$

15. C. To solve for x, you must isolate the x variable. In order to do this, move all the other variables to the right side of the equation.

$2x + 3y - 9z = 243$

$2x + 3y - 9z + 9z = 243 + 9z$

$2x + 3y = 243 + 9z$

$2x + 3y - 3y = 243 + 9z - 3y$

$2x = 243 + 9z - 3y$

$2x \div 2 = (243 + 9z - 3y) \div 2$

Therefore, $x = (243 + 9z - 3y) \div 2$

16. D. Using the formula to calculate the area of a parallelogram, you would plug in the length (120 miles) and the width (75 miles) to have A = (120miles)(75miles), which produces the answer 9,000 square miles.

17. B. According to the table, the lowest wind chill is −31 and the highest is 90. The range (difference) between the two values is 90 − (−31). Remember when subtracting a negative number, the negatives cancel out and you need to add the values together: 90 + 31 = 121.

18. C. To solve, convert all fractions to decimals by dividing the numerator by the denominator. When that is done, look for the decimal that is closest in value to the batting average. $0.3333 \left(\frac{1}{3}\right)$ is the closest in value to 0.342.

$1 \div 2 = 0.5$

$1 \div 4 = 0.25$

$1 \div 3 = 0.33333$

$2 \div 5 = 0.4$

19. D. The key terms to focus on are *times* (multiply), *increased by* (add), and *distributed equally* (divide). Therefore, the correct answer is $(4x + 2) \div 3$.

20. A. First combine the poppy seed scones and the cranberry scones to see how many scones have no icing (9 + 24 = 33). Then find the total number of scones baked (15 + 9 + 24 = 48).

$\frac{33}{48} = \frac{11}{16}$ To find the percentage of non-icing scones, create a ratio and divide the numerator by the denominator.

$11 \div 16 = 0.6875$ Multiply by 100 to get the percentage.

$0.6875 * 100 = 68.75\%$ Round to the nearest whole number (the 7 tenths moves the 8 units up to 9 units.)

69% of the scones are not iced.

21. B. To solve, change the percentage into a decimal (divide by 100) and then multiply by the total amount of money earned.

$5 \div 100 = 0.05$

$0.05 * 120,000 = \$6,000$

22. A. There are two ways to solve this problem. First, calculate the total income made over the next 5 years (120,000 * 5 = \$600,000). Then multiply that value by the percentage saved (600,000 * 0.10 = \$60,000). The second way is to calculate the yearly amount saved by multiplying the yearly income by the percentage of money saved (120,000 * 0.10 = \$12,000). Then take the money saved per year and multiply it by the number of years the family is saving for (\$12,000 * 5 = \$60,000).

23. D. To solve, multiply the value of the raise by the percent of the mortgage and bills (15,000 * 0.32 = \$4,800). The question asks for the amount from the raise that will go toward the mortgage and bills, not the amount from the total income.

24. C. This equation requires you to follow the order of operations law in mathematics (PEMDAS). The order is as follows: parenthesis, exponents, multiplication, division, addition, and subtraction. It is best to make all terms in the same format, so change the fractions and percentages into a decimal format. $\frac{4}{5} = 0.8$ and $89\% = 0.89$

$(0.8 + 123.8) + 7^2 * 0.89$ Parenthesis must be simplified first.

$124.6 + 7^2 * 0.89$ Exponents must be simplified next ($7^2 = 7 * 7 = 49$).

$124.6 + 49 * 0.89$ Multiplication is the next step.

$124.6 + 43.61$ Addition is the final step in this equation.

168.21

25. B. The mean of a set of values is the average. To find the mean, add up all values in the set and then divide by the number of numerals found within the set.

$$328 + 347 + 442 + 298 + 400 + 323 + 287 + 315 = 2{,}740$$

$$2{,}740 \div 8 = 342.5$$

Social Sciences

1. B. The motto of the country, when it was first established as the United States in 1776, was "E Pluribus Unum." It was found on documents, coins, and other memorials. Its translation is "out of many, one" meaning that there are many people from diverse backgrounds and many states, all of whom make up one unified country. In 1864, a different motto was being used, but not until 1956, was it officially approved by President Eisenhower to change the motto of the United States to "In God We Trust." It is now evident on currency, in Congress, and other noted places.

2. A. The white color used in the 13 stripes on the American flag stands for the hope, purity, and innocence of this nation's people. Red represents courage, and blue signifies justice.

3. A. Both President Washington (1st) and President Lincoln (16th) were memorialized with monuments in Washington D.C., but both were *not* assassinated while in office. They are both honored in the rock formation carving of Mount Rushmore and are both found on U.S. currency: Washington is on the one dollar bill, and Lincoln is on the five dollar bill.

4. B. The four presidents designed in rock on Mount Rushmore were selected for the themes they represent. They are Thomas Jefferson (expansion), Abraham Lincoln (unification), Teddy Roosevelt (conservation), and George Washington (independence).

5. B. The 19th Amendment of the U.S. Constitution implements women's suffrage and now allows female citizens of America to vote in elections held in this country.

6. D. A representative democracy is one in which a small group makes decisions for others in the total population. The United States uses a form of representative democracy by electing politicians in the House of Representatives and in the Senate to represent the people living in the 50 states.

7. D. The First Amendment of the Constitution of the United States indicates that all individual's who are citizens of this country have the right to freedom of expression. This includes the freedom of religion, of speech, of the press, of assembly and the right to petition the government.

8. A. The Mississippi River is an important feature in the United States. Many large rivers such as the Ohio and the Missouri flow into it. It contributed to the rapid movement of settlers from the Midwest traveling westward as it aided in the transportation of people, goods, and services.

9. C. Kansas is the state identified by the box with the number 1. It is located centrally in the continental United States and considered to be in the region of the Midwest.

10. C. The Rio Grande River, the longest river in North America, starts in southwestern Colorado and flows southeast through New Mexico. It forms the boundary between Texas and Mexico and empties into the Gulf of Mexico. This river is much too shallow for commercial navigation, but is used extensively for irrigation projects.

11. D. The Appalachian Mountains are about 1,500 miles in length, with the highest peak at over 6,600 feet, extending from central Alabama in the United States northward through the New England states and three of the Canadian provinces. There are significant ranges known within that include the Cumberland Mountains, the Blue Ridge Mountains, the Allegheny Mountains, the Catskill Mountains, the Green Mountains, and the White Mountains.

12. A. The order of the given wars on a timeline should appear as follows: the American-Indian War (1587–1890), the American Revolution (1775–1783), the Civil War (1861–1865), the Korean War (1950–1953) and the Persian Gulf War (1990–1991).

13. B. As a result of WWII, several global organizations were started and these included: The United Nations (UN), the World Bank, the World Trade Organization (WTO), and the International Monetary Fund (IMF).

14. B. The Cold War began as a non-violent conflict between the Soviet Union and the United States regarding communism and moved into ending the use of nuclear arms and missiles. Both John F. Kennedy, President of the United States, and Nikita Khruschev, President of the Soviet Union, were in office during the Cold War. They worked together to prevent another major war from occurring. Not until the presidency of Ronald Reagan and the soviet leader Mikhail Gorbachev did the Cold War finally come to a halt.

15. A. There are 100 Senators in Congress. This number is based on two seats per state, and with 50 states in America there are 100 seats representing the citizens.

16. C. The Supreme Court is situated in the judicial branch of government, as it interprets and explains the laws. Congress is in the legislative branch. If the Supreme Court denies or rejects a law that Congress has already decided upon, it demonstrates a form of checks and balances with the Supreme Court (the judicial branch), reviewing the action of Congress (the legislative branch).

17. B. The Andes Mountains located in South America are the longest in the world (4500 miles). They were created by movement of the continental and Pacific plates. The Spanish once conquered the native Incas and the minerals continue to be mined as valuable natural resources. The Rocky Mountains of the United States also offer rich mineral resources.

18. B. The Gulf Stream moves warm water from the Gulf of Mexico northward past Florida and east across the Atlantic Ocean to Western Europe. It produces warmer weather for the people even though they are located at a cooler latitude.

19. A. The numbers on this world map represent the prime meridian, the equator, a line of latitude, and a line of longitude.

20. A. The Tigris-Euphrates Civilization was known for designing laws and establishing an effective government with a standard legal system.

21. C. Athens contributed a form of government based on the rule by the people called democracy during which every male in the society had the chance to vote on how the city might be managed. Today, for most democratic societies, the vote is offered to all citizens of a nation.

22. D. Communism was a part of the German life for many years, and in 1961, a wall was built to separate East Germany from West Germany. It kept families separated and divided the country. Finally in 1989, it was removed due to the change in government philosophy, which was the collapse of communism there.

23. A. The economy was significantly affected by the construction and completion of a transcontinental railway system. Products could be moved and sold in various parts of the country, and people could emigrate to other areas of the country in the west. This was a boom to the economy.

24. A. A natural economy is one in which the individuals function within a trade system rather than using a monetary foundation for the exchange of goods and services. Using beads to trade for fruits is an example of this economic system.

25. B. Cultural diffusion describes how a formed culture spreads into other parts of the world. It occurs over a period of time and changes the area. When people of strong cultural heritage migrate to other lands, they want to keep their traditions, so they may spread their culture or create new communities that reflect their cultural values and practices.

Science

1. A. Opaque objects such as wood, metal, rocks, or mirrors do not let light pass through, since the light that reaches this type of object is not absorbed. The light is either stopped or bounced back into the air.

2. C. The invention of the light bulb by Thomas Edison in 1879 fell between the invention of the telephone in 1875 by Alexander Graham Bell and the invention of the motorized airplane in 1905 by the Wright Brothers.

3. C. Symbiosis is the process of two or more living organisms existing in the same environment each making evolutionary changes to benefit each other. Lichens are an example of organisms that function with symbiosis.

4. A. This is the law of Gradualism by Darwin. He believed that changes in a species, such as those that occur in order to adapt to new environments, take a long and gradual period of time, rather than happening suddenly with the new generations.

5. A. Nature versus nurture refers to human development. It suggests that through the genes, a human gains natural behaviors, but those behaviors learned in the environment may be different based on the individual's nurturing.

6. D. Charles Darwin developed the theory of evolution that resulted in defining Natural Selection. It is explained as *the individual organisms with favorable traits are more likely to survive and reproduce.*

7. D. An instinctive behavior is one that is genetically inherited and remains constant in the entire species. Bears hibernate in the winter months due to instinct, even if the weather is warmer than usual. The other three examples are learned behaviors, as they are modeled or imitated or the species is adjusting according to the environment.

8. B. The visible spectrum is defined as the colors seen in the rainbow. Although ultraviolet light has the most energy of those possibilities given, ultraviolet light is not part of the visible spectrum (a rainbow). Therefore, violet is the correct answer.

9. C. Einstein developed the theory of relativity ($E = mc^2$) in 1905 about 4 years after Curie discovered radium in 1901 and prior to Sabin's discovery of the origin of blood and cell development in 1917. The answer is between 3 and 4 on the timeline.

10. A. Water boils at a temperature of 212 degrees Fahrenheit when it becomes a vapor. When water is subjected to an increased temperature that reaches this degree, it changes to a gas.

11. A. Light travels faster than sound, so it is common for people to see the light from a lightning strike prior to hearing the sound made by the thunder that the lightning causes.

12. D. The human eye can perceive color (yellow in a banana) due to the way the given object reflects the light it receives (a banana reflects the yellow and absorbs the other colors).

13. D. During both the vernal equinox (spring) and the autumnal equinox (fall), the length of the days and the nights are the same. During the solstice, the nights and days are different. An eclipse is a pattern caused by the moon, the sun, and the Earth, and a phase refers to the stages of the moon each month.

14. D. A wedge is a simple tool that is used to push things apart or secure things together. It magnifies the force at the site of placement allowing the ease of use. The student could use a wedge to pry the mud and stones apart so the glob would be dismantled. He could then determine if an animal lived inside!

15. A. The Earth orbits the sun in 365 days but it takes only 24 hours to spin once on its axis.

16. C. The larger the number of cycles per second shows the greatest frequency or highest Hertz. In diagram 3, the sound waves are moving rapidly and therefore producing faster and higher energy.

17. D. Reproduction is the only basic life function of a species that will guarantee the survival of that particular species. All other systems are critical to the existence of the living organism, but reproduction is the system that will create more of the same kind of species.

18. D. The product rubber does not carry a current, as it is not a material that may be used as a conductor. It is an insulator, which prevents the flow of electrons through it. The students will surmise that using a paper clip or a copper wire would be a better conductor.

19. B. The skydiver is only sitting and has not yet employed full energy. She, therefore, has potential energy. Once the sky diver jumps and begins to float to the ground with an open parachute, she will produce kinetic energy.

20. D. An ecosystem must have balance in order for it to fully function. Although an ecosystem is impacted by the food, reproduction rates, and climate, the most critical area that affects the balance is the species interactions. If all species are interacting to the fullest, then the Earth's systems and cycles (Water Cycle, Food Cycle, Weather Cycle, Heat Cycle, and so on) are working to ensure food, climate, and reproduction.

21. B. An earthquake is the result of a transform boundary. When two or more plates rub or slide against each other the result is an earthquake. This rubbing causes the plates to crumble along the fault line and back down into the mantle where the portions of crust are recycled.

22. A. The zygote appears just after the egg and before the embryo (egg, zygote, embryo, fetus, newborn). A zygote is a fertilized egg (formed by two gametes) and, therefore, occurs as soon as the reproduction of the parents has affected the egg.

23. A. The nucleus of a plant or animal cell is the control center of the cell's functions such as reproduction and protein synthesis. It contains the chromosomes that have the DNA.

24. A. The most important reason to teach students health education under the science curriculum is to educate them to attain and maintain a healthy lifestyle. Critical to being healthy as youngsters and later as adults is to employ behaviors and establish conditions that ensure proper health and reduce at-risk behaviors. Students should be exposed to the attitudes and values of a proper healthy lifestyle, as well as be provided with opportunities to practice and acquire appropriate skills.

25. D. The unifying processes of science are fundamental to science instruction and understanding science as a world topic. In this scenario, the teacher is focusing on the process of *classification*. This process utilizes the commonalities of objects to logically group them. As students group the plants they will be better able to make inferences and predictions on the outcomes of the dye solution, as well as observe the differences or similarities in the plants as the experiment proceeds.

Answer Sheet for Practice Exam 2

(Remove This Sheet and Use It to Mark Your Answers)

Language Arts

1 Ⓐ Ⓑ Ⓒ Ⓓ
2 Ⓐ Ⓑ Ⓒ Ⓓ
3 Ⓐ Ⓑ Ⓒ Ⓓ
4 Ⓐ Ⓑ Ⓒ Ⓓ
5 Ⓐ Ⓑ Ⓒ Ⓓ
6 Ⓐ Ⓑ Ⓒ Ⓓ
7 Ⓐ Ⓑ Ⓒ Ⓓ
8 Ⓐ Ⓑ Ⓒ Ⓓ
9 Ⓐ Ⓑ Ⓒ Ⓓ
10 Ⓐ Ⓑ Ⓒ Ⓓ
11 Ⓐ Ⓑ Ⓒ Ⓓ
12 Ⓐ Ⓑ Ⓒ Ⓓ
13 Ⓐ Ⓑ Ⓒ Ⓓ
14 Ⓐ Ⓑ Ⓒ Ⓓ
15 Ⓐ Ⓑ Ⓒ Ⓓ
16 Ⓐ Ⓑ Ⓒ Ⓓ
17 Ⓐ Ⓑ Ⓒ Ⓓ
18 Ⓐ Ⓑ Ⓒ Ⓓ
19 Ⓐ Ⓑ Ⓒ Ⓓ
20 Ⓐ Ⓑ Ⓒ Ⓓ
21 Ⓐ Ⓑ Ⓒ Ⓓ
22 Ⓐ Ⓑ Ⓒ Ⓓ
23 Ⓐ Ⓑ Ⓒ Ⓓ
24 Ⓐ Ⓑ Ⓒ Ⓓ
25 Ⓐ Ⓑ Ⓒ Ⓓ

Math

1 Ⓐ Ⓑ Ⓒ Ⓓ
2 Ⓐ Ⓑ Ⓒ Ⓓ
3 Ⓐ Ⓑ Ⓒ Ⓓ
4 Ⓐ Ⓑ Ⓒ Ⓓ
5 Ⓐ Ⓑ Ⓒ Ⓓ
6 Ⓐ Ⓑ Ⓒ Ⓓ
7 Ⓐ Ⓑ Ⓒ Ⓓ
8 Ⓐ Ⓑ Ⓒ Ⓓ
9 Ⓐ Ⓑ Ⓒ Ⓓ
10 Ⓐ Ⓑ Ⓒ Ⓓ
11 Ⓐ Ⓑ Ⓒ Ⓓ
12 Ⓐ Ⓑ Ⓒ Ⓓ
13 Ⓐ Ⓑ Ⓒ Ⓓ
14 Ⓐ Ⓑ Ⓒ Ⓓ
15 Ⓐ Ⓑ Ⓒ Ⓓ
16 Ⓐ Ⓑ Ⓒ Ⓓ
17 Ⓐ Ⓑ Ⓒ Ⓓ
18 Ⓐ Ⓑ Ⓒ Ⓓ
19 Ⓐ Ⓑ Ⓒ Ⓓ
20 Ⓐ Ⓑ Ⓒ Ⓓ
21 Ⓐ Ⓑ Ⓒ Ⓓ
22 Ⓐ Ⓑ Ⓒ Ⓓ
23 Ⓐ Ⓑ Ⓒ Ⓓ
24 Ⓐ Ⓑ Ⓒ Ⓓ
25 Ⓐ Ⓑ Ⓒ Ⓓ

Social Studies

1 Ⓐ Ⓑ Ⓒ Ⓓ
2 Ⓐ Ⓑ Ⓒ Ⓓ
3 Ⓐ Ⓑ Ⓒ Ⓓ
4 Ⓐ Ⓑ Ⓒ Ⓓ
5 Ⓐ Ⓑ Ⓒ Ⓓ
6 Ⓐ Ⓑ Ⓒ Ⓓ
7 Ⓐ Ⓑ Ⓒ Ⓓ
8 Ⓐ Ⓑ Ⓒ Ⓓ
9 Ⓐ Ⓑ Ⓒ Ⓓ
10 Ⓐ Ⓑ Ⓒ Ⓓ
11 Ⓐ Ⓑ Ⓒ Ⓓ
12 Ⓐ Ⓑ Ⓒ Ⓓ
13 Ⓐ Ⓑ Ⓒ Ⓓ
14 Ⓐ Ⓑ Ⓒ Ⓓ
15 Ⓐ Ⓑ Ⓒ Ⓓ
16 Ⓐ Ⓑ Ⓒ Ⓓ
17 Ⓐ Ⓑ Ⓒ Ⓓ
18 Ⓐ Ⓑ Ⓒ Ⓓ
19 Ⓐ Ⓑ Ⓒ Ⓓ
20 Ⓐ Ⓑ Ⓒ Ⓓ
21 Ⓐ Ⓑ Ⓒ Ⓓ
22 Ⓐ Ⓑ Ⓒ Ⓓ
23 Ⓐ Ⓑ Ⓒ Ⓓ
24 Ⓐ Ⓑ Ⓒ Ⓓ
25 Ⓐ Ⓑ Ⓒ Ⓓ

Science

1 Ⓐ Ⓑ Ⓒ Ⓓ
2 Ⓐ Ⓑ Ⓒ Ⓓ
3 Ⓐ Ⓑ Ⓒ Ⓓ
4 Ⓐ Ⓑ Ⓒ Ⓓ
5 Ⓐ Ⓑ Ⓒ Ⓓ
6 Ⓐ Ⓑ Ⓒ Ⓓ
7 Ⓐ Ⓑ Ⓒ Ⓓ
8 Ⓐ Ⓑ Ⓒ Ⓓ
9 Ⓐ Ⓑ Ⓒ Ⓓ
10 Ⓐ Ⓑ Ⓒ Ⓓ
11 Ⓐ Ⓑ Ⓒ Ⓓ
12 Ⓐ Ⓑ Ⓒ Ⓓ
13 Ⓐ Ⓑ Ⓒ Ⓓ
14 Ⓐ Ⓑ Ⓒ Ⓓ
15 Ⓐ Ⓑ Ⓒ Ⓓ
16 Ⓐ Ⓑ Ⓒ Ⓓ
17 Ⓐ Ⓑ Ⓒ Ⓓ
18 Ⓐ Ⓑ Ⓒ Ⓓ
19 Ⓐ Ⓑ Ⓒ Ⓓ
20 Ⓐ Ⓑ Ⓒ Ⓓ
21 Ⓐ Ⓑ Ⓒ Ⓓ
22 Ⓐ Ⓑ Ⓒ Ⓓ
23 Ⓐ Ⓑ Ⓒ Ⓓ
24 Ⓐ Ⓑ Ⓒ Ⓓ
25 Ⓐ Ⓑ Ⓒ Ⓓ

CUT HERE

Language Arts

Directions: Read the following multiple-choice questions and select the most appropriate answer. Mark the answer sheet accordingly.

1. Dale's grandparents were born in Germany and came to the United States when her mother was a little girl. They told Dale's mother many stories as she was growing up and then Dale's mother shared the stories with her. Dale enjoyed the interesting and mysterious legends about creatures that lived in the forest and animals that could fly. She hopes to tell these stories to her children when she grows up.

   Dale's grandparents shared stories from their generation to her mother and then her mother shared them with her. This is an example of what type of literature genre?

   A. epics
   B. fantasies
   C. folktales
   D. mysteries

Read the following passage and answer questions 2–4.

   Fred Johnson, a 20th century artist, was a famous circus banner painter. He met many of the original circus performers of the world renowned circus families such as the Ringling Brothers, Barnum & Bailey, and the Mills Brothers. He earned a reputation at a period in history when the circus was the most popular form of amusement and entertainment in the country. Although he was not formally trained, his talent was the forerunner to his career. His work was used as advertising for the upcoming circus shows and remained in place at the side shows while a circus was set up in town. Once the show was over and the circus packed up, the banners were left to blow in the wind or were tossed in the trashed. Painting banners required special talent and "tricks" as the work had to be done on very large pieces of canvas and completed very quickly. Not many could keep up the pace or do the work that Johnson did. He was best known for the "flash" he used to create his images. One might be at a loss for words in describing his work. Finding a piece of his art now is rare, but exciting!

2. If a person were to summarize this piece, what might be the main theme?

   A. Johnson led other artists in the field of circus painting.
   B. The circus was once the most common amusements in the country.
   C. Early historical forms of advertising included painters who were not trained.
   D. Johnson had talent in art that pertained to a cultural period of American history.

3. What did the author mean when she wrote this sentence?

   One might be at a loss for words in describing his work.

   A. It would be difficult to express the uniqueness of his art.
   B. A person might not understand the art that was presented.
   C. Circus art and performers use a completely different lingo.
   D. Some of the art terms are new to the reader and incomprehensible.

4. Which of the following words might best describe the character of this piece?

   A. fast
   B. unique
   C. excitable
   D. uneducated

GO ON TO THE NEXT PAGE

5. Anne Frank was a young girl who lived a life of fear during World War II in Germany. She was one of the Jews who lived in secrecy during the Nazi reign. During her short life, she wrote in her diary to keep a record of what had occurred and how she felt. Her memoirs are known as *The Diary of Anne Frank,* and it is an example of
_____.

   A. poetry
   B. fiction
   C. research
   D. non-fiction

6. A fifth grade teacher presented this passage to her students and asked them to look at the underlined word and decide what type of noun it is.

The geese flew south shortly after the first freeze of the year. The <u>flock</u> consisted of hundreds of birds.

The word flock is a _____ noun.

   A. plural
   B. abstract
   C. common
   D. collective

7. A third grade student has decided that she will construct a survey for her science project and ask family and friends several questions about the solar system. She is puzzled at the spelling of the word she wants to use as the title of her paper. Which of the following is correct?

   A. questionare
   B. questtionair
   C. questonaire
   D. questionnaire

Read the following passage.

Shirley cut some flowers from the garden and chose a vase from the cabinet. She ran into the kitchen to fill the vase with water, but dropped it. Instead, she went to get the broom and dustpan.

8. Select the sentence that demonstrates the best inference.

   A. The vase was made of glass.
   B. The flowers had dirt on them.
   C. The vase was too full of water.
   D. The flowers spilled on the floor.

Read the poem and answer questions 9 and 10.

The first snow fell softly around her feet.

It covered the sidewalk and most of the street.

It glistened and twinkled under the light.

And hurried the children to see the sight!

9. What is the tone that the author chooses to express in this poem?

   A. anger
   B. danger
   C. sadness
   D. excitement

10. What does the author mean by the last line of the stanza?

   A. The character needed help through the snow from the children.
   B. The beauty of the snow made the children want to rush to see it.
   C. The snow was so deep that the children had to hasten through it.
   D. The landscape was covered in snow and the children had to move in it.

11. Marci read a story about a grandfather who owned a ranch and let the neighbor children ride a special horse everyday. Marci loved the story, and it reminded her of her own grandfather who was a cowboy in Arizona. She loved to ride horses on his ranch when her family visited on vacation. Marci is showing a connection to the story she read that is best described as

   A. text-to-text
   B. text-to-self
   C. text-to-home
   D. text-to-world

Read this paragraph and answer questions 12–13.

A group of hikers roamed in the desert on their way to the base of the mountain. The sun was deadly hot and the breeze stilted. They surveyed their options for retreating to a shady place, but found that the only tree for miles was being used. They slowly approached the shaded portion of the scorched landscape to find a family of javelina snoozing soundly.

12. In what point of view is this paragraph written?

    A. first person
    B. second person
    C. third person
    D. fourth person

13. Which literary element does this passage, the *scorched landscape,* describe?

    A. tone
    B. mood
    C. theme
    D. setting

14. Personification is a type of figurative language in which words are used to give human characteristics to a nonhuman thing, such as an object, idea, or animal. Which of the following sentences is an example of personification?

    A. The cat licked her paws like a child with an ice cream cone.
    B. The chimney roared with laughter as the smoke blew out the top.
    C. The mother hen gathered her chicks before the hungry fox appeared.
    D. The road swerved and curved through the valley and up the mountainside.

15. Children need direct instruction to understand the various multiple meanings of vocabulary words. In this sentence, what is the meaning of the homophone *ball*?

Cinderella made a mad dash to get to the *ball* by midnight.

    A. a toy
    B. a dance
    C. a program
    D. a round sphere

16. Which word in this sentence is considered an adjective?

As the sun set behind the thunderous clouds, the rain began to fall lightly in patterns on the sidewalk.

    A. lightly
    B. patterns
    C. sidewalks
    D. thunderous

17. Choose the BEST sentence to summarize this passage.

Jesse James is an infamous American outlaw who showed ruthless abandonment and extreme violence. He and his older brother, Frank, lead the James Brothers, a band of outlaws, in many robberies and hold-ups. Jesse James was said to have robbed from the rich and given to the poor. However, this was more myth than truth. He robbed others and kept the money for himself and his band. He was known for his ruthless treatment of those he robbed, using extreme force to obtain that which he desired. In 1874 Jesse James had two children. He waited 2 more years until he and his gang attempted their most daring heist. After this robbery of the First National Bank Frank and Jesse were the only members of the gang left alive or not apprehended. Jesse James was murdered by Robert Ford, as he was attempting to clean a photograph on the wall. Robert Ford shot him in the back of the head as he stood upon a chair to reach the dusty photograph.

    A. Jessse James was shot in the back of the head by Robert Ford as he cleaned a dusty photograph.
    B. Jesse James and his brother were involved in many robberies and murders, the most famous and daring was the theft at the First National Bank.
    C. Jesse James did not give the riches he stole to the poor as many people once believed but kept them for himself instead.
    D. Jesse James was a ruthless and violent American outlaw who led the James Brothers Gang in many robberies with his brother Frank.

GO ON TO THE NEXT PAGE

179

18. The word "yesterday" in the following sentence is what part of speech?

Yesterday, Oddie went to the ice cream store to have a malt and read the paper.

    A. adverb

    B. noun

    C. adjective

    D. preposition

19. In this paragraph the pronoun 'it', refers to

_____.

Justin, a photographer in Chicago, worked on a restaurant layout about Mexican food. It contained a series of photos that included guacamole, salsa, enchiladas, and tacos. The client was pleased with the piece and offered Justin a substantial raise for doing it.

    A. food

    B. client

    C. layout

    D. restaurant

Read the passage and answer questions 20–22.

Flowers are the reproductive organs of plants and have male and female structures. The male part is called the stamen and generates the pollen. The female organ is called the pistil, which contains the stigma, the styles, and the ovary. When the pollen joins in the ovary, seeds are created.

20. This passage is an example of what type of writing?

    A. narrative

    B. expository

    C. persuasive

    D. descriptive

21. What inference could be made about the method in which the pollen leaves the stamen and arrives at the ovary?

    A. The wind carries the pollen to the ovary.

    B. The rain moves the pollen from one plant to another.

    C. The sun directs the pollen from the male to the female.

    D. A person must remove the pollen from one plant and place it in another.

22. What is the main idea of this passage of informational text?

    A. Flowers are reproductive organs.

    B. Pollen is important to male plants.

    C. Seeds are created in a simple manner.

    D. There are several different parts to plants.

23. In the sentence "Jesse James was an infamous American outlaw," which of the following words would be the BEST synonym for "infamous?"

    A. honorable

    B. lowdown

    C. shameful

    D. notorious

24. The series of events in a story is known as the

    A. inciting force

    B. exposition

    C. plot

    D. climax

25. In the sentence "Screaming is pointless" the word *screaming* is what part of speech?

    A. noun

    B. verb

    C. adjective

    D. adverb

Math

Directions: Read the following multiple-choice questions and select the most appropriate answer. Mark the answer sheet accordingly.

1. Suki has taken a job as a delivery boy. He makes $9.25 per hour plus tips. Suki must work around his school schedule and works 5 hours Monday, Wednesday, and Friday but only 3 hours on Tuesday and Thursday. He works a 7-hour shift on Saturday and 6 hours each Sunday. How much more money does Suki make during the week than on the weekend? (Do not calculate tip, only shift work.)

   A. $27.36
   B. $46.40
   C. $64.33
   D. $74.00

2. Eric's kayak team has 6 members, who weigh 205, 195, 210, 180, x, and 198 pounds. If the average weight of these players is $198\frac{1}{3}$ pounds, what is the value of x?

   A. 206 lbs
   B. 202 lbs
   C. 195 lbs
   D. 190 lbs

3. Which of the following is the greatest in value?

   A. 5% of 500
   B. 18% of 140
   C. 33% of 90
   D. 12% of 250

4. How many inches are in $5\frac{1}{3}$ feet?

   A. 60 inches
   B. 63 inches
   C. 64 inches
   D. 66 inches

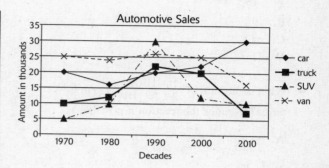

Use the preceding graph to answer questions 5–7.

5. In what decade was there a rise in all types of vehicle sales?

   A. 2000
   B. 1990
   C. 1980
   D. 1970

6. What sentence best describes the trend in car sales over the decades, according to this graph?

   A. Car sales have dropped and risen equally.
   B. Car sales have steadily declined since 1970.
   C. Car sales have continually risen since the 1980s.
   D. Car sales have declined once but then rise equally after that.

7. In 1970 how many of the total vehicles sold were not cars?

   A. 40,000
   B. 30,000
   C. 20,000
   D. 10,000

GO ON TO THE NEXT PAGE

8. Find the range of the following set of values (a range is the difference between the highest and lowest value).

−90, 34, 17, −4, 56, 24, −45, 89

- **A.** 179
- **B.** 93
- **C.** 72
- **D.** 1

9. What is the sum of $\frac{1}{2}$, $\frac{1}{5}$, $\frac{3}{10}$, $\frac{7}{15}$ in lowest terms? (Reduce the fraction if possible.)

- **A.** $1\frac{7}{15}$
- **B.** $\frac{3}{8}$
- **C.** $\frac{21}{15}$
- **D.** $2\frac{5}{8}$

Use the illustration that follows for questions 10–11.

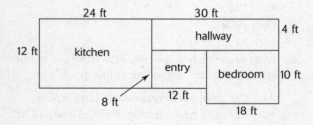

10. Mabel wants to tile her entryway, kitchen, and hallway. If each square foot of Spanish tile costs $5.20, and no partial tiles are sold, how much money will Mabel spend to tile these three areas? (A = b ∗ h)

- **A.** $452.40
- **B.** $1092.00
- **C.** $1868.60
- **D.** $2620.80

11. Haley teaches 7 classes of middle school students every day for 55 minutes each. On average it takes each class 11 minutes to change into their PE clothes and meet in the gym. What percentage of Haley's day is spent waiting for the students to get ready for class?

- **A.** 5%
- **B.** 10%
- **C.** 15%
- **D.** 20%

12. A swimmer swims in a 50-meter pool. If the swimmer completes 4 laps (50 meters each), how many feet has the swimmer traveled? 1 meter = 3.28 feet (Round the answer to the nearest whole number.)

- **A.** 164 ft
- **B.** 328 ft
- **C.** 492 ft
- **D.** 656 ft

13. A 25 lb child has strep throat. If the pharmacist gives the appropriate amount of medicine at 25 mg per pound, how much medicine will the child receive?

- **A.** 25 mg
- **B.** 350 mg
- **C.** 625 mg
- **D.** 700 mg

14. Solve the following equation, reduce to lowest terms.

$$\frac{1}{2} * \frac{3}{4} + 6.5 - \frac{1}{8}$$

- **A.** $6\frac{5}{18}$
- **B.** $6\frac{3}{4}$
- **C.** $3\frac{1}{2}$
- **D.** $3\frac{7}{8}$

15. If it takes Kris 2 pedal turns to make her bike tire complete one full rotation, and the circumference of the tire is 3 ft, how many pedal turns will she have to make to travel one mile? (1 mile = 5280 ft)

- **A.** 880 turns
- **B.** 1,760 turns
- **C.** 2,640 turns
- **D.** 3,520 turns

16. Place the following set of values in numerical order from least to greatest.

78.2, $78\frac{3}{5}$, 78.8, 780 %, $78\frac{2}{5}$

A. 780%, 78.2, $78\frac{2}{5}$, $78\frac{3}{5}$, 78.8

B. 78.8, $78\frac{3}{5}$, $78\frac{2}{5}$, 78.2, 780%

C. 78.2, 780%, $78\frac{2}{5}$, $78\frac{3}{5}$, 78.8

D. $78\frac{2}{5}$, $78\frac{3}{5}$, 780%, 78.2, 78.8

17. What number comes next in the pattern?

2, 4, 16, 256, 65536, _____

A. 2147483648
B. 4294967296
C. 6637843984
D. 8589934592

18. Which equation represents the statement "8 less than a number divided by the number increased by 20"?

A. $(8 + y) \div y - 20$
B. $(8 - y) \div 20y$
C. $(y + 8) \div 20y$
D. $(y - 8) \div y + 20$

19. Andrea has a caseload of clients 2 times the amount of Poppy's caseload. Poppy has a caseload that is 55 more than Shirley has. What equation best represents Andrea's caseload? (A = Andrea, P = Poppy and S = Shirley)

A. $S + P = 2A$
B. $A = 2(S + 55)$
C. $A = 2(P + S + 55)$
D. $55S + 2P = A$

Use the following chart to answer questions 20–21.

Accessory	Cost
tires	$68.50 each or $260 for a set of 4
fuzzy dice	$4.00
seat cover	$25.00 each
mud flaps	$55.00 each
floor mat	$22.50 each or $42.00 for a pair

20. Ken needs to buy 4 new tires for his truck and also a pair of mud flaps. He has $402.00 in his savings. After he purchases the tires and mud flaps, how many fuzzy dice could he purchase?

A. 4
B. 6
C. 8
D. 10

21. How much money would it cost Alan to replace 4 floor mats and 4 seat covers?

A. 180
B. 184
C. 190
D. 194

22. Basta saves 10% of her income every month and places it into a bank account for future use. If she makes $2284 per month, how much money will she save after 6 months?

A. $137.40
B. $3710.40
C. $370.40
D. $1370.40

GO ON TO THE NEXT PAGE

23. Judy can write a lesson plan in 2 hours. She is planning to go on vacation for 2 weeks and needs to have lesson plans ready for each class she will miss. She teaches 2 classes at night, 3 times a week and 3 during the day, 2 times a week at the university. If she needs a lesson plan for each class meeting, how many hours will she need to spend writing?

A. 10 hours
B. 12 hours
C. 24 hours
D. 48 hours

24. What is the value of '*x*' on the following number line?

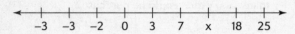

A. 12
B. 13
C. 14
D. 15

25. Charles finds a pair of hiking boots on sale for 30% off the regular price of $120. He also finds a pair of shorts for 10% off the original price of $45 and a pair of sock for $12. How much money will Charles spend on his purchase?

A. $106.20
B. $123.60
C. $130.70
D. $136.50

Social Sciences

Directions: Read the following multiple-choice questions and select the most appropriate answer. Mark the answer sheet accordingly.

1. When students read historical documents such as speeches, essays, and interviews, they should use critical thinking skills to determine

   A. fact from opinion
   B. their involvement
   C. the historical period
   D. the type of document

2. Each President has had a special group of people that support and advise the position. What is this group called, and how are they comprised?

   A. The Congressional Aides are decided upon by the nation's Secretary of State.
   B. The Cabinet is a group of representatives voted on by the people of the 50 states.
   C. The Congressional Aides include a select group of senators chosen by the Supreme Court.
   D. The Cabinet is made up of the executive department leaders or Secretaries so chosen by the President.

3. The Appalachian Mountain range significantly contributed to the United States' status _____.

   A. as a transportation hub
   B. as an industrialized nation
   C. of Native American reservations
   D. of settlers reaching the Mississippi

4. The United States is located in the

   A. Eastern and Northern Hemispheres
   B. Eastern and Southern Hemispheres
   C. Western and Northern Hemispheres
   D. Western and Southern Hemispheres

5. Which of the following women was the primary reason that the United States became so involved in the Civil Rights Movement?

   A. Rosa Parks
   B. Mother Teresa
   C. Harriet Tubman
   D. Susan B. Anthony

6. The system that best reflects the global market and use of a world system is

   A. gift economy
   B. dual economy
   C. open economy
   D. mixed economy

7. What was the most important decision made by the government in the United States regarding the monopolies of the oil and steel industries of the 1880s?

   A. Launched the stock markets
   B. Guidelines of capitalism used
   C. Passage of laws for regulation created
   D. Established planned economy system

8. Rivers naturally begin in

   A. seas
   B. lakes
   C. valleys
   D. mountains

GO ON TO THE NEXT PAGE

Answer question 9 using the following map.

9. Using the map provided, which bodies of water are represented by the letters A, B, and C?

- **A.** Adriatic Sea, China Sea, Red Sea
- **B.** Persian Gulf, Caspian Sea, Black Sea
- **C.** Arabian Sea, Mediterranean Sea, Aral Sea
- **D.** Mediterranean Sea, Black Sea, Caspian Sea

10. How did the Egyptian Civilization and its significant architectural structures impact the Indian and Chinese River Valley Civilization? The Indian and Chinese River Valley people

_____.

- **A.** built waterways and transportation hubs and ports.
- **B.** created large structures in the center of their cities.
- **C.** designed university programs in mathematics and sciences.
- **D.** developed advanced engineering and architectural technology.

11. When teaching students to recite the Pledge of Allegiance, which of the following would be an appropriate introduction to its meaning?

- **A.** all people should be treated equally
- **B.** support is necessary in war and conflicts
- **C.** religion has no place in the country's heritage
- **D.** the country is based on a government of separate states

12. Symbols used to represent a country demonstrate the _____ of the land.

- **A.** Ideals
- **B.** Structure
- **C.** Economy
- **D.** Population

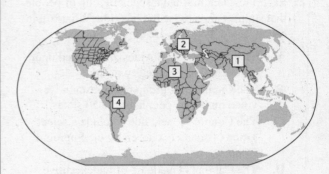

13. Which region of the world were these structures found?

- **A.** 1
- **B.** 2
- **C.** 3
- **D.** 4

14. The voyage of Ferdinand Magellan was long and complicated. Although he attempted to circumnavigate the world, he died prior to the end of the voyage. Only a few men survived to continue this mission. However, Magellan established the need for the

- **A.** Equator
- **B.** Prime Meridian
- **C.** Continental Divide
- **D.** International Dateline

15. Which of the following historical events occurred when President John F. Kennedy and the Cuban leader Fidel Castro were in power in their respective countries?

    A. The Cold War
    B. The Bay of Pigs
    C. The Vietnam War
    D. The Invasion of Panama

16. The section in the Constitution that briefly describes the purpose of the government to protect the rights of the people and known as the introduction is called

    A. The Preamble
    B. The Bill of Rights
    C. The Federalist Paper
    D. The Mayflower Compact

17. Which of the following Amendments outlines a citizen's right to a trial by jury for civil cases?

    A. Amendment 5
    B. Amendment 7
    C. Amendment 9
    D. Amendment 11

18. A dictatorship is a specific form of government related to the general type called

    A. Anarchism
    B. Democracy
    C. Republicanism
    D. Authoritarianism

19. The _____ branch of the U.S. government includes the president, the vice president, the cabinet and the departments and agencies.

    A. Judicial
    B. Executive
    C. Legislative
    D. Democratic

20. How did people immigrate from the continent of Africa to America?

    A. by transcontinental railway systems
    B. by land bridge from Asia to North America
    C. by boats and ships across the Atlantic Ocean
    D. by wagon train parties of settlers moving west

21. Which of the following events occurred chronologically last?

    A. Mayan Indians construct Palenque.
    B. President Lincoln is assassinated while watching a performance at *Ford's Theatre.*
    C. Lewis and Clark begin an expedition to explore the west.
    D. The Revolutionary War begins.

22. The Non-European civilization noted for developing metallurgy, designing irrigation, road, and agricultural systems was the

    A. Inca
    B. Islam
    C. Mayan
    D. Mongolian

23. Although they provide limited data, students should use _____ to make interpretations and record statistical and specific historical information.

    A. timelines
    B. political maps
    C. graphs or tables
    D. reference resources

24. The Woman's Suffrage movement supported women around the world in their attempt to

    A. buy and own homes
    B. gain the right to vote
    C. run for political office
    D. obtain similar jobs as men

25. The first transcontinental railroad, which was constructed to move people and goods across the country, was funded by

    A. the settlements
    B. private companies
    C. a group of explorers
    D. a law passed in Congress

GO ON TO THE NEXT PAGE

Practice Exam 2

187

Science

Directions: Read the following multiple-choice questions and select the most appropriate answer. Mark the answer sheet accordingly.

1. Which of the following occurred after Darwin created his theory of evolution?

   A. discovery of frictional heat
   B. discovery of static electricity
   C. theory on the conservation of matter
   D. theory of microbes and pasteurization

2. Studies were done on reproduction, genetics and the survival of certain traits in species that brought knowledge to the scientific world, enabling us to better understand our origins. Which scientist is considered "The Father of Genetics?"

   A. Albert Einstein
   B. Gregor Mendel
   C. Charles Darwin
   D. Sir Issac Newton

3. What is the correct order of the visible color spectrum, which is considered a rainbow?

   A. blue, violet, indigo, green, red, yellow, orange
   B. yellow, orange, red, blue, green, indigo, violet
   C. red, orange, yellow, green, blue, indigo, violet
   D. violet, indigo, blue, green, orange, yellow, red

4. Scientists have discovered differences in the rocks found around the world and each rock found falls into one of three primary categories. The three types of rocks are called

   A. intrusive, extrusive, fossil
   B. carbons, minerals, volcanic
   C. continental, tectonic, glacial
   D. sedimentary, metamorphic, igneous

5. Chromosomes are important to reproduction and are passed along through the genes of the parents. How many pairs of chromosomes are most humans born with?

   A. 21
   B. 23
   C. 25
   D. 28

6. There are three states of matter, which are characterized by molecular movement. Which state of matter shows the characteristic of having both distinct shape and volume?

   A. gas
   B. solid
   C. liquid
   D. energy

7. Models have intrinsic value in science education. There are several types that help students understand objects or processes better. A model that shows a bacteria or virus in 3-D that a student can handle is an example of a _____ model.

   A. physical
   B. objective
   C. conceptual
   D. mathematical

8. The Earth is comprised of large land masses and bodies of water. How much of the Earth's surface is covered specifically by water?

   A. two-thirds
   B. half
   C. three-fourths
   D. five-eighths

9. When a female tiger and a male tiger mate, they each deliver certain genes to the developing offspring. As this occurs, cells go through a process to aid in developing and growing. When a cell divides and creates two nuclei, each having the same number of chromosomes as the original, the process is called

   A. mitosis
   B. meiosis
   C. pruning
   D. selection

10. A kayaker is stalled at the top of a waterfall planning her descent. This may be considered a form of potential energy. After the kayaker begins to move down the waterfall, this potential energy has changed into _____ by virtue of the movement.

   A. kinetic energy
   B. caloric energy
   C. metabolic energy
   D. conductive energy

11. A cub scout on a camping trip is roasting a hotdog using a bent coat hanger. He notices that after a short time holding the hotdog over the campfire that his fingers are getting warmer from the small handle he made out of the metal hanger. The leader warns that he could burn his hand, as this is most likely the result of _____.

   A. radiation
   B. expansion
   C. convection
   D. conduction

12. A fifth grade teacher includes students in a food demonstration to make hard candy. Through this process, the students will observe the various states of matter and the changes in the substances, as well as learn how to measure. To make hard candy the teacher uses a liquid combination of water and sugar along with coloring and flavoring. When the liquid is boiled and then dropped into ice water, the students will hear a crack, see the liquid harden and therefore learn the concept of

   _____.

   A. boiling point
   B. freezing point
   C. saturation point
   D. calculation point

13. In the law pertaining to the relationship of mass and energy, often known as the Theory of Relativity by Einstein, the formula he developed was $E = mc^2$. The letter E means energy; the letter m pertains to mass; and the letter c stands for

   _____.

   A. speed of light
   B. power of heat
   C. circumference
   D. centrifugal force

14. An important Earth process in the balance of an ecosystem is the Oxygen Cycle. If plants expel oxygen for animals to breathe, how do animals break it down into energy?

   A. through exercise
   B. by digesting food
   C. through respiration
   D. by eliminating waste

15. A system of the body that is responsible for the maintenance and regulation of all other systems is called the

   A. endocrine system
   B. circulation system
   C. assimilation system
   D. reproductive system

16. Based upon the data in the following chart, what hypothesis makes the most sense?

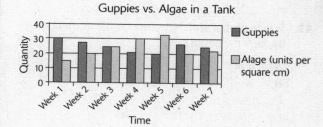

   A. Guppies do not live very long in a tank.
   B. The amount of algae is steadily increasing until the guppies increase.
   C. Algae grows quickly in a tank community.
   D. The number of guppies is dependant upon the amount of algae present.

GO ON TO THE NEXT PAGE

17. A third grade teacher has introduced the concept of simple machines to the class. She is trying to help students understand how these simple machines can be useful in daily life. She asks the students to look around and point out a simple machine in the classroom that is an example of a lever. Which of the following do the students choose?

    A. a stapler
    B. an eraser
    C. a computer
    D. a pencil sharpener

18. In order for an ecosystem to be considered in a balanced state it must have the following three characteristics: constant source of energy, energy converted to glucose, and nutrients and matter recycled successfully. Which of the following is an example of a disruption of the food chain equilibrium of a river ecosystem?

    A. The near extinction of a small river guppy, which feeds the primary consumers of the river community.
    B. An increase in the river's current, which pushes supplies through the water at a faster speed.
    C. A rock eroding into sediment at the bottom of the river, which causes sediment to settle at the mouth of the river.
    D. There is a flooding of the river, which pervades the nearby village and causes mass destruction.

19. Which part of a plant transports the nutrients through the entire plant?

    A. root
    B. stem
    C. leaves
    D. flower

20. Insulin was a discovery of monumental proportions of its time. It has helped to manage the health of people with diabetes for many years. During what decade was it discovered?

    A. 1920
    B. 1930
    C. 1940
    D. 1950

21. A bicyclist is pedaling down a hill, but does not know how fast he is traveling, however he knows he traveled 825 feet in 25 minutes. If he were to implement the formula to determine his speed, what would the answer be? (Assume there is no friction or outside force acting upon him.)

    A. 33 miles per hour
    B. 25 miles per hour
    C. 25 feet per minute
    D. 33 feet per minute

22. Which of the following is the correct classification name for the Kingdom in which Humans are listed?

    A. Animalia
    B. Mammalia
    C. Hominadae
    D. Homo Sapiens

23. It is believed that the first hominids roamed the Earth in the period of _____

    A. 570–280 million years ago—Paleozoic
    B. 250–135 million years ago—Mesozoic
    C. present time to 66 million years ago—Cenozoic
    D. between 50 and 100 million years ago—Proterozoic

24. If a male parent carried the dominant genes for a specific trait identified as BB, and the female parent carried the dominant and the recessive genes for the same trait (Bb), what would their 4 offspring most likely demonstrate?

A. All four would have dominant genes.

B. Two would have dominant and two would have recessive genes.

C. Three would have dominant and one would have recessive genes.

D. One would have dominant and three would have recessive genes.

25. A teacher is sharing information about the Food Pyramid with her students in order for them to understand the format of a science principle. Which of the following unifying process categories would this belong?

A. form and function

B. evidence, models, explanation

C. systems, orders, organizations

D. change, constancy, measurement

IF YOU FINISH BEFORE TIME IS CALLED, CHECK YOUR WORK ON THIS SECTION ONLY. DO NOT WORK ON ANY OTHER SECTION IN THE TEST.

Answer Key

Language Arts

1. C
2. D
3. A
4. B
5. D
6. D
7. D
8. A
9. D
10. B
11. B
12. C
13. D

14. B
15. B
16. D
17. D
18. A
19. C
20. B
21. A
22. A
23. D
24. C
25. A

Math

1. D
2. B
3. D
4. C
5. B
6. C
7. A
8. A
9. A
10. D
11. D
12. D
13. C

14. B
15. D
16. A
17. B
18. D
19. B
20. C
21. B
22. D
23. D
24. A
25. D

Social Sciences

1. A
2. D
3. B
4. C
5. A
6. C
7. C
8. D
9. D
10. D
11. A
12. A
13. C

14. D
15. B
16. A
17. B
18. D
19. B
20. B
21. B
22. A
23. C
24. B
25. D

Science

1. D
2. B
3. C
4. D
5. B
6. B
7. C
8. A
9. A
10. A
11. D
12. C
13. A

14. C
15. A
16. D
17. A
18. A
19. B
20. A
21. D
22. A
23. C
24. A
25. C

Answer Explanations

Language Arts

1. **C.** Folktales are stories that are passed down from one generation to another generation and may include fables, myths, legends, folktales, and tall tales. Dale's grandparents shared stories with her mother and then her mother shared them with her. These stories were told from one generation to the next.

2. **D.** The main theme of this paragraph refers to the talent of Fred Johnson and the fact that he contributed to an art form that is no longer common, but reflective of a great period in our country's history.

3. **A.** The idiomatic expression, *at a loss for words*, means that a person might be in a state of uncertainty and not be able to say exactly what they mean. It appears that the author believes that Johnson's work was unique and someone might have trouble explaining it.

4. **B.** It seems that the author reflected on the interesting and unusual talent of Johnson. The word unique best describes the character, as he had talent for a lost art and was considered well-known.

5. **D.** A memoir or diary is considered non-fiction as it is presented with factual aspects about an author's life. It is considered a literary piece that is true from the perspective of the author.

6. **D.** A collective noun names a group or collection of people, things, places, concepts, or characteristics, such as family, team, flock or herd.

7. **D.** The correct spelling for the word that the student wants to use that means a survey of questions is questionnaire.

8. **A.** The most probable selection is that the vase was made of glass. An inference is made by a reader based on his previous experience. In reading this passage, a reader should understand that if the vase was dropped and Shirley went to get a broom, the vase must have broken. It was most likely made of glass.

9. **D.** The author is sharing the excitement of the first snow of winter. As it falls, it covers a person's feet, then the sidewalk and finally the street. It is a wonder for the children to see.

10. **B.** The last line of the poem is *And hurried the children to see the sight!* It means that the snow is "calling" to the children to come and see how it glistened and twinkled and covered the sidewalk and street.

11. **B.** Marci is making a text-to-self connection as she is relating something that is important in her life to something that occurred in the story. She made a personal connection about her grandfather to the character of the grandfather in the story. This story reminded her of the horse riding activity she participates in at her grandfather's ranch with the horse riding activity in the story.

12. **C.** The author is relating the story in the third person. In this form of point of view, the author tells the story using an outside voice, as the narrator is not one of the characters.

13. **D.** The setting of a story includes the time, the place, the physical details, and the circumstances or events in which a situation occurs. The setting of this story is the desert, and it is described as the *scorched landscape* which helps the reader better relate to the physical details of the story.

14. **B.** The example of personification is the sentence about the chimney, as it gives human characteristics to the chimney. Chimneys are not capable of laughter, yet this sentence allows the reader to visualize the smoke. *The chimney roared with laughter as the smoke blew out the top.*

15. **B.** The word *ball* has a variety of meanings; however, in this sentence the most likely answer is a dance.

16. **D.** The word *thunderous* describes the clouds and is, therefore, considered an adjective. Adjectives describe nouns. The other words mentioned are lightly, an adverb; patterns, a noun; and sidewalks, a noun.

17. **D.** The passage relays much information about Jesse James, a famous American outlaw. Summarizing requires readers to take the large information and condense it into the general main idea. The general idea of the passage above is that Jesse James was a ruthless outlaw that led the James Brothers Gang.

18. **A.** Adverbs are words that modify a verb, an adjective, or another adverb. Adverbs tell how, when, where, why, how much, and how often. "Yesterday" is a time adverb.

19. **C.** The pronoun 'it' is used twice in this paragraph, both times referring to the *restaurant layout*.

20. **B.** An expository method of writing provides information about a topic in an objective and non-emotional manner. Expository text can be found in textbooks, pamphlets, guidebooks, and research documents.

21. **A.** A student should be able to infer, from previous experience and knowledge, that the wind is one of the factors that helps to carry pollen from the male to the female plant. Other ways that pollen moves from the stamen of the male to the ovary of the female is by bees, birds or animals.

22. **A.** The main idea of this paragraph is that flowers are the reproductive organs of plants. This main idea is supported by various details about the organs and how reproduction occurs.

23. **D.** The word *infamous* has many synonyms but it depends upon how the word is used. Although *infamous* also can mean shameful and lowdown, the best synonym to replace it in the sentence is *notorious*.

24. **C.** The *plot* tells the events of a story; the *inciting force* tells the events that lead to the central conflict; the *exposition* is the initial understanding of a story, in which the characters, setting, tone, and initial understanding of the story are presented to the reader; and the *conclusion* ends the story by wrapping up all actions.

25. **A.** Screaming is a type of verbal known as a gerund. A verbal is a word that is made from a verb, has the power of a verb, but acts like another part of speech. A gerund is a verb ending in –ing that is used as a noun. Therefore, screaming is a noun in this sentence.

Math

1. **D.** First calculate how many total hours Suki works during the week by adding $(5 + 5 + 5 + 3 + 3 = 21$ hrs). Then find the amount of money he makes over that amount of time by multiplying the hourly wage by the total hours worked $(21 * 9.25 = \$194.25)$. Now calculate the amount of time worked on the weekend by adding $(6 + 7 = 13$ hrs). Then find the total money made by multiplying the hourly wage by the total hours spent $(13 * 9.25 = \$120.25)$. The problem asks for the difference in wages ("how much more does Suki make during the week than on the weekend?"). The difference requires the operation of subtraction $(\$194.25 - \$120.25 = \$74.00)$.

2. **B.** The average is given $\left(198\frac{1}{3}\right)$ along with 5 of the weights. Let x represent the missing weight and calculate using the equation of averages. There are 6 total weights that must be added together and then divided by 6 to achieve the average of $\left(198\frac{1}{3}\right)$ pounds.

$(205 + 195 + 210 + 180 + 198 + x) \div 6 = \left(198\frac{1}{3}\right)$

$(988 + x) \div 6 = \left(198\frac{1}{3}\right)$

$(988 + x) \div 6 * 6 = \left(198\frac{1}{3}\right) * 6$

$988 + x = 1190$

$x = 202$ lbs.

3. **D.** To solve change each percentage into a decimal by dividing it by 100. Then multiply the "value of" numeral by its corresponding decimal. Last, compare the numbers to find the greatest in value (30 or 12% of 250).

$5 \div 100 = 0.05$ $0.05 * 500 = 25$

$18 \div 100 = 0.18$ $0.18 * 140 = 25.2$

$33 \div 100 = 0.33$ $0.33 * 90 = 29.7$

$12 \div 100 = 0.12$ $0.12 * 250 = 30$

4. **C.** There are 12 inches in every foot. To calculate the inches in 5 feet simply multiply $5 * 12 = 60$. For $\frac{1}{3}$ of a foot you must set up a proportion. $\frac{1}{3} = \frac{12}{1}$. Cross multiply and reduce to get 4 inches ($\frac{12}{3}$). Add 60 and 4 to get the amount of 64 inches. Remember that it asks for $\frac{1}{3}$ of a foot, not just 3 inches of a foot.

5. B. The graph shows an increase in all vehicle sales in 1990 from that of the previous decade. Cars increase from 16,000 (1980) to 20,000 (1990); Trucks increase from 12,000 (1980) to 22,000 (1990); SUVs increase from 10,000 (1980) to 30,000 (1990); and Vans increase from 24,000 (1980) to 26,000 (1990).

6. C. The question asks only for the description of the trend in car sales. The graph shows a small decline in car sales from 1970–1980 but after that the sales have gradually and steadily increased each decade.

7. A. Look at the values of the other vehicles sold besides cars. Trucks = 10,000; SUV = 5,000; and Van = 25,000. Add these amounts together to get the total vehicles sold that were not cars. 10,000 + 5,000 + 25,000 = 40,000.

8. A. The range is the difference (subtract) between the highest value and the lowest value in a set of numbers. In the set –90 is the lowest value and 89 is the highest value. 89 – (–90) will give the range of 179; remember that when subtracting a negative number the negatives cancel out, and it becomes an addition problem.

9. A. To solve addition of fractions, the denominators must be the same. Start with $\frac{1}{2}$ and $\frac{3}{10}$ to obtain like denominators. Next, combine $\frac{1}{5}$ and $\frac{7}{15}$.

$\frac{1}{2} = \frac{5}{10}$ and this allows it to be added to $\frac{3}{10}$: $\left(\frac{5}{10} + \frac{3}{10} = \frac{8}{10}\right)$.

$\frac{8}{10}$ is able to be reduced to $\frac{4}{5}$.

$\frac{1}{5} = \frac{3}{15}$ and this allows it to be added to $\frac{7}{15}$: $\left(\frac{3}{15} + \frac{7}{15} = \frac{10}{15}\right)$.

Finally, combine $\frac{4}{5}$ and $\frac{10}{15}$. (Obtain the same denominators by changing $\frac{4}{5}$ into $\frac{12}{15}$.)

$\frac{12}{15} + \frac{10}{15} = \frac{22}{15}$ (Convert this improper fraction to a mixed number by dividing the numerator by the denominator and placing the remainder in fraction format.)

$22 \div 15 = 1$ with a remainder of 7

$1\frac{7}{15}$ (This cannot be reduced any further as it is in the lowest terms.)

10. D. This problem requires a calculation of the area of each room to be tiled. Use the formula A = b * h. Calculate each room separately, and then add the areas together to get the total area to be tiled. After calculating the total area multiply by the cost of each square foot.

$A_{kit} = 24 * 12 = 288$ ft^2

$A_{entry} = 12 * 8 = 96$ ft^2

$A_{hall} = 30 * 4 = 120$ ft^2

$288 + 96 + 120 = 504$ ft^2

$504 * 5.20 = \$2,620.80$

11. D. Calculate the total time in Haley's day by multiplying the class time by the number of classes (55 * 7 = 385 min). Then calculate the approximate time it takes the students to get ready throughout the day by multiplying the average time by the amount of classes (11 * 7 = 77 min). To find the percentage of time Haley spends waiting for students, divide the time the students take getting dressed out by the total time of class throughout the day (77 ÷ 385 = 0.2). To find the percentage, multiply the decimal by 100 (0.2 * 100 = 20%).

12. D. Determine the total distance traveled in meters first by multiplying 4 * 50 = 200 meters. To calculate feet traveled multiply the total meters by 3.28 (200 * 3.28 = 656 ft).

13. C. The child weighs 25 lbs, and the medicine is given per pound. Calculate the total medicine given by multiplying the dosage per pound by the total weight of the child (25 * 25 = 625).

14. B. Convert all numbers to common terms, in this case fractions $\left(6.5 = 6\frac{1}{2}\right)$. Remember to follow the order of operations law (PEMDAS—parenthesis, exponents, multiplication, division, addition, subtraction).

$\frac{1}{2} * \frac{3}{4} = \frac{3}{8}$ (Multiply the fractions first.)

$\frac{3}{8} + 6\frac{1}{2} - \frac{1}{8}$ (To add or subtract fractions, the denominators must be the same.)

$\frac{3}{8} + 6\frac{4}{8} - \frac{1}{8}$ ($\frac{1}{2}$ is equal to $\frac{4}{8}$.) Addition comes next.

$6\frac{7}{8} - \frac{1}{8}$ (Subtract the fractions; make sure they have the same denominators.)

$6\frac{6}{8} = 6\frac{3}{4}$ (Reduce to lowest terms.)

15. D. First divide 5280 ft by the circumference of the tire (3 ft) to determine how many times the tire must rotate in a mile. $5280 \div 3 = 1760$. Then multiply that rotation by the number of times Kris must pedal to make the tire revolve one full rotation to get the total number of pedal turns she must make to travel a mile. $1760 * 2 = 3520$.

16. A. Change all numbers into common units to work with, in this case use decimals. For fractions divide the numerator by the denominator to get the decimal form. For percentage, divide the percent by 100 to get the decimal form. $78\frac{2}{5} = 78.4$ and $780\% = 78$ and $78\frac{3}{5} = 78.6$. After all numbers are in a common format, compare to determine the order of least to greatest. 780%, 78.2, $78\frac{2}{5}$, $78\frac{3}{5}$, 78.8.

17. B. The pattern requires that the previous number be squared. $2^2 = 4$, $4^2 = 16$, $16^2 = 256$, $256^2 = 65536$, and so $65536^2 = 4294967296$.

18. D. The key terms to focus on are *less than* (subtract), *divided by* (division), and *increased by* (add). Therefore, the correct answer is $(y - 8) \div y + 20$.

19. B. Set up equations for each caseload. Then plug in the equations for the appropriate variable.

S = Shirley's caseload   P = Poppy's caseload   A = Andrea's caseload

$P = S + 55$

$A = 2P$ (The question asks for Andrea's caseload.)

$A = 2(S + 55)$ (Plug in the value of P.)

20. C. First calculate how much money Ken will spend on the 4 tires and mud flaps by adding ($260 + $55 + $55 = $370). Then subtract the total spent from the total amount he has in savings ($402 − $370 = $32). Since fuzzy dice cost $4, divide the amount of money left by the cost of one set of fuzzy dice ($32 ÷ $4 = 8). Therefore, Ken can buy 8 fuzzy dice.

21. B. Calculate the cost of 2 pairs of floor mats by multiplying $42 * 2 = $84. Then calculate the total cost of 4 seat covers ($25 * 4 = $100). Now add up the two answers to get the total amount needed ($84 + $100 = $184).

22. D. There are two ways to calculate the money Basta will save after 6 months. First, calculate how much money she saves per month by multiplying 10% (0.10) by her monthly income of $2284, which yields $228.40. Then multiply that amount by the time she is saving (6 * 228.40 = $1370.40). The second way is to calculate the total money Basta will make over 6 months and then multiply that by 10% (6 * $2284 = $13704 * 0.10 = $1370.40).

23. D. First calculate how many classes Judy teaches per week. 2 night classes 3 times a week equals 6 classes at night and 3 classes 2 times a week equals 6 classes in the day. The total number of classes she teaches per week is 12 (6 + 6). She will be gone for 2 weeks, multiply 12 * 2 = 24. Judy must write 24 lesson plans for the class meetings she will miss during vacation. Since it takes her 2 hours for each lesson plan multiply 24 * 2 for the total hours she will spend writing (24 * 2 = 48 hours).

24. A. The pattern in the number line is to increase each value by one more than the last number was increased by.

$-3 + 0 = -3$

$-3 + 1 = -2$

$-2 + 2 = 0$

$0 + 3 = 3$

$3 + 4 = 7$

$7 + 5 = 12$ (This is the missing value.)

$12 + 6 = 18$

$18 + 7 = 25$

25. D. Calculate the sales discounts by multiplying the percentage by the original price ($0.30 * 120 = 36$; $0.1 * 45 = 4.5$). Take these values and subtract them from the original price to obtain the sale price. $120 - 36 = \$84$ and $45 - 4.5 = \$40.50$. Now add these two sale prices with the original price of the socks. $\$84 + \$40.50 + \$12 = \$136.50$.

Social Sciences

1. A. When students are reading historical documents that have personal perspectives evident in the content, it is critically important that they understand how to decipher fact from opinion.

2. D. The U.S. Constitution allows for the leaders of the executive departments to advise the President. These leaders are called Secretaries and make up the advising Cabinet, which is selected by the President based on the departments currently in existence.

3. B. The Appalachians, located in the eastern United States provide natural resources such as iron, gas, coal and oil as well as power for electricity from the waterways. It was a major influence on the establishment of industry in the U.S.

4. C. The United States is part of the continent of North America, which also contains Canada and Mexico. North America is located in the northern half of the world, above the equator and west of the prime meridian; therefore, the United States is found in the Western and Northern Hemispheres.

5. A. Rosa Parks was a black woman who lived in Alabama. She refused to give up her seat on the bus to a white man and move to the back as was the custom for black people in the South. She was arrested and put in jail for disobedience, which ignited a period in history known as the Civil Rights Movement.

6. C. An open economic system, presently in use throughout the world for most major countries, allows the export and import of goods and services from the global market.

7. C. When Roosevelt held a monopoly over the oil industry and Carnegie had a monopoly on the steel industry, capitalism began to rise, which was not acceptable to many in the country. Through the urging of businessmen and government officials, regulations were finally passed into law to end monopolies in the country.

8. D. Mountains are the initial starting place for rivers, as the water is collected from the rains and snows at the top and flow down the sides into river valleys.

9. D. The bodies of water represented on the map of Europe include the Mediterranean Sea, the Black Sea, and the Caspian Sea.

10. D. The Indian and Chinese River Valley Civilization developed advanced engineering and architectural technology, and built massive tombs and palaces. It is reflected that they prospered from the knowledge gained from previous work done.

11. A. The Pledge of Allegiance indicates that this nation represents the liberty and justice for **all** people. The Pledge is a form of support that people demonstrate to ensure that fairness and freedoms are guaranteed.

12. A. When a country utilizes a symbol to represent the land and its people, the symbol demonstrates their ideals. For example, a symbol for America is the bald eagle, which represents the ideals of freedom, courage, strength, and immortality, all significant to the nation and the citizens.

13. C. The structures created to honor deceased pharoahs, known as the Great Pyramids, are found in the area of Egypt on the continent of Africa. They were constructed in about 2500 BCE.

14. D. Upon the return from the journey, the survivors of the expedition found their calendars were one day behind, even though they clearly maintained the ship's log. However, at this time in history, they did not have clocks that were accurate enough to measure the lengthening of each day. Since they had traveled westward completing a circum-navigation, they had actually rotated the Earth's axis one time less. It caused commotion and was a mystery to the people, but it also established the International Dateline.

15. B. In April 1961, the United States invasion by the CIA, headed by President John F. Kennedy was done to try to overthrow Cuba leader, Fidel Castro. The invasion began in the bay named Bahia de Cochinos at the south coast of Cuba, which may be named after the triggerfish. It was a failed mission, Castro felt victorious in his revolution, and the event was termed the Bay of Pigs Invasion.

16. A. The Preamble is the introduction to the Constitution and it briefly states the governments' role to protect the citizens. It also explains the values and beliefs of the U.S. government system. The Bill of Rights is the first ten amendments and is a part of the Constitution, but not the introduction.

17. B. Amendment 7 was designed to secure the right to a trial by a jury of peers for citizens accused of crimes related to civil infractions.

18. D. Authoritarianism is a form of government that secures obedience through strict control through coercion and oppressive measures. Communism is also a type of authoritarianism.

19. B. The Executive branch guarantees the laws of the United States are followed and includes the president, vice president, cabinet members, department members, and agencies.

20. B. People began to immigrate early in the history of the world searching for safe places and hunting for food. At this time, there was land that covered the ocean between Asia and North America where the Bering Strait now appears. It was known as a land bridge and people moved north in Africa through Asia and then walked across this area of Asia into North America (now Canada and Alaska).

21. B. President Lincoln was assassinated on April 14, 1865, at the end of the Civil War well after the Mayan Civilization had fallen, after the Revolutionary War, and after the exploration of the West had begun. The Mayan Indian Civilization was in existence from 250 A.D. until 900 A.D. and responsible for many art, architectural, and mathematical systems still in place today. The Revolutionary War began in 1776. Lewis and Clark began their expedition in 1804 after President Jefferson commissioned them to explore the western United States.

22. A. The Incan civilization is best known for the development of metallurgy and the systems they established for their society. They designed irrigation systems and road and agricultural systems that aided future civilizations.

23. C. Graphs and tables are tools used to record historical data. These require that students interpret data that is limited in content but may offer specific statistical and historical information.

24. B. During the 1830s political reform allowed men the right to vote, but women were not yet allowed or even considered. A movement to allow women this right began in America and spurred other women around the world to focus their efforts on obtaining this right.

25. D. In the 1850s, Americans wanted a railroad system that would stretch transcontinental to move people and goods. It was very expensive, so Congress passed a law to help. They gave federal land and loaned money to two companies so they could build a railroad in hopes that the economy and population of the west would be increased.

Science

1. **D.** Louis Pasteur discovered the existence of microbes and developed the method of pasteurization in 1858, more than 50 years after Darwin's theory of evolution was announced (1835). The other three possible answers were all set in the 1700s (static electricity—1750, conservation of matter—1771, frictional heat—1790).

2. **B.** Gregor Mendel is known for his study of genetics. In 1865, he surmised through a series of experiments using pea plants that reproduction of two different types of plants results in changes to the later generations that reflect each of the parent plants.

3. **C.** The correct order of the visible color spectrum, a rainbow, is taught by using the acronym ROY G BIV which stands for red, orange, yellow, green, blue, indigo, violet.

4. **D.** The three categories of rock are sedimentary (hardened by compression), metamorphic (made of igneous sedimentary or metamorphic), igneous (cooled magma).

5. **B.** Most humans have 23 pairs of chromosomes, which amount to a total of 46. A child receives 23 chromosomes from the father and 23 from the mother, which pair up during reproduction. If there is a change in the pairing a deformity or disability may occur.

6. **B.** In a solid, the molecules are formed tightly together, as the energy decreases. A solid maintains its shape and volume unless some force is imposed upon it to change that. A liquid has volume but it takes the shape of the container that holds it. Gas has no volume and no definite shape.

7. **C.** A conceptual model provides an abstract or replicate of a model of an object or system that is too large to study or too small to see otherwise. Examples include: a model of the watershed system, a model of tectonic plates that cause an earthquake, or a bacteria or germ that is found in the human eye.

8. **A.** Two-thirds of the Earth's surface is covered by water in the form of lakes, streams, oceans, and seas and only one-third is land mass (continents).

9. **A.** Mitosis is the cell reproductive process in most animals that occurs in the nucleus of a cell during division. It creates two new nuclei, each having an equal number of chromosomes.

10. **A.** Potential energy is defined as that possessed by an object that is capable of movement. After the object begins to move, it creates kinetic energy and is measured by the force and speed of the object.

11. **D.** Metal is a strong conductor of heat. When this cub scout holds the metal hanger over the flame, the heat that is gathered from the hotdog and the part of the hanger exposed to the flame begins to warm up rapidly. The heat travels (is conducted) up the length of the coat hanger and begins to warm the scout's hand. The longer he leaves the hanger near the heat source, the hotter it will get. He could potentially burn his hand.

12. **C.** A saturation point is the point at which something can no longer be absorbed, or dissolved. In this case, the boiled liquid became a solid during the process of cooling, but it cracked at the point that the substance could no longer be cooled any further, the saturation point.

13. **A.** The letter c in Einstein's theory stands for the speed of light, which is about 3000,000 kilometers per second. Basically, his theory proved that when particles of matter move fast enough, they can gain in mass.

14. **C.** In the Oxygen Cycle, plants expel oxygen, which animals need to sustain life. Animals break down the oxygen into energy for their cells through the process of respiration.

15. **A.** The endocrine system, which is comprised of the thyroid gland, the lymph system, and hormones in the human body, is responsible for the regulation of the body. This system controls all other life processes.

16. **D.** The best hypothesis, based upon the data, is that the more algae there is, the fewer guppies there will be. It appears, based upon the graph, that as the algae increases the guppies decrease and then as the algae decreases the guppies increase. This is an example of a community finding equilibrium.

17. **A.** A stapler is an example of a class 2 lever. It places the fulcrum at one end, so the load is between the fulcrum and the effort.

18. A. There are numerous things that can disrupt an ecosystem and its equilibrium. The disruption in the food cycle occurs when producers become scarce or consumers become too many. The near extinction of a guppy can affect the food chain by decreasing the amount of energy available for the higher consumers, which can lead to starvation and even death. Likewise, too many guppies would put a strain upon the plankton or plant life of the river and also cause an impact upon the ecosystem.

19. B. It is the stem that transports the nutrients to the leaves, after the root has absorbed the minerals and water.

20. A. Insulin was discovered in the 1920s and has been used since that time to help people with diabetes. It was discovered by a Toronto physician, Frederick Grant Banting, in 1921. He received the Nobel Prize in Medicine for this discovery.

21. D. The formula used to determine speed is $s = d/t$, which stands for speed = distance divided by time. Using this to calculate his speed, he could figure $s = 825$ ft / 25min, which equals 33 ft / min. (Remember to check the units of measurement when calculating speed!)

22. A. The human classification under Kingdom is Animalia, while Mammalia is the Class, Hominadae is the Family, and Homo Sapiens is the Species.

23. C. The Cenozoic period is the period in which the humans were first thought to exist, sometime between present time and 66 million years ago. Other suspected animal forms included primates, horses, mastodons, whales, alligators, and saber-toothed tigers.

24. A. Using the chart that Gregor Mendel developed, according to the genes BB and Bb, the four offspring would have the following patterns: BB, BB, Bb, and Bb. Therefore, all four would have the dominant genes for that trait even though they carry the recessive gene as well.

25. C. The example of a Food Pyramid falls under the unifying process of systems, orders, and organizations. Constructing this chart is a method of organizing scientific information.

Final Thoughts and Tips

Exam day is approaching, so you should be sure to take all the preparatory and necessary steps to be properly registered and to complete your studying. Following the set guidelines and using quality study periods will help ensure satisfactory success on this Praxis II exam. You will be much closer to obtaining your teacher certification or the licensure required in your state.

Registration

Some examinees are required to complete more than one Praxis II examination in the field of education. This will depend on their specific area of teaching. The department of education in the specific state may provide the necessary information for testing based on the requirements for certification and licensure. If a mandatory exam is one other than that specified in this study guide, check the other guides developed by Wiley Publishing, Inc as these might be helpful.

When planning to take multiple examinations, it is recommended that only one exam be taken each day to optimize study time and to focus on the specific content included in the separate exams. The Praxis II exams can be physically and mentally draining, as they can be complicated and fast-paced. To maximize your performance, consider your individual learning style as you prepare for the exam.

Review registration guidelines:

- Confirm exam dates and locations online at http://www.ets.org/.
- Check accommodations if you are an individual with a disability.
- Register at least one to three months ahead of the test date to secure a seat at the preferred location.
- Save proof of registration (admission ticket) to bring to the testing center on the day of the exam.

Studying

Personal methods of studying that are comfortable, and effective, providing a level of confidence, are essential for examinees. Examinees should prepare and study ahead of the scheduled test date and not try to cram information the week or day before the test. This exam includes content knowledge and application so retention and skill are a necessity.

The two practice tests available should help examinees address the types of questions that will appear on the actual exam and provide the opportunity to pace answering the questions. For examinees who desire additional study information, a few select websites have been included, but a general search on the Internet for specific topics is also possible.

Recommended study tips:

- Review the table of contents to determine the topics covered on the exam.
- Assess individual strengths and needs regarding content knowledge.
- Read information about the exam format to become familiar with the questions.
- Design the most effective methods and strategies to study and prepare for the exam.
- Develop an individualized study plan based on your strengths and needs.
- Ensure a comfortable study environment with accessible materials.
- Study every day prior to the exam, reviewing the previous day's information.
- Take the sample practice exams either before or after using the study guide materials.
- Use the answer explanations as additional study information.

Testing Time

The day before the exam:

- Participate in activities that will not distract from studying, as the effects of some activities may exhibit on test day and affect performance.
- Eat well and drink adequate water.
- Organize the items needed at the testing location: proof of registration, identification, pencils, pens, clothing, etc.
- Obtain directions for the testing center and determine the travel time.
- Try not to stay up late to cram for the exam.
- Choose an evening of rest and a get a great night of sleep.

The day of the exam:

- Awake early to avoid rushing around.
- Eat a healthy breakfast that includes protein and water or juice.
- Remember to pack all the important items needed for the exam.
- Arrive 15 to 30 minutes early to the exam location.
- Breathe, relax, and be confident!

You have worked hard to begin the journey toward an enriching career. The outcome of this examination is very important to securing your certification/licensure to teach in your desired state. Congratulations on your accomplishment.

The trusted guides to a higher score on Praxis II® exam —from the experts at CliffsNotes®.

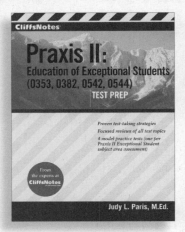

978-0-470-23844-8

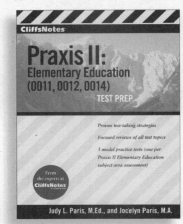

978-0-470-25956-6

978-0-470-44855-7

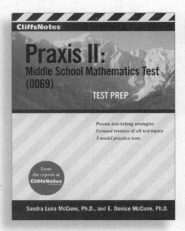

978-0-470-27822-2

978-0-471-75212-7

978-0-470-39728-2

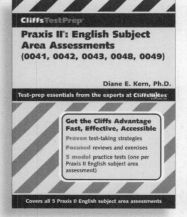

978-0-471-78506-4

978-0-471-78767-9

978-0-470-23842-4

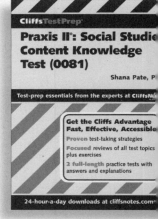

978-0-471-79412-7

Available wherever books are sold or visit us at CliffsNotes.com®

CliffsNotes
A Branded Imprint of WILEY
Now you know.